A Heterodox Marxist and His Century: Lelio Basso

Historical Materialism Book Series

Editorial Board

Loren Balhorn (*Berlin*)
David Broder (*Rome*)
Sebastian Budgen (*Paris*)
Steve Edwards (*London*)
Juan Grigera (*London*)
Marcel van der Linden (*Amsterdam*)
Peter Thomas (*London*)

VOLUME 216

The titles published in this series are listed at *brill.com/hm*

A Heterodox Marxist and His Century: Lelio Basso

Selected Writings

By

Lelio Basso

Edited by

Chiara Giorgi

Translated by

Matteo Mandarini
David Broder

BRILL

LEIDEN | BOSTON

Library of Congress Cataloging-in-Publication Data

Names: Basso, Lelio, author. | Giorgi, Chiara, editor. |
   Mandarini, Matteo, translator. | Broder, David, translator.
Title: A heterodox Marxist and his century: Lelio Basso : selected writings / by
   Lelio Basso ; edited by Chiara Giorgi ; translators, Matteo Mandarini
   and David Broder.
Description: Leiden ; Boston : Brill, [2021] | Series: Historical materialism book
   series, 1570-1522 ; volume 216 | Includes bibliographical references and index. |
Identifiers: LCCN 2020030864 (print) | LCCN 2020030865 (ebook) |
   ISBN 9789004321687 (hardback) | ISBN 9789004432123 (ebook)
Subjects: LCSH: Socialism–Italy–History–20th century.
Classification: LCC HX288 .B329 2021 (print) | LCC HX288 (ebook) |
   DDC 320.53/2092 [B]–dc23
LC record available at https://lccn.loc.gov/2020030864
LC ebook record available at https://lccn.loc.gov/2020030865

Typeface for the Latin, Greek, and Cyrillic scripts: "Brill". See and download: brill.com/brill-typeface.

ISSN 1570-1522
ISBN 978-90-04-32168-7 (hardback)
ISBN 978-90-04-43212-3 (e-book)

Copyright 2021 by Koninklijke Brill NV, Leiden, The Netherlands.
Copyright for the original, Italian publications by La Fondazione Lelio e Lisli Basso-ISSOCO.
Koninklijke Brill NV incorporates the imprints Brill, Brill Hes & De Graaf, Brill Nijhoff, Brill Rodopi,
Brill Sense, Hotei Publishing, mentis Verlag, Verlag Ferdinand Schöningh and Wilhelm Fink Verlag.
All rights reserved. No part of this publication may be reproduced, translated, stored in a retrieval system,
or transmitted in any form or by any means, electronic, mechanical, photocopying, recording or otherwise,
without prior written permission from the publisher. Requests for re-use and/or translations must be
addressed to Koninklijke Brill NV via brill.com or copyright.com.

This book is printed on acid-free paper and produced in a sustainable manner.

Contents

Acknowledgements   VII

Introduction   1
    Chiara Giorgi

PART 1
In Search of Marx: The Writings of the Young Lelio Basso

1   Socialism and Philosophy, *Avanti!*, 2 March 1924   31

2   Term of Comparison, *Conscientia*, 9 May 1925   35

3   The Reformation and European Thought: Marx, *Conscientia*, 25 July 1925   39

4   Socialism and Idealism, *Il Quarto Stato*, 10 April 1926   42

PART 2
Marxism and the History of Italy

5   The Working Class in the Social Republic, Istituto di studi Socialisti-Libreria Editrice *Avanti!*, Rome-Milan 1944–5   49

6   Training Cadres. Problems of the Party, *Unità proletaria*, 15 April 1945   58

7   Democracy and Legalism, *Avanti!*, 23 February 1947   64

PART 3
The Interpretation of Marxism After Rosa Luxemburg

8   Rosa Luxemburg, *Il Quarto Stato*, 15 January 1949   69

9   The Contribution of Rosa Luxemburg to Marxist Thought, in *Rosa Luxemburg e lo sviluppo del pensiero marxista*, Franco Angeli, Milano 1976   76

10 The Dialectical Nature of the State According to Marx, in G. Carandini, *Stato e teorie marxiste*, Mazzotta, Milano 1977   93

11 Society and State in the Thought of Marx, *Problemi del socialismo*, 1973, 13–14, pp. 115–48   108

12 Marxism and Revolution, *Problemi del socialismo*, October, 1966, no. 11   137

13 Lenin and Marx, Revolutions in the Centre and Revolutions in the Periphery of Capitalism, *Il Segnalatore*, June 1971, no. 1   146

14 Marx, Lenin and Rosa Luxemburg, *Rinascita*, 7 January 1972, no. 1   154

15 The Transition to Socialism, *Problemi del socialismo*, January–March 1977, no. 5   161

PART 4
Marxism, a Science of Revolution
(*Selected Writings Drawn from Lelio Basso,* Socialismo e rivoluzione, *Feltrinelli, Milan, 1980*)

16 Socialism as the Emancipation of Man   173

17 The Scientist and the Revolutionary   186

Bibliography   199
Index   202

Acknowledgements

I want to thank Anna Basso for supporting this project, as well as the wonderful staff at the Fondazione Lelio e Lisli Basso. I also thank the translators Matteo Mandarini and David Broder. This book is dedicated to those who struggle for radical change.

Chiara Giorgi

Introduction

Chiara Giorgi

1   Lelio Basso, a Twentieth-Century Socialist

Lelio Basso is a major, but little known, twentieth-century socialist. His interpretation of classical socialism is at times heretical, combining different elements of Marxist thought (while remaining faithful to it), the intellectual tradition of the labour movement, and early twentieth-century socialism. He is also a Marxist who developed out of an early twentieth-century 'humanist' reading of Marx (which had been advanced in particular by Rodolfo Mondolfo) – one that he would continue to elaborate, with somewhat unorthodox additions and interpretations.

Until his death in 1978 Basso continued to be inspired by Marx's thought, in his political activity and in his passion for intellectual enquiry that was never divorced from 'practice'. In his early years these qualities served to actively engage the young generation of anti-fascist Italians, and subsequently to instigate large-scale theoretical and political endeavours. His peculiar neo-Protestant sympathies in the 1920s, his close ties – personal as well as intellectual and political – with Piero Gobetti, his fascination with the ideas of Rosa Luxemburg, his predilection for history and later for the field of human rights, all these make of Basso a unique activist and intellectual.

Lelio Basso belongs to a 'special' generation who grew up in the aftermath of the First World War; a war that was experienced as a historical watershed: a revolution in behaviours, customs and thought, the real turning point of the century. What bound him to the 'youths' of this generation was a radical view of politics as a pedagogy, as education and culture, as historical consciousness.

Reacting against the reformist deviations prevailing in Second International socialism of the time, his is an uncompromising socialism. His socialism was revolutionary and critical in tone, as materialist in its view of reality as it was 'voluntarist' and subjectivist in its commitment to a new society – one that had yet to be fully imagined and built. His criticism of the philanthropic and paternalistic tendencies of nineteenth-century socialism is accompanied by a vision of the proletarian striving to acquire human dignity (*'proletariato'* was a term used with particular frequency in his early writings).

The theme of working-class consciousness is the fundamental theme of Basso's thought and politics: how the working class becomes aware of its historical role and its constitution as a political entity capable of acting incisively on material processes so as to implement concrete and radical change. What today would be understood in terms of 'subjectivisation' is a constant in Basso's thought, an aspect of his commitments both *in* the party and *for* the party. It is no coincidence that he is most keen to emphasis Marxism's concentration on the proletariat's acquisition of its own class consciousness in opposition to another class. He also highlights 'Marx's dialectical conception', understood as the perennial succession of contradictions and problems to be resolved and overcome, which then progressively generate new and greater problematics. From his early days to his mature years, Basso always stressed Marx's view on the importance of keeping together the development of the contradictions of capitalist production and the organisation of the working class, which he considered the main objective conditions for revolution. Equally, for Basso the working class was the universal subject of liberation, the only class capable of social action, which alone was capable of emancipating society as a whole. He frequently reaffirmed the conscious participation of the working class in processes *already* taking place in capitalist society.

We encounter here one of the key elements of Basso's interpretation of Marx, as well as evidence of his great debt to Rosa Luxemburg, of whom he is one of the major Italian interpreters. He draws upon many aspects of her thought and was particularly influenced by her processual view of revolution. Basso often repeated that, so long as they retained the capacity to proceed to undermine the existing relations of production, there was no incongruity between the daily struggles of the workers to improve their conditions and political actions aimed at overturning capitalism. Hence, for example, his rejection of the superficial distinction between reformers and revolutionaries that in his view was typical of the Second International. For Basso, revolution (he entitled his last work *Socialism and Revolution*) is not the violent and abrupt seizure of power, but – in the light of the materialist conception of history – a historical process which produces a radical transformation in social relations. In this sense, he saw the socialist party as the party of the revolutionary class, a well-organised party able to educate and guide workers, the active vehicle of class-consciousness. With this in mind, in the mid-1930s he directed his efforts at reconstructing the 'party, but in Italy' (as he writes in one of his most famous articles),[1] aiming

---

1 S.D., 'Il partito, ma in Italia (consensi a Veturio)', in *Quaderni di Giustizia e Libertà*, June 1933, 7. S.D. was one of Basso's many pseudonyms.

particularly at the political and cultural education of the younger generation who had been led astray by twenty years of fascism. With these intentions he was to lead the newly founded Socialist Party between January 1947 and 1948, when it was Italy's largest left-wing party.

The originality of Basso's notion of socialism is to be found in three concepts that are of equal power: equality, freedom and dignity. Equally original is his peculiar interpretation of constitutional issues and of the field of tensions of social and civil rights. In Basso, there is an immediate 'discovery' of freedom, linked to a desire for revolution and ethical renewal. This was due to his Marxist education, and it accompanies his neo-Protestant sympathies. From Marx he derives a conception of man immersed in the material conditions of social life, a conception of the human essence as a totality of social relations. From neo-Protestantism he acquires a conception of man's inner freedom: a deep spiritual need that is immanent to the universal human essence and to the ethical significance of Basso's socialism. Even in his earliest writings, Basso's notion of freedom was an expression not of natural rights but of the rights enjoyed by citizens as members of a political community. After the Second World War he reiterated time and again the relation between freedom and participation, opposing to freedom understood as the absence of any prohibitions the inalienable importance of freedom as active involvement in the self-government of a community.

According to Basso's historical analyses, it was the nineteenth century changes that followed from the social pressures and battles of the subaltern classes that led to a critique of the idea that true freedom consists of the autonomy of the individual from the political community. At the same time it led to a new conception of humankind and of freedom in relation to the collective dimension: to the idea that freedom is the point of equilibrium between individuality and sociality. In the post-war years, he developed his own approach to democracy and how best to achieve it: above all it meant actual participation of the popular masses in the running of the economic and social life of the country and their involvement in every institution, every space and form in which new social life, or associated and free living was realised; a democracy as the union of equality and freedom, where workers become aware of their rights and dignity through the experience of conflict and active participation. In the context of the new Italian republic, socialism and democracy are viewed as one and the same. Genuine and profound democracy, the aim of socialism, can only be achieved through it; and it is the working class that plays a leading role in a new experiment in democratic life without losing sight of the ultimate goal of radical transformation. From the mid-1940s onwards, Basso continued to think in terms of building a socialist society as a qualitative leap beyond fascism and its foundation, capitalist society. Although socialism remains, for Basso, the final goal, it will not come about immediately or suddenly, it requires a constant effort to create the concrete conditions for its ultimate triumph. As we said, in his reinterpretation of Marx, Basso combines a revolutionary spirit inspired by a processual view of change with the dialectical unity of the subjective element and objective dynamics of a given historical context, which for him were the key drivers of the transition to socialist society.

2   The Early Writings: Marxism as a Philosophy of Human Action

The generation to which Basso belonged grew up in the 1920s. It experienced the immediate post-war years as the true turning point of the twentieth century. Its attitude was one of moral rebellion against fascism's totalitarianism. The philosophy that could best express this turn was, for Basso, Marxism, a philosophy that would remain his reference point and of which he would be one of the most significant proponents in that troubled period of historical transition.

Rodolfo Mondolfo's 'humanist' interpretation of Marxism was one of the fundamental elements that Prometeo Filodemo (a nickname Basso used in his youth) shared with the generation of young Marxists of the early twentieth century. What was particularly valued in it was its critique of the dominant reformist tendencies of Second International socialism. In the early years of his intellectual life, Basso drew inspiration from the lectures of Ugo Guido Mondolfo, the essays of Rodolfo Mondolfo, his friendship with Piero Gobetti and Gentile's interpretation of Marxism, described as 'idealistic', 'subjectivist and voluntarist'.[2] Increasingly frequent references to philosophy and to action followed 'the long slumber of late nineteenth-century evolutionary and determinist materialism'[3] and were some of the principal elements of a response to the general and prolonged 'crisis of Marxism'.[4] The new reading of Marx is permeated with humanist (and no longer naturalist) historicism and an interpretation of Marxism as a 'philosophy of praxis'. Mondolfo's overcoming of positivism leads to the valorisation of the conscious and voluntary elements in his writings, as it does in those of the young Basso. This new interpretation

---

2   N. Bobbio, note in R. Mondolfo, 'Né materialismo né idealismo ma realismo critico-pratico', in Mondolfo 1975, pp. 260–1.
3   Marramao 1971, p. 273.
4   For more on this crisis and the various responses developed in the broader context, see Laclau and Mouffe 1985.

of Marx as a 'philosophy of human action' (as described by Basso in February 1924)[5] is based on a reassessment of man's ethical and ideal autonomy, and – via Gentile – there lies at its core an activist approach to Marxism as a 'philosophy of praxis'.[6] Basso's early writings reveal the source of this idea, which was first expounded by Gentile and then by Mondolfo, as that of a 'praxis that overturns itself'. The source of the young Basso's 'activist-spontaneist views' is Gentile's erroneous translation of Marx's 'umwälzende Praxis' (third thesis on Feuerbach), which was first taken up by Mondolfo.[7] This concept of a 'praxis that overturns itself' as opposed to Marx's original of 'overturning praxis',[8] or 'praxis that overturns', involves a hypostatisation of the activity of the subject and of the ethical ideal (as well as the primacy of consciousness-formation), which will later result in Mondolfo's and Basso's theories being accused of subjectivist idealism.[9] Despite belonging to this ideological context, which was typical of a specific historical period of Italian and European culture, Basso later distanced himself from his spiritual master (in his review of Mondolfo's book *Sulle orme di Marx*, 1924). The break happens on the basis of the practical ineffectiveness of Mondolfo's doctrine, its ultimate moderation and reformism, which was far from revolutionary. What he had in common with his first teacher, however, was a critical attitude both to 'self-styled revolutionaries' – spontaneists convinced they could establish socialism by force regardless of any objective conditions – and towards the 'collaborationist reformists', who sought to achieve socialism 'by collaborating with the existing regime'. It is precisely this critique that would lead Basso to distance himself from Mondolfo, while both retained a strong affinity with Antonio Labriola.

In late nineteenth-century Italy, Labriola had shed light on the core of Marx's thinking, namely historical materialism (as opposed to naturalistic materialism and idealism). This was seen as a realistic conception of historical processes in their objectivity, an instrument capable of providing a full understanding of historical reality. Labriola saw historical materialism – with the philosophy of

---

5 Prometeo Filodemo, 'Un anno di critica marxista', in *Critica sociale*, 15–29 February 1924, 4, pp. 58–61.
6 Giovanni Gentile (1875–1944), was a neo-Hegelian philosopher whose thinking develops a notion of thought as a 'pure act', which exists never as result but always as practice, always in-becoming.
7 G. Marramao, 'Mondolfo Rodolfo', in Andreucci and Detti (ed.) 1975, p. 527. On Gentile's on the 'reduction of the object to the activity of the subject', see Garin 1955, pp. 230 ff.
8 This is translated as 'revolutionising practice' in the Progress Publishers translation of the 'Theses on Feuerbach', in Marx and Engels 1969, p. 13. In the 'Theses on Feuerbach' in Marx and Engels 1975, p. 4, and in Marx 1992a, p. 422, it is translated simply as 'revolutionary practice'.
9 On Gentile's idealistic interpretation of Marx's words, see also Favilli 1996, pp. 273 ff.

praxis at its 'heart'[10] – as a 'philosophy of life', an understanding of reality, of the hardness and historicity of things, of their generation and becoming (he frequently refers to the *genetic* conception and method).[11] Labriola interpreted praxis not as pure activity but as 'work done by the *determinate*-historical subject upon an objective structure of *determinate* relations'. He saw praxis as 'an element arising from *within theory* and its entire *genetic-morphological* dimension'. Thus, the philosophy of praxis was conceived as a 'general world-view' and conception of history from the standpoint of the proletariat; that is, 'from the point of view of *work*, as an action exerted on nature by history and by its major force of production (the working class)'.[12] Theoretically, Labriola's polemic was levelled against positivist and idealist historians and, politically, at the founders of the Socialist party. Labriola's revolutionary conception of the historical process had led him to criticise the moderation and reformism of the early Italian socialists, and to reject the demagogy of those who thought the revolution could take place suddenly and in the absence of objective conditions. Basso was to adopt similar ideas in the early 1920s, in writings that were full for praise for Labriola.[13]

Basso will often refer to the revolutionary aspect of Labriola's Marxism, emphasising the centrality of subjectivity (the need for the working class to acquire consciousness and *autonomy*).[14] For this reason, Basso, like Gramsci, thinks that Labriola should be circulated amongst working-class forces: for this generation, Labriola was a fundamental resource to be exploited in the political and intellectual battles of the time, and his thinking was a key element in the interpretation of Marx's philosophy as a philosophy of praxis.[15]

Notwithstanding this background, Basso's subjectivist interpretation of Marxism – his humanist approach to Marxism and socialism – divorce him from some fundamental precepts expounded by Labriola (who, despite his limits,[16] showed a deep understanding of *Capital* and, crucially, incorporated into

---

10   Garin 1965, p. liii.
11   'Discorrendo di socialismo e di filosofia', in Labriola 1976.
12   G. Marramo 1971, pp. 111 and 118.
13   L. Basso, 'Sulle orme di Marx', in *Critica Sociale*, 15–30 April 1924, 8, pp. 123–7.
14   Cf. for example Labriola, 'Discorrendo di socialismo e di filosofia'.
15   As Garin writes (in Garin 1965, p. lxiv), Labriola's legacy lies above all in his idea that 'political struggle is not detached from theoretical reflection'. Thus, a generation of young people 'began to react to Croce's and Gentile's reductionism', rediscovering Labriola and, 'through the personal experience of political struggle combined with philosophy, they rediscovered the sense of the philosophy of praxis'.
16   Marramao notes that Labriola remains a Second International Marxist, lacking a 'vision of the autonomous movement of the class *within* capital, an interpretation of class struggle

his own thinking some of Marx's postulates that revolutionised the preceding philosophical tradition, including his own 'new materialism').[17] In this sense, it has been said that Basso, in common with other young intellectuals of the time, did not fully appreciate Labriola's contributions to Marxism, being still rooted in the prevailing idealism and 'Gentile's actualism'.[18]

Basso's early Marxist works are intent on giving new meaning to the idealist source of Marx's writings, which was to be found in Hegel. His aim was to curb the excesses of early twentieth-century positivism by opposing to it a conception of Marxism revitalised by ethical idealism and a spiritual tension that would be able to guide young socialists to confront and overcome their inner limits and those of the nation. Basso makes himself into the proponent of a philosophy of socialism based on this reading of Marxism.

The philosophy he advocates is of a new kind, stemming from the actions of the proletariat 'fighting for its emancipation'. It is a philosophy that can satisfy the needs of new social forces, developing in tandem with the new working-class consciousness because, as Basso says, 'socialism must not only be an outlet for the conscious proletarian revolution but also the realisation of proletarian philosophical thought'. It is they alone who can lay claim to their own philosophy. This reference to the idealist foundation of Marxism is a constant refrain of Basso's early writings. He never misses an opportunity to refer to Hegel (against Kant) and especially Hegelian dialectics, which Marx had first developed into a unified vision of subject and object, of nature and humanity, and of the individual's social rootedness. Neither – writes Basso – 'Kant's abstract individual, nor Hegel's Absolute Spirit, but the social individual, whose consciousness is reducible to the ensemble of social relations'.[19] Basso goes on to claim that the union of subject and object is the 'work of praxis', understood here as human activity and consciousness, which in turn

---

as being antithesis of the system' (Marramao 1971, p. 121). While it is true that we find in him a certain '"fetishism of the forces of production", connected to a certain tendency to "mechanism" and an insistence ... on the *technico*-material moment of production' (p. 117), this is not accompanied by any political indications, or any positive articulation of the link between theory and praxis. However, Labriola shows a much more advanced understanding of Marxism than many social democrats of the times (Turati, Kautsky, Bernstein), though his contributions to Marxism are nowhere near as fundamental as those made by Lenin. See pp. 80 ff., in relation to Tronti's *Operai e capitale*.

17 Balibar 1995, p. 41. See also Mezzadra 2018, pp. 27 ff.
18 Luporini 1973, p. 1604. As pointed out (Garin 1965, cit., p. lxi) it was Gentile who first saw praxis as a pure act, 'uncoupling human action from any *hardness* of things (from all "materialism")'.
19 Prometeo Filodemo, 'Valore morale del socialismo', in *Critica sociale*, 1–15 January 1925, 1, pp. 25–8.

is the ensemble of 'social relations directed at the production process' (the reference to the sixth of the *Theses on Feuerbach* seems to be quite clear here, although for Marx it was human essence, and not consciousness that was 'the ensemble of the social relations').[20] Moreover, Basso sees Marx as 'the Teacher and Educator of proletarian consciousness',[21] and Marxism as the expression of an activist and uncompromising philosophy, while historical materialism is – and remains in these early writings – above all a *philosophy* of history. In an article with the evocative title of 'Marxismo e liberazione proletaria' (Marxism and proletarian liberation), published in *La Rivoluzione Liberale* in April 1925, Basso clearly outlines the development of his Marxism and highlights the centrality of class struggle – 'a general principle of history' – from which alone can come a new kind of ethics, one which 'from the Marxist standpoint' does not lie outside concrete human action. Through class struggle, which negates – because it overcomes – capitalist society, the proletariat 'becomes conscious of itself' and achieves freedom.[22]

This emphasis on the need for working-class consciousness, for the proletariat (and humanity as a whole) to achieve autonomy, and moral and spiritual dignity, as well as his focus on the importance of freedom, will draw Basso to neo-Protestantism. From the very beginning, socialism appeared to him as a drive for human redemption and liberation that is capable of expressing new values that are antithetical to the bourgeois world, morally as well as economically. He is particularly receptive to socialism's emancipatory charge: its role as theoretical and practical instrument for the acquisition of new working-class consciousness and, more generally, as being foundational to humanity's road to liberation.

Members of this young generation of intellectuals shared an ethical and political interest in historical events as well as a sense of the impossibility of a theory that was not also a practice, and a commitment to the construction of 'a new political culture'. There was much 'material' to work upon: the interpretation of events since the October Revolution; the 'crisis of the liberal state in Italy, and the prospects for working-class struggles within this crisis'; and new definitions of socialism and liberalism, the 'revision of [existing] cultural and philosophical currents'. All of this was subjected to 'impatient research'[23] by this young generation that was intent on involving the old 'masters' in this process (Croce, Gentile, Salvemini, and many more), reinterpreting them, distancing themselves from them, but unable to take their place or escape them.

---

20   Marx 1975, p. 5.
21   'Termine di paragone', in *Conscientia*, 9 May 1925, 19, p. 1. See Part One of this book.
22   'Marxismo e liberazione proletaria', in *La Rivoluzione Liberale*, 26 April 1925, 17, p. 69.
23   Cf. C. Luporini, 'Il marxismo', cit., p. 1590.

In the years of fascism's rise and consolidation, Basso strengthens his anti-fascist activity and consolidates his Marxist orientation. In 1925 he defends his undergraduate dissertation at the University of Milan – *La concezione della libertà in Marx* (*The concept of freedom in Marx*) – in which he develops some key elements of his own theoretical thinking. In it we find a reappraisal of Hegel, which is contrasted with positivist interpretations of Marx. He also lays claim to a conception of freedom that lies 'within man', as a product of 'human consciousness'.[24] His reference point remains the class struggle and the need for political action that can transform society by leveraging the highpoint of Marx's contradiction between the forces and the relations of production. For Basso the proletariat that is educated by the most 'intransigent class struggle' becomes the bearer of a new kind of freedom, one which is no longer abstract and fragmented, like that of the *citoyen* criticised by Marx, but is 'general' and inclusive, encompassing all concrete aspects of man's life. What Italy needs is 'a love of freedom', and this can only come about 'through a resolute spiritual education, a sense of human dignity' that is drawn from the most intransigent of class struggles.[25]

It is this pronounced sensibility for the formative processes of consciousness, within a vision of 'Marxist revolution' as a process of 'spiritual regeneration',[26] that led Basso to a keen interest in neo-Protestantism. In a number of articles he highlighted the link between 'Marxist revolution' and 'Protestant revolution', their common search for truth and action as a formative process, thereby championing a more comprehensive need for renewal.[27] In an important article entitled 'La riforma e il pensiero europeo: Marx' (Reformation and European thought: Marx), Basso sees Marxist revolution 'as redemption, as palingenetic effort', and class struggle as an 'awareness of the tragic split ... that everyone reflects internally that is translated into a working faith, into a tenacious will to overcome oneself by overcoming the object, in a religious effort of renewal, of purification'. He concludes that a conception such as this could not develop from 'a soil that had not previously been fertilised by the Protestant Reformation'.[28] Finally, in 'Difesa del protestantesimo' (Defence of Protestantism) – in which he makes a scathing attack on reformist socialists like Claudio

---

24   Prometeo Filodemo, 'Le fonti della Libertà', in *La Rivoluzione Liberale*, 17 May 1925, 20, pp. 81–2.
25   Ibid.
26   Prometeo Filodemo, 'Rivoluzione protestante', in *Critica sociale*, 1–15 July 1925, 13, pp. 153–4.
27   Ibid.
28   'La riforma e il pensiero europeo: Marx', in *Conscientia*, 25 July 1925, 30, p. 2. See Part One.

Treves, outlining conflicts that are not only personal but that express the difference between two generations that developed in different spiritual environments – he asserts that 'the Reformation we have in mind is not the mechanical repetition of the Reformation of Luther and Calvin', but 'a continuous process of negation and overcoming of Catholicism':

> Luther and Calvin, like Hegel and Marx, are the terms of this process. Therefore, our Protestantism is at one with our Marxism.[29]

In his opinion the revolutionary significance of Marxism, equal to that of the Reformation, lay in the autonomy acquired through the process of proletarian emancipation. The proletariat is indeed the 'autonomous class' that struggles for economic and moral redemption with only its own resources to rely upon. Basso's neo-Protestantism was always aimed at promoting socialism, or rather a 'faith in socialism' that can create a new world, one no longer dominated by the particularism of the bourgeois era, one that can uplift 'the downtrodden masses so that they may achieve their hard fought human dignity and state it proudly'.

3 Mature Writings: Marxism, the Science of Revolution

Basso continued to develop his interpretation of Marxism throughout his political and intellectual life, systemising his thoughts in a major posthumous publication, tellingly entitled *Socialismo e rivoluzione* (Socialism and Revolution) (1980). From the middle of the 1960s, when he became less involved in party politics, his study of Marxism became increasingly intense and achieved a certain degree of completion, though not to the extent that he would have wished. In this period he further explores issues already present in the years of his development as a Marxist, focusing in particular on the 'transition to socialism', the concept of revolution, the theory of the 'two contradictory logics', alienation, and free human development.

In one of his most significant later Marxist articles, Basso writes:

> It should be stressed, explicitly, that what distinguishes a real revolutionary from a reformist is not … the struggle for the violent seizure of power but the capacity for subjective intervention in the objective processes of

---

29 'Difesa del protestantesimo', in *Il Quarto Stato*, 19 June 1926, 13, p. 3.

the development of society, the use of the socialising forces of production against the privatising relations of production.[30]

In restating his reading of Marx, Basso combines a view of revolution in which change is seen as a process, with a dialectical unity of the subjective components and objective dynamics in a given historical context; these he sees as deciding factors in the transition from a capitalist to a socialist society. On several occasions he distinguishes various periods of Marx's activity and thought, identifying the third and final period as the one he feels the greatest affinity to. As regards the first period, which includes the formative years and the drafting of the *Manifesto*, Basso criticises Marx for his focus on the violent seizure of power, which Basso ascribes to the influence of the French Revolution. Not only does Basso consider this perspective insufficiently 'reflective', too concerned with giving an immediate response to the political events of the time, but he argued that Marx made a serious error of historical judgement, ignoring his own most valuable contribution, namely the dialectical method.[31]

Indeed, taking up the theme of a great interpreter of Marx, Rosa Luxemburg (whose works Basso started translating in the 1920s),[32] he stresses the fact that the heart of Marx's entire doctrine is 'the dialectical-materialist method of examining the problems of social life'.[33] What Basso values most in Marx is this reading of reality, which alone can bring about a socialist revolution against capitalist development and hence allow us to see the contradictions within the historical process and the *need* to overcome them. In this theoretical and practical setting – where we can find the legacy of his early criticisms of self-styled revolutionaries and reformist collaborators – revolution is not a single sudden clash between the proletariat and capitalism, 'an act of a single given moment', 'a definitive violent confrontation'; it is rather 'something that is inherent in capitalist development itself, when the contradictions and tensions' it gener-

---

30 L. Basso, 'L'utilizzazione della legalità nella fase di transizione al socialismo', in *Problemi del socialismo*, 1971, 5–6, p. 843.
31 Cf. 'Appunti su Lelio Basso interprete di Marx', in Guastini 1981, pp. 117 ff.
32 As will be seen, Basso begins translating the writings of Rosa Luxemburg in exile, which he then continued to do throughout his life. See: L. Basso, 'Rosa Luxemburg', in *Il Quarto Stato*, 15 January 1949, 2, pp. 3–5 (see Part Three of this book); Luxemburg 1967; 'Il contributo di Rosa Luxemburg allo sviluppo del pensiero di Marx', in Basso 1976a (see on this book, Part Three); 'Socialismo e rivoluzione nella concezione di Rosa Luxemburg', in Basso 1971, 1, pp. 40–65; Luxemburg 1971; Basso 1973a, pp. 5–20; Basso (ed.) 1977; and various other articles published in newspapers. See also G. Bonacchi, 'Lelio Basso e Rosa Luxemburg: due battaglie minoritarie?', in Ajmeni (ed.) 1981, pp. 177 ff.
33 L. Basso, 'Introduzione', in Luxemburg 1967, p. 40.

ates reach their peak.[34] According to Basso, Marx's complex vision of historical change is developed in a number of stages: after an initial revolutionary voluntarism, he discovers through a careful study of the 1848 revolutions that revolution can only happen if the objective conditions are in place, i.e., if the existing regime and ruling class are in a state of crisis, having exhausted their positive historical function. Under capitalist conditions, when there is a conflict between the forces of production and relations of production – the former a socialising force, the latter a privatising one – then we have the objective prerequisites for change. During these years, between 1850 and the founding of the International, Marx writes, among other things, the 'Preface to the *Critique of Political Economy*' (1859), a text repeatedly referred to by Basso. According to Basso, in this text Marx recognises that the bourgeoisie still has the strength to consolidate its power, going on to illustrate the dynamics that would be needed to bring about 'revolutionary upheaval'.

Basso freely quotes from Marx:

> No social formation is ever destroyed before all the productive forces that it is able to contain have developed, and new superior relations of production never replace it before the material conditions for their existence have matured within the womb of the old society. Mankind thus only ever sets itself those tasks that it is able to solve, since closer examination will always show that that same task arises only when the material conditions for its realisation are already present or at least in the course of formation.[35]

In the dialectical conception of the historical process, the objective conditions for a new society arise when there is a conflict, rather than a correspondence, between the ever-expanding forces of production, 'because man has ever greater needs', and the existing social relations. At this point there is a need for new social relations that correspond to the new mode of production in which the advanced level of the forces of production is expressed. Thus, a new social order arises slowly and gradually within the old, overturning it and replacing it.[36]

While it is clear that, as they develop, the forces of production come into conflict with a determinate set of relations of production, objectively direct-

---

34 L. Basso, 'Introduzione', in Luxemburg 1967, p. 97.
35 L. Basso, 'Marxismo e democrazia', in *Problemi del socialismo*, 1958, 1, p. 16. Basso here confuses the dates of the 'Preface' (1859) and the 'Introduction' (1857).
36 Basso 1980, p. 109.

ing change towards a new social formation, the decisive factor is subjective intervention. The objective formation of the conditions for the new, superior relations of production must be accompanied by a process of subjective awareness, wherein the more advanced classes begin to realise the role they are to play. This further step forward is to be found, according to Basso, in Marx's *Herr Vogt* (1860). Basso frequently referred to this book, though it is not often visited by Marxist scholars, and forms a reference point for his views on the formation of class-consciousness in the workers' movement, an issue that absorbed him from his early writings. It is the duty of the workers' movement to exploit the contradictions of the system, to participate in 'the objective revolutionary processes and direct them towards a socialist outcome'.[37] For Basso, as for the Marx cited by Basso, the proletariat must act in parallel with the 'spontaneous forces of capitalist society stemming from the social development of the forces of production'.[38] Although Basso bases his arguments on Marx's fundamental and well-known 1859 Preface, an element of Basso's youthful idealism still seems to linger.

As we have seen, what was missing in the young Basso – and in his intellectual group – was a full awareness of the novelty of Marx's materialism. While accepting Marx's criticism of human activity not being conceived as *objective* activity in the First Thesis on Feuerbach,[39] they had in fact fallen into analogous errors. They had taken the element of subjectivity and made it absolute, conceiving 'the significance of "revolutionary", of "practical-critical", activity' in voluntarist terms. Although from Marx they certainly learnt that the proletariat was the practical subject that would dissolve the existing order of things and, in the process, would change itself – by changing the world – they remained within the perspective of idealism.[40] What is missing in the view of this generation of early twentieth-century Marxists to which Basso

---

37   Basso 1980, p. 122.
38   Ibid. See L. Basso, 'Marx e i problemi della transizione al socialismo', in *Ipotesi*, 1978, 3–4, pp. 29–33.
39   Marx says that Feuerbach 'does not conceive human activity itself as objective activity ... he regards the theoretical attitude as the only genuinely human attitude ... Hence he does not grasp the significance of "revolutionary", of "practical-critical", activity'.
40   Balibar 1995, pp. 26–7. It is no coincidence, says Balibar (pp. 65–7), that Marx derived his new materialism from a fundamental theoretical innovation: the 'genesis of subjectivity (a form of determinate historical subjectivity) as part (and counterpart) of the social world of objectivity'. Subjectivity loses its transcendental nature and becomes a result of the social process. The concept of subjectivity is reformulated by Marx (in *The German Ideology* and *Capital*), though a reconsideration of the constitution of social objectivity (this is where he introduces a new element 'into the discussion of the relations between "subjectification", "subjection" and "subjectivity"').

belongs, is what for Marx (the Marx of *The German Ideology* and *Capital*) is encompassed by the identification of theory with the production of consciousness, that is of *praxis* and *poiêsis* (*free action* and *necessary action*).[41]

More than a gap – that which characterises Marx's reflections on the 'production of subjectivity'[42] – this is a reading of Marx's texts that aims above all to emphasise and actualise *praxis*, as that which is capable of realising change through the activist negation of the old world. It is the subjective aspect, which establishes itself on the grasp of social processes (and dynamics) that it constitutes and produces. The crucial point concerns the genesis of subjectivity vis-à-vis the social world of objectivity and the sphere of production in relation to the subjective and political choices of the historical referents of the project of change (the proletariat as a universal class). In terms of class-consciousness, it involves 'installing the materialism/idealism dilemma – the perennial question of their difference – at the very heart of the theory of the proletariat and of its privileged historical role'.[43]

What is critically important is a specific intellectual development that aims to privilege the education of the exploited masses, their acquisition of class-consciousness, as well as the active involvement of the antagonist class in relation to the concrete opportunities present in the material context. The coexistence of the two terms of the revolutionary process is interpreted as man's subversive activities vis-à-vis the objective conditions.

This focus on the processes of subjectification – understood in terms of the formation of class consciousness, of the construction of subjectivity and the organisation of the working class – influences Basso's reading of Marx's *Capital* (and the *Grundrisse*). In his analysis of the links between the forces of production and the relations of production, Basso seems to overlook – as did Labriola[44] – the complex co-implications and feedback of capitalist development and the subjective aspects (labour and capital) which determine the *social relation* of capital.[45] The key issue here is the 'production of subjectiv-

---

41 As Balibar notes: it is in his 'revolutionary thesis that *praxis* constantly passes over into *poiêsis* and vice versa' (Balibar 1995, p. 41) that Marx goes beyond the radical distinction between the one and the another which is characteristic of traditional philosophy, thus ridding himself of this distinction between *free* action and *necessary* action.
42 For an analysis of Marx in these terms, see Mezzadra 2018.
43 Balibar 1995, cit., p. 27.
44 Marramao 1971, cit., p. 117.
45 As Marx wrote, capital 'is not a *thing* but a *social relation* between persons established by the instrumentality of things'. This fundamental assertion is found in the first book of *Capital*.

ity', linked to capital's valorisation process that 'produces the subjective figures of the capitalist and the wage-labourer' which appear 'at the same time as its precondition'.[46]

3.1 The Influence of Rosa Luxemburg

Rosa Luxemburg is, without question, central to Basso's Marxist theoretical elaborations. And indeed, the next step in his reflections is to be found in the well-known theory of the 'two contradictory logics'. Marx's most original contribution, which gives the subaltern class the tools for its revolutionary praxis is, according to Basso, his identification of the conflict objectively present in society between two opposing tendencies. The first one expands progressive forces, in the direction of a '*socialising* logic of the development of the forces of production'; the second one stems from the logic of profit and conservation, and is intent on resisting and blocking the development of socialising forces. The workers' movement was tasked with responding to this 'dialectical tension', to consciously take up a position within the antagonistic logic and use 'this objective drive to bit-by-bit realise achievements that can be grasped' by it.[47]

From this stems Basso's new way of considering democracy and its tools, the law and the organisation of the state. As we said, Basso believes that Marx's greatest achievements as a scientist of revolution are to be found in his third and final period, when he comes to the realisation that the political struggle of the working class must make use of the new instruments of bourgeois democracy, which can lead to a peaceful conquest of power. Basso explains that the democratic institutions themselves were either obtained through struggles from the ruling class, or were the result of an often painful compromise. Hence democracy gives workers an 'effective, albeit partial, way of participating in power' and of limiting the bourgeoisies' conservative reaction.[48] This leads him to make an assessment of democracy's legal and institutional terrain in the light of Marx's analyses. For if one considers the Marxist doctrine of the state in the more general terms of the history of class struggle and of the materialist conception of the relationship between the economic and social structures, we must arrive at a consideration of the legal and political superstructures. As Basso explains:

---

46 Mezzadra 2018, p. 37. For an expanded discussion of Basso's reading of Marx see C. Giorgi, 2018.
47 L. Basso, 'Giustizia e potere. La lunga via al socialismo', in *QUALEgiustizia*, 1971, 11–12, pp. 648–9.
48 Basso 1976b, p. 23.

political power and state organization tend to reflect the structural aspects of society and therefore also the balance of forces between classes as they are gradually modified ... under the pressure of the oppressed classes' struggle for emancipation.[49]

The development of relations of force open up new opportunities for the subaltern classes on the legal-institutional terrain as well. The state is not just an instrument by which the ruling class exerts its dominion, a monolithic block that is independent of social relations of force and their modifications, but also a tool that can be used by the subaltern classes to achieve social transformation. Equally law, which is commonly conceived as an inert and passive instrument of the bourgeoisie, is an expression of society as a whole with 'its struggles, its divisions, which includes the working class' and its antagonisms.[50]

Basso's idea of transformation is based on a reality that he believes 'is necessarily contradictory' and that uses 'an aspect of the contradiction that is found in society, in the institutions and, consequently, also in human consciousness, as a starting point for renewal'.[51] It is not by chance that Basso quotes a passage from *Capital* as the epigraph to his book *Socialism and Revolution*:

> The only royal road along which a mode of production and the social organisation that corresponds to it travel en route to their dissolution and their transformation, is that of the historical development of their immanent antagonisms. This is the secret of the historical movement that doctrinaires, optimists or socialists, do not want to understand.[52]

Basso harks back to the Marx of *Capital*, the 'mature' Marx, who in his opinion observed the struggles of English workers and saw the advantages that could be gained by the conscious intervention of the working classes through their main 'instruments' (unions, cooperatives, party, International, but also universal suffrage, parliamentary participation, factory legislation, structural reforms). It is not the strategy used by 'Blanquist type revolutionaries, who aim to directly seize power' but calls instead for the 'mediation of structural reforms', which

---

49 Basso 1976b, p. 24. Also 'Società e Stato nella dottrina di Marx', in Basso 1971, 13–14, pp. 115–48 (See Part Three of this book) and Basso's 'La natura dialettica dello Stato secondo Marx', in Carandini (ed.) 1977, pp. 17–35. See Part Three of this book.
50 L. Basso, 'Giustizia e potere. La lunga via al socialismo', in *QUALEgiustizia*, 1971, 11–12, pp. 648–9.
51 Ibid., p. 641.
52 Basso quotes from the 1872–5 French edition of *Capital*. See Basso 1980, pp. 11 and 102.

can lay 'the foundations of socialism'. Equally, however, it excludes reformism 'understood as the mere accumulation of reforms that are not directed towards a socialist project, not consistently embedded within a coherent picture of transformation, but that aim merely at correcting or mitigating the inescapable evils of capitalist society'.[53]

Here we find a key passage in Basso's interpretation of Marx, one which owes a great debt to Luxemburg. Starting with what he considers the main value of Marxism, i.e. the dialectical method, embedded 'in the heart of class struggle', one comes to grasp that 'the socialist future is already there in the capitalist present', in the awareness that 'the true essence of each moment appears only if we consider that moment within the continuity of history', what Basso identifies as the 'totality of the historical process'. This well-known concept of 'totality' is central to Luxemburg's thinking.

This conception of totality as a method, totality that exists as an awareness of the unity of each historical moment with the totality of the historical process – according to Lukács' interpretations of the early 1920s – [54] was immediately taken over by Basso. In particular, the standpoint of totality (totality as a method) is to be found in the notion that all partial phenomena are moments of the whole. The point of view of the totality establishes the need of social revolution, of 'the total transformation of the totality of society'.[55]

In this interpretation of totality (which can be found in the young Basso, as well as in the adult who carefully studied Marx's entire works, with particular attention to the social formation as a totality and to the totality of the historical process in dialectical terms),[56] the proletariat is the universal class, the subject of transformation – thinking and operating on 'a different level from the existing order'.[57] At the same time, the party is the form taken

---

53 Basso 1980, p. 229.
54 'Rosa Luxemburg als Marxist', in *Kommunismus*, 15 January 1921, 1–2 ('The Marxism of Rosa Luxemburg', in Lukács 1971, pp. 27 ff.).
55 'The Marxism of Rosa Luxemburg', in Lukács 1971, p. 51.
56 As Basso points out (Basso 1980, p. 110), the dialectical conception of the totality of the historical process includes both the existing state of things, and its negation, i.e. the process of both formation and dissolution. See the chapter on *revolutionary praxis* in Basso 1980, pp. 103 ff., especially the sections significantly entitled 'Formazione sociale come totalità, Unità di totalità e processo genetico, Il sorgere delle nuove formazioni sociali: concezione dialettica della totalità del processo storico' (Social formation as a totality, unity of totality and the genetic process, the emergence of new social formations: dialectical conception of the totality of the historical process).
57 L. Basso, 'Sulle orme di Marx'.

by proletarian *class* consciousness. Hence Basso's constant focus on both the organisation of the party, the ethical vehicle for proletarian struggle, and the relationship between reform and revolution, i.e. the relationship between the single goals of everyday struggle and the perspective of revolution – the 'final goal'. Basso's commitment to the totality of the process means that he never separates 'the single moments and the single objectives of everyday struggle from the overall vision of the struggle itself, the daily struggle for reform from the prospect of revolution, from the final goal'.[58] Rosa Luxemburg had criticised reformism and revisionism in favour of 'revolutionary Marxism', the essence of which involved grasping contradictions within the historical process, that is to say, understanding it in its totality in view of its overcoming, with 'the triumph of socialism'.[59] Basso's political activity, especially after World War II, centred on this interpretation of Marxism: emphasising the need to link the daily struggle to the final goal, preventing the former from degenerating into reformism and thereby becoming part of an authentic revolutionary process. The long-standing dispute between the interpreters of Marxism as everyday reformist activity, passively awaiting the revolution, and those who interpreted Marxism as subjectivism and adventurism is resolved in the dialectical unity of daily action and final goal.[60]

3.2 *From Capitalist Dehumanisation to Complete Socialist Humanisation*

The other recurrent 'classical' theme in Basso's reading of Marx concerns his reflections on alienation, or more *specifically* 'dehumanisation' in relation to the 'human condition' and free human development.[61] Basso sees the 'problem of alienation as one of "dehumanisation"', with reference to all those phenom-

---

58 L. Basso, 'Introduzione' a R. Luxemburg 1967, p. 29. Equally, in *Socialismo e rivoluzione* (Basso 1980, p. 230), Basso says that it is only in reference to the totality of the revolutionary process, i.e. 'the root causes of social phenomena found in the very heart of capitalism, that single partial objectives, single reforms acquire revolutionary value, thus leading to the ultimate goal of revolution'.

59 Ibid.

60 Basso 1980, p. 159. As was recently noted (Luca Basso 2012), in principle Marx sees no conflict between the daily struggles of workers to better their working conditions (for example, shorter working hours) and political actions aimed at overturning capitalism. The determining factor for Marx is whether the reforms achieved by the workers' struggle corresponds to a practice that can change and overturn the existing relations of production. See also Mezzadra 2018, pp. 73–4.

61 Basso states explicitly that he wishes to analyse the problem of alienation in terms of 'dehumanisation', which is nevertheless theoretically and politically in line with his analysis of Marx.

ena that involve the 'reversal of the relation of producer to product'. He is particularly focused on highlighting the dynamic that underlies this reversal: where the product is no longer subordinated to the producer, the product is 'separated from [the producer], is objectified in the form of an autonomous entity which opposes and dominates him, preventing him from achieving full self-realisation'.[62]

This reversal of relations is evident in both religion and work. Though different, these phenomena both contain conditions of 'dehumanisation', in that they can transform man 'from being the conscious agent of a process with an end in view to being the object of a mysterious process'.[63] Capitalism is responsible for this reversal and for generating the greatest degree of dehumanisation, as described by Marx in *Capital*, while the revolution has the task of re-humanisation.[64] It is not by chance that Basso focuses on what he calls political alienation, in its quintessential form of bureaucracy. Bureaucracy develops into 'a separate body, estranged from the community', above it and in opposition to it. It is, in short, a case of Marx's demystification of the mechanism whereby 'every common interest is immediately severed from society, opposed to it as a higher, *general* interest', snatched from the activity of society's members and presented as a separate objectivity (and transformed, as stated by Marx in the *18th Brumaire* and quoted literally by Basso, into 'an object of government activity').[65] Political power constitutes the space for individual participation to the community and to social activities, which is expropriated, alienated, and opposed to the individuals themselves in the form of a 'sovereign', a prince, or an abstraction of the state personified by those in power. And as Marx explained this alienated participatory moment is only apparently restored in representative forms: electoral participation in a society based on reified and anonymous relations is but a caricature of participation in social life.[66]

The dynamics of political alienation or dehumanisation that are present in political representation are the same as those found in commodity fetishism – the very 'reversal produced by capitalism' – transforming 'living labour into dead labour' in appropriation, exploitation, and the valorisation of the sur-

---

62　Basso 1980, p. 59.
63　Basso 1980, p. 62.
64　Basso 1980, p. 72. One of the chief reasons for Basso's favourable reception in Germany in the 1970s would seem to lie in his affinity with some of the themes dear to the Frankfurt School.
65　K. Marx, *The Eighteenth Brumaire of Louis Bonaparte*, in Marx and Engels 1975–2005, vol. 11, p. 186.
66　Basso 1980, p. 68.

plus generated by 'living workers'. It is this dehumanisation mechanism that Basso wishes to stress in Marx's analysis of surplus labour and surplus value: which 'by stripping workers of their control over the production process, transforms living labour into dead labour, "fetishises" commodities, "reifies" human relationships, and tends to perpetuate them so as to safeguard and consolidate the dominion and oppression of capital, of dead labour over living workers'.[67] Pursuing this current in Marx's thought, throughout *Socialismo e rivoluzione* Basso focuses on the many passages – in *Capital* and elsewhere (especially the *Grundrisse*) – that deal with dehumanising processes of 'every aspect of the workers'. Echoing the pages on commodity fetishism, on the origins of capitalism, and on the function and the effects of the introduction of machines, Basso comes to what he considers the heart of Marx's analysis of capitalism: 'a historical process that has its roots in the social formation that preceded it and begets the social formation that will follow'. The contradictoriness of the system means that 'on the one hand capitalism has produced the greatest degree of dehumanisation, while on the other it has fulfilled a historical task of primary importance', laying the foundations for a complete humanisation. Basso identifies these foundations especially in the socialisation of labour and the reduction made possible in working hours by science and technology. Social work and free time are the conditions for moving on to the next stage, the communist stage, whose 'distinctive feature' is precisely humanisation, 'achieved by means of the conscious control of the process of production, creation and self-creation'. Re-humanisation, therefore, is achieved by planned 'conscious control in accordance with a plan', to the 'realisation of a project' and 'praxis's work towards an end'.[68] Basso argues that now that capitalism has created 'the conditions for social, collective production', it is now necessary to gain 'the collective control of social (and not just individual) life'.[69]

Here the emphasis is again firmly placed on the importance of demystifying *consciousness*, liberating it 'from the enslavement brought about by the reversal of producer-product relations'. Through these stages (including the phase of 'capitalist hell' and the experience of class struggle), we come to grasp what for Marx – in Basso's view – is the nature of the new 'communist or socialist society': the 'conscious reconstruction of human society', or the 'effective suppression of ... the self-alienation of man'. It is because of this 'real *appropriation* of

---

67 Basso 1980, p. 72.
68 Basso 1980, pp. 75, 92, 87.
69 Basso 1980, p. 91.

human essence', this 'complete return of man to himself', assigned to the realm of freedom, to communist society, that Basso is led to refer frequently to the Paris Commune and to focus on the various moments of the *revolutionary process*.[70]

One of the most impassioned speeches Basso made in the 1970s is dedicated precisely to the Paris Commune. He saw it as a significant revolt against the early manifestations of capitalism's typical tendency to destroy man's world, isolating her from society and reducing humanity to a simple instrument of a distant and extraneous power. Conversely, the Parisian experience also highlights the message of 'autonomy', the 'exaltation of personality as a liberation from all forms of oppression, and as the concrete and effective capacity for self-management' – of 'participation' and 'responsibility'.[71]

The deepest significance of the Commune, as the 'government of the working class',[72] lies in its 'effort to create a society on a human scale', where we all share in 'a group, in a community, in our tangible personal relations with other human beings'. This is the best way to counter the spread of the 'anonymous and impersonal relations of the market', a 'system of anonymous and reified relations'.[73]

Similarly, analysing 'the leap from the realm of necessity to the realm of freedom', Basso emphasises the condition that he believes will be reached through socialist revolution: where all men will have the opportunity 'to control the forces of production together, to build their future together, each individual developing according to their own abilities, to in short overturn the dehumanising process that capitalism is currently imposing to its greatest degree'.[74]

In the same way as for Marx, the goal is the realm of freedom, where 'personality can be developed as an end in itself'. For Basso communist society and socialism exist as one, with no temporal differentiation.[75]

---

70   Basso 1980, pp. 94 ff. Basso cites from Marx's *Economic and Philosophic Manuscripts of 1844*, MECW 3, p. 296. For Basso's analysis of the various moments of revolutionary dynamics and the strategy of the revolutionary process, see chapters three and seven of Basso 1980.
71   L. Basso, 'La Comune di Parigi, Comune' (1972), now in Sala (ed.) 2005, pp. 190 ff.
72   The complete definition given by Marx of the Commune is that it is 'essentially a working class government, the product of the struggle of the producing against the appropriating class, the political form at last discovered under which to work out the economical emancipation of labor'. See K. Marx, *The Civil War in France*, MECW 22.
73   Basso, *La Comune di Parigi*, in Sala (ed.) 2005.
74   Basso 1980, p. 99.
75   Basso 1980, p. 98. See Giorgi 2015a, pp. 149–64.

4 Strategy and Revolutionary Praxis

As we have already outlined, Basso sees the revolution as a process. In *Socialismo e rivoluzione* he illustrates what, in his reading of Marx, is one of the most decisive elements of revolutionary strategy: the 'intervention of the labour movement in the development of capitalist contradictions', in the conflict between the two contradictory logics discussed above.[76] What we need, says Basso, is:

> a long term effort, a long march through the contradictions of society that are present everywhere, not only in the factory where they are most visible, but also in all the crucial areas of social life, in all institutions and in all superstructures because they form the immanent and irrepressible contradictions of capitalism that are reflected in all its forms. They must be tackled everywhere and defeated by the workers' movement through an antagonistic spirit and by implementing the alternative solutions provided by socialist society.[77]

As the fundamental aim of socialism is to help alienated human beings gain control of the process of social production (i.e. the 'transformation of alienated men into free, conscious and responsible builders of a common future'),[78] this can only be achieved through revolutionary praxis. Such a praxis has two aims:

> The first is to transform society by intervening in the objective process … in order to effectively organise all the collective elements that it produces, directing them towards a new socialist social formation. The other is to transform man so that he is able to freely manage this new society.[79]

The presupposition for the transition to socialism is revolutionary praxis understood as subjective intervention. In Basso's view, it was Marx himself who assigned such a decisive role for revolutionary practice to the formation and development of class consciousness.

Basso organised the ranks of Italian anti-fascism and the socialist movement in the 1920s and '30s in light of these convictions. And once Italy became

---

[76] Basso 1980, p. 39.
[77] Basso 1980, p. 24.
[78] Basso 1980, p. 210.
[79] Ibid.

INTRODUCTION   23

a democratic republic, he continued his work on numerous initiatives inside and outside the Socialist Party.

In the early 1940s, after twenty years of Fascism, the possibility seemed to emerge for revolution in Italy and Europe, although this would have required 'a period of rapid and intense education of the proletariat, which could only take place through encouraging as far as possible initiative from below'.[80] At this historical moment Basso echoes the rallying cries of Rosa Luxemburg: occupy the factories and create workers' councils (Basso was to waver between 'workers' councils', repeatedly calling for the creation of institutions from below, while also having absolute faith in party democracy).

In April 1943, as a member of the MUP (Movement of Proletarian Unity for Socialist Edification)[81] and then at the helm of the socialists in northern Italy, Basso left his mark in two important documents of this period. The objectives in the document issued after the first Congress of the MUP called for: the establishment of a socialist workers' republic based on the principle of socialisation; the creation of a peaceful European community opposed to 'narrow-minded nationalism'; socialisation of the means of production, exchange and agriculture; establishment of socialised distribution institutions and suppression of any kind of 'capitalist market manoeuvres'; elimination of all forms of capitalist property and guarantee of 'comfortable and healthy accommodation for all workers' families'; respect and 'equality of all faiths and races before the law'; and the strengthening of spiritual and cultural values by giving 'special attention' to education. The goal was to construct a new social order that could 'finally realise the long held hope that the free development of each individual could be the condition for the free development of all'. This goal could be achieved by transforming the economic structure through the 'effective participation of all workers in the administration of the state, so as to realise a true and profound democracy, which is the goal of socialism and that can only be achieved through socialism'.[82]

In August 1943 MUP and PSI merged in the new Italian Socialist Party of Proletarian Unity, PSIUP and Lelio Basso was among its leaders. His calls for proletarian revolution and socialism became even more forceful. He believed that the situation in Italy and Europe towards the end of 1943 and the begin-

---

80   Basso to the Secretary of the Italian Socialist Party of Proletarian Unity of northern-central Italy, in June 1944, in Annali della Fondazione Lelio and Lisli Basso-Issoco, *L'archivio Basso e l'organizzazione del partito* (1943–45), Franco Angeli, Milan 1988, pp. 40 ff.
81   The MUP was founded in January 1943 as a prototype for a new united party of the Italian proletariat.
82   MUP, Programme declaration, (Udine, 24 April 1943), in F. Amati, *Il Movimento di unità proletaria (1943–1945)*, in Monina (ed.) 2005, pp. 159 ff.

ning of 1944 was clearly an invitation for revolution. These themes recur in the articles he wrote in this period. He also called for the creation of institutions for worker self-government (workers' councils) and party democracy. Basso believed that the party had a key role in forming consciousness, preparing revolutionaries for 'self-control and self-government'.[83] In terms of revolutionary praxis, between 1944 and 1945 Basso focused on the task of strengthening the party, which he believed needed to be more efficient and democratic. It also required reorganisation in terms of sociological composition, a clear definition of its political orientation in accordance with strictly revolutionary objectives and to engage in the task of forming party cadres. He set out a roadmap for the transformation of the country, creating the 'foundations for a true government of the people, a genuine workers' democracy'. This, for Basso, was what socialism was all about. He envisaged a historical process that could change 'men and national institutions' profoundly, producing 'a truly radical revolution not only in economics and social relations, but also in customs and morality'. Processes that the party – above all others – had to engage in to the highest degree.

Writing in the journal *Politica di classe*, he advocates the creation of Factory Agitation Committees [*Comitati d'agitazione di fabbrica*], as forms of autonomous workers' organisations with a role similar to that played by the workers' councils in the years after the First World War. It is on the theme of work that Basso reformulates a particular idea of democracy, advocating – in a major essay of 1945 entitled 'La classe lavoratrice nella Repubblica Sociale' – the urgent foundation in Italy of 'a true democracy of the working class'. Based on a historical view of democracy (one in which all members are socially equal, which 'is not the same thing as liberal democracy') and a non-static conception of the law (reminding us that law itself is meant to serve social needs), he wrote of a different and novel function for democracy. It was time to consider a reconfiguration of the democratic state, one in which 'the working class can finally show itself to be the central element of the life of the state'. The real democracy to which he refers is founded on the secure democratic consciousness of citizens, the awareness of individual rights and upon the ground of economic security. The key elements sanctioning the foundation of this true democracy include: the guarantee of economic security for all workers (right to assistance, fair remuneration and the right to existence); access to culture; workplace democracy and control of production. He was particularly concerned with the last two points, affirming the need for management councils and, above all, insisting on their function as schools of self-government, which 'serve

---

83   Basso, 'Bandiera Rossa', *Socialismo*, 18 March 1944.

INTRODUCTION   25

to prepare party executives for the future socialisation'.[84] Between 1945 and 1946 Basso dedicated an increasing number of speeches to the role of the political party and its profound bond with the working class, which in accordance with vanguardist conceptions was to guide 'the working classes in their struggle for the establishment of a new social order'.[85] With the passage of time, Basso became increasingly convinced that the birth of a socialist society in Italy was not imminent. Therefore, work had to continue within bourgeois society to exploit its objective contradictions so that concrete premises could be established to overturn capitalist social relations. At that historical moment there was no point thinking about the *sudden* advent of socialism in Italy; rather it was necessary to create the conditions, the premises 'for development in a socialist direction'.

From this perspective there is a very close link between the struggle for democracy and the struggle for socialism. Basso contrasts moderate solutions and purely formal interpretations of democracy (typical of social democrats) to a more substantive conception:

> which presupposes that the masses have attained adulthood, that is a higher level of material and intellectual existence achieved through struggle. As long as the Italian proletariat is forced to fight every day against unemployment, poverty, hunger and disease, democracy will remain an illusion, whatever laws are established.[86]

He realises that 'illegalities will inevitably occur' during the great agrarian unrest (in the occupations of uncultivated lands and other agrarian struggles). However, unlike those who 'are opposed to unrest to avoid any possible illegalities', Basso gives his backing to the ongoing conflicts. Thus democracy is understood as 'a surge that comes from below', as 'the workers becoming conscious of their role' as the new ruling class. That is to say, 'the realisation of this consciousness through increasingly effective participation in leagues, cooperatives, management councils, mass organs and local administrations up to the political leadership of the country'.[87] The way out of the crisis that Italy finds itself in, 'the taking of power by the working class' itself, can take

---

84   L. Basso, 'La classe lavoratrice nella Repubblica Sociale', edited by Istituto di Studi Socialisti, Milan, Libreria editrice Avanti! (1945?). See section 2.
85   In Basso (signed Spartaco), 'Unità proletaria', in *Unità proletaria. Organo della Federazione lombarda del PSIUP*, 15 April 1945, 1, pp. 2–4.
86   Basso, 'Democrazia e legalitarismo', in *Avanti!*, 23 February 1947. See section 2.
87   Ibid.

place democratically provided the state does not re-establish itself 'in accordance with the old capitalist structures', without undergoing profound renewal in a socialist direction.[88] The realisation of true democracy (not bourgeois democracy) is not acquired by formally complying with laws but via 'the living experience of class struggle'. It is achieved in the 'awakening' of agricultural workers, of the working class and the humble labourers from centuries of oppression.

> We believe that democracy is not just the application of certain forms or the exercise of certain rights entrusted to people who have no awareness of their position in society. On the contrary, it is the ever more effective and concrete participation of all the masses of the people in the administration of the economic and political life of the country ... in all the forms established by the new social life.
>
> As law was created to serve social needs – in some circumstances, such as the struggle of the 'masses' for dignity, the violation of certain formal legalisms can be 'legitimate'. What matters most is the reawakening of 'proletarian consciousness', the development of political capacity as opposed to the petty orthodoxy of law.[89]

The party envisaged by Basso is also class conscious and revolutionary, but *most of all* it is a party of the masses. Its aim is the *democratic* accession to power by 'a class of workers mutually consenting to and prepared for the exercise of power'. The party must not only be able to deal with political issues but must also be able 'to confront any practical problems that must be resolved by a ruling party'.[90] It is in the interests of workers, farmers and intellectuals for 'the masses to participate more effectively and concretely in the administration of politics and the national economy'; the final goal of this unity is the realisation of a socialist society.[91] As regards the situation in Italy, Basso believes that the only alternative is between a new bourgeois dictatorship and socialist democracy. The latter can be achieved 'only if the proletarian parties can mobilise all the strata of the working class around a common platform for struggle'.

---

88   L. Basso, 'Tre punti da chiarire', in *Quarto Stato*, 30 Jan.–15 Feb. 1947, 25–6, pp. 18–23.
89   Ibid.
90   L. Basso, 'In ogni paese c'è una sola via per l'affermazione del socialismo', *Avanti!*, 14 January 1947.
91   L. Basso, 'Tre punti da chiarire'.

INTRODUCTION 27

The democracy to which Basso alludes, one that exists as a union of 'justice and freedom understood in socialist manner', can be achieved through the practice of class struggle, which is able to provide 'workers with a consciousness of their rights and their personality'.[92]

On the basis of these convictions, Basso continued to conduct his battles in a variety of fields in the post-war years: as the general secretary of the Italian Socialist Party from January 1947 to the summer of 1948, as a lawyer involved in defending former partisans, trade unionists, strikers involved in a long series of political trials in the 1950s, as a key figure in the Russell Tribunal and as a leading intellectual, radical, militant and Marxist.[93]

5 Conclusions

Basso belongs to the history and times of the twentieth century, which his life largely spans: from the experience of the First World War and the post-war years – the former experienced in its global and collective form, as the experience of general mobilisation involving a 'mass' of individuals, the latter as a yearning for a new form of life, a new form of human co-existence; this was followed by the tragic events of fascism; the subsequent years of democratic reconstruction; and the first warning signs of globalisation. Basso represents another, dissonant voice within the socialist tradition. The silences that have at times marginalised his work can be linked to the originality of his – never orthodox – thinking, as well as to the unfortunate later history of the Italian Socialist Party.[94]

However, his ideas are still germane to the present day and the challenges of creating a better society. As he said in his impassioned speech on the Paris Commune:

---

92 Ibid.
93 The Russell Tribunal was formed in November 1966 with the aim of investigating the violations of international law carried out by the United States government and military in the Vietnam War. Basso played an extremely important role in this and the following Second Russell Tribunal (1972–6) that focused on the repression in Brazil, Chile and Latin America. Indeed, it was Basso who chaired the Second Russell Tribunal, which was investigating the violation of civil rights and the use of repression and torture in Central and Southern American dictatorships. He put his stamp on the organisation, turning the opinion-making tribunal into a vector for processes of participation and mobilisation that he considered to be indispensable for the development of individual and collective consciousness and responsibility (see Monina, 2016).
94 Italian socialism has had a bumpy ride, degenerating badly in the final years of the twentieth century. This decline and shift to the right is most evident in the figure of Bettino Craxi,

> If I had to summarise in one sentence what I consider the most profound meaning of the Commune, I would say that it represents an endeavour to create a society worthy of man, to save threatened human values, to prevent all beings, men and women, the elderly and children from being reduced to anonymous machines operated by a Kafkaesque power, and to help them live a human life. It is precisely this humanity that capitalism, on account of its internal contradictions, could not allow ...[95]

This view of socialism is drawn from the history of the subaltern classes, and has been put in practice by Lelio Basso in his own life. It is a lesson that today seems more relevant than ever.[96]

---

the leader of the Italian Socialist Party, one of the principal authors of this tragic epilogue and of the abandonment of any revolutionary standpoint or affinity with the interests of the working class.

95   L. Basso, 'La Comune di Parigi', cit., p. 192.
96   TN: In the rest of this book, most Marx's citations are drawn from K. Marx. F. Engels, *Collected Works*, Lawrence & Wishart, London, 1975–2004, vol. 1–50. These will be indicated in the text as MECW followed by a volume number.

PART 1

*In Search of Marx: The Writings
of the Young Lelio Basso*

∵

CHAPTER 1

Socialism and Philosophy

The poet from Arquà [Francesco Petrarch] called upon the philosophers to be poor but independent, naked but free: philosophy, the science of sciences, he placed above governments and lords, out of reach of the beguiling powers of gold, because only in this way could it remain the unprejudiced search for truth.*

It is not my task here to enquire whether philosophers have obeyed Petrarch's exhortation, or if they deserve the scorching epithet given to them, not long ago, by the author of *Nova Polemica*.[1] What is certain is that public opinion tends far more towards the latter and we would be lucky to find anyone taking the more kindly view of philosophy as a pointless waste of time rather than an odious mystification. What is sure is that everywhere today, and especially in Italy, respect for philosophy is far below what it was. The blame for this lies primarily with historical events and also, perhaps, partly with those who do not take an interest in it but, more significantly, with those who have been involved in it.

Today, philosophy in Italy has been reduced to a meagre existence: no more fruitful debates, no elevated discussions, no considered analyses. No longer are the different currents of thought in the struggle that is the source of truth: the few who still remain, unaccustomed now to what was once the raison d'être of philosophy, repeat Benedetto Croce and Giovanni Gentile, wrongly considered to dominate the field. Indeed, if there are no rivals, who can they dominate?

Indeed, if we do not even have the phalanxes of idealists, Croce has not formed a school and Gentile appears to be the leader of a so-called spiritualist revival, a pitiful pseudo-philosophy that boasts among its greatest exponents those true defenders of church and country, Papini and Giuliotti.[2]

Certainly, this decay of philosophy in Italy can be attributed in no small measure to its recent politicking: absolute idealism has lost its way in the cor-

---

* Prometeo Filodemo, 'Socialismo e filosofia' in *Avanti!*, 2 March, 1924. EN: *Avanti!* was the original newspaper of the Italian Socialist Party (*Partito socialista italiano* or PSI).
1 EN: Lorenzo Stecchetti, pseudonym for Olindo Guerrini, was of the Carducci school of poetry. His *Nova Polemica* published in 1878, Guerrini, took issue with a number of idealist authors.
2 CG: Domenico Giuliotti (1877–1956) and Giovanni Papini (1881–1956) together wrote the *Dizionario dell'omo salvato* (Vallecchi, Florence 1923), which was inspired by an intransigent, anti-modern and traditional Catholicism.

ridors of Minerva, the philosophy of the pure act has been contaminated by the impurities of politics. Praxis has negated theory; herein lies the perpetual condemnation of this philosophical system that wanders in its search for absolute and universal values, the more of which it asserts in its writings the more it is forced to misrecognise them in its activities.

Will philosophy be able to rise again and recover from this deserved disrepute? Of this there is no doubt, because philosophy is the immortal need of human thought in its aspiration to penetrate reality. It is the very image of immanent and concrete reality. From this need new philosophical currents will spring forth tomorrow, new ideas will sprout, like sparks new thoughts will break out. Philosophy will undoubtedly live and never will die as long as human kind survives.

Philosophy – which is one thing only, with its history, the history of human thought and affairs – will have changed its content to respond to the needs of the new social forces.

New consciousness and new philosophical thought will necessarily be proletarian. Indeed, I say that the one and the other will have one birth, from the proletariat's own struggle for emancipation; a proletariat, that is, that is uncompromising in its fight and does not allow itself to become confused with the bourgeoisie or allow itself to be tinged with bourgeois values; a proletariat that can find within itself, using its own energy, its own initiative, the weapons to rise up and triumph. Socialism must not only be the outlet of the conscious proletarian revolution but also the realisation of proletarian philosophical thought.

Today this philosophy that is immanent to the proletariat is barely sketched in the doctrine improperly called historical materialism, which should rather be called historical realism. It does not combat bourgeois idealist philosophy as the opposite that excludes its opposite, as non-experts like to imagine, but supersedes it as its dialectical negation and, thus, in a sense, realises and continues it. In short, bourgeois ideologies are the conceptual premise for proletarian ideologies, in the same way that the bourgeois regime is the de facto condition for the triumph of socialism. To disregard these ideologies means refuting historical understanding; to study them means penetrating the intimate essence of proletarian doctrines, which are at one with the history of the proletariat.

The time has then come to cease this affected contempt for philosophy, which is principally due to ignorance, inasmuch as it mistakes philosophy itself with a specific philosophical current and fails to grasp its great historical significance. It is time for the proletariat to start elaborating its doctrine based upon its own action, but this doctrine then sheds light upon that activity by placing it within the broader framework of the movement of history. This elaboration requires – as I said – a long and patient labour. These elaborations are – as I have said – only beginning and require long and patient work. Did not Karl Marx call philosophy the 'material weapon of the proletariat'?[3] Did not Friedrich Engels assign it the noble task of realising Hegel's idealism, the same idealism which through the teachings of Bertrando Spaventa inspired Gentile – who, it should be noted, wrote a book called *The Philosophy of Marx*, which deserves to be read, especially for its fine chapter on the 'The Philosophy of Praxis'.[4]

Can we really know anything about Marxism without having previously studied Hegel, from whom it derives? How can anyone know about Hegelianism without first studying Schelling, Fichte, Kant, in turn influenced by Rousseau and the theorists of natural law, Locke and English empiricism, and by Wolff and the early idealist philosophers? And how much can we really know about this philosophy unless we see it in relation to other systems that came before it? In short, we should conduct a general reappraisal of philosophy in all its aspects. Otherwise, why should we prefer Marxism to facile revolutionary socialism (which achieved a certain degree of success in the past), or to idealistic socialism, humanitarian socialism, utopian socialism, abstract socialism, or whatever other socialism we wish to call upon?

In this mental labour, this considered comparison of philosophical systems, in the striving to reconnect them to the social conditions from which they arose and in which they found their *raison d'être*; that is, the proletariat's critical habit, which is its most powerful weapon, is forged through the study of philosophy or – which is the same thing – of reality philosophically understood. Because critique means independence, means freedom of judgement and action; it signifies self-awareness and rebellion. Unfortunately only few are conscious of the proletariat's duty to renew bourgeois culture and ideology – amongst whom I particularly wish to mention one (who suggested these thoughts to me), the bold theoretician of syndicalism, Enrico Leone: an indefatigable scholar and writer, whose book *Anti-Bergson* has just been published.[5]

It would be futile to deny the importance of Bergson's philosophy and the powerful influence it exercised on his contemporaries. Rarely have philosophers sparked such fiery enthusiasm and violent hostility, which is a clear demonstration of the deep impact he made on new currents of thought. Marxism itself

---

3   TN: Marx actually writes, 'Just as philosophy finds its *material* weapons in the proletariat, so the proletariat finds its *intellectual* weapons in philosophy'. See 'Critique of Hegel's *Philosophy of Right*. Introduction' in Marx 1975, p. 257.
4   Gentile 1899.
5   Leone 1923.

has revealed its influence in the revolutionary syndicalist revision. What else is Sorel's thinking but a superimposition of Bergsonism on Marxism, both of which are muddled and transformed into a kind of social pragmatism? What else is myth for him if not Bergsonian intuition transported into the sphere of social competition? And is not his campaign against intellectualism and positivism the same battle, the same impulse as Bergson's against science – which is perhaps heroic, but otherwise futile? Does not the revolutionary enthusiasm of the proletariat perhaps replicate the impulse of creative evolution?

This is precisely what Leone senses. Having recently defended Marx against Sorel in a fine speech (at the Railwaymen's Union in Bologna), he now focuses on a general battle against the philosophy of intuition. Through a concise, sharp and yet lively critique, he attempts to demonstrate the bourgeois and democratic origins of Bergson's attempt to destroy science and reason in favour of common wisdom. This is not to deny the genius of Bergson's work by reducing it to a fashionable dilletantism and to a mere dinner party philosophy, as someone might think who lingered too superficially over Leone's readily drawn caricature. He is to be seen as interpreting a given historical moment, a time of demagogic democracy. He encapsulates and develops in his undoubtedly vast and profound work the feelings and thoughts of that time.

This is how Leone concludes his combative monograph: 'Popular knowledge, despised by Kant, has regained its lost prestige: democratic in life, it becomes intuitionistic and unreasoning in philosophy. So the Philistine merchant makes peace with his good conscience. However, standing between Kant who deposes an elect group of Masters of their philosophical knowledge and Bergson, and similar anti-philosophers who exalt popular knowledge absolved of wisdom, there is Marx. He begins to reconcile philosophy (which is no longer for the few) with the capacity of the people who lay claim to it as the search for a universal wisdom that elides classes, and that provides them with the power that arms them and makes them stronger'.[6]

The proletariat has finally understood that it has a duty to lay claim to philosophy.

---

6 Leone 1923.

CHAPTER 2

Term of Comparison

About eighty years ago, in a context that in some respects reflects certain situations today, Karl Marx entered the political arena.* His early writings – that the socialists of our country have never reflected upon because they were unable to penetrate their spirit – deserve to be remembered today. After the painful effort to develop a new self-consciousness in these years, they deserve to be read and experienced so that they become the blood of our blood.

At that time Germany was reduced to a state of wretched servitude, which she bore with resignation and indeed even satisfaction, patriotically satisfied because the Restoration was anti-French. Arnold Ruge, writing about the situation to Marx in March 1843, paints a bleak picture. 'I can feel the exact same sense of oppression and humiliation as during the time of Napoleon's conquest, when Russia imposed a strict censorship on the German press. If some wish to find comfort in the fact that we now show the same frankness as then, for me this offers no consolation'. The Germans are the same people who welcomed Napoleon to Erfurt with a murmur of applause, who congratulated him and called him *notre prince*, to which he replied: '*je ne suis pas votre prince, je suis votre maître*'. They are the same as those the King of Prussia referred to in 1813 when he said: 'look how the people fight for us'. Ruge says, 'Germany is not the heir that survives but the inheritance to which we must appeal. The Germans do not count for the fighting parties but for the number of souls that must be sold there ... Fifty years after the French Revolution we again feel the same the shame as during the days of despotism, which we have lived long enough to experience. Do not tell me that the nineteenth century will not put up with it: the Germans have resolved this problem. Not only do they put up with it, they bear it with patriotism; and we, who blush at it, we know very well that they deserve it ...' And this bleak diagnosis leads to the bleak conclusion: 'In effect this race is not born to be free ... The German spirit has shown itself to be contemptible'.[1] But where does this slavery come from?

For Marx, the problem is eminently spiritual, a question of consciousness. Hölderlin wrote in Hyperion: 'It is a hard saying, and yet I speak it because it is the truth: I can think of no people more at odds with themselves than the

---

* Prometeo Filodemo, 'Termine di paragone', *Conscientia*, 9 May, 1925.
1 A. Ruge to Marx, March 1843.

Germans. You see artisans but no men, thinkers, but no men ... masters and servants, but no men, minors and adults, but no men'.[2] And Marx agrees:

> 'that would imply thinking beings, free men, republicans. The philistines do not want to be either of these. What then remains for them to be and to desire? What they want is to live and reproduce themselves (and no one, says Goethe, achieves anything more), and that the animal also wants; at most a German politician would add: Man, however, *knows* that he wants this, and the German is so prudent as not to want anything more'.[3]

Therefore, this spiritual unity, this consciousness must be formed, moulded, but it must be formed and moulded anew; it should be unencumbered with the dross of the past. Hence the wound that lacerated the Germanic spirit should not be allowed to close too quickly, before equalisation has been achieved. 'The longer the time that events allow to thinking humanity for taking stock of its position, and to suffering mankind for mobilising its forces, the more perfect on entering the world will be the product that the present time bears in its womb'.[4] No hasty solution then, no half measures. The disease must run its course; but equally the people must become aware of it, feel intimately their own spiritual tragedy, reflect in their soul what only to superficial thinkers appears as a limitation of freedom. 'The point is not to let the Germans have a minute for self-deception and resignation. The actual pressure must be made more pressing by adding to it consciousness of pressure, the shame must be made more shameful by publicising it. Every sphere of German society must be shown as the *partie honteuse* of German society: these petrified relations must be forced to dance by singing their own tune to them! The people must be taught to be *terrified* at itself in order to give it *courage*'.[5]

Here is the rebellion against nationalistic patriotism, which presumes to impose silence so as not to compromise Prussia's credit abroad. Marx wishes to proclaim loud and clear his country's shame. 'Germany is sunk deep in the mire and will sink still deeper. I assure you, even if one has no feeling of national pride at all, nevertheless one has a feeling of national shame'.[6] This shame must be proclaimed loud and clear, so that it penetrates the flesh of the German people so that they make it their own, feel it burning in their chest and burning

---

2 F. Hölderlin, 'Hyperion', in Hölderlin 1990, p. 128.
3 Marx to Ruge, May 1843, MECW 3, pp. 134–7.
4 Marx to Ruge, May 1843, MECW 3, p. 141.
5 Marx, 'A Contribution to the Critique of Hegel's Philosophy of Right', in MECW 3, p. 178.
6 Marx to Ruge, March 1843, MECW 3, p. 133.

in their enslaved souls, so as to find the nourishment to fashion a new soul, a new consciousness, the consciousness of a free man.

So what is being asked? Not a well thought out plan of reforms that will ensure the rule of law and freedom: this purely external freedom, a freedom in law but not in consciences, not in the most intimate and deepest part of the people is not true freedom. Similarly, a real liberal is not someone who defends freedom as a purely rational concept, a logical conclusion of certain principles, or as an institution to be preserved because other countries have it, but as 'the feeling that man has of his being'. It is for this reason, argues Marx, that the protests of the liberals in defence of freedom of the press fall on deaf ears. 'They have never come to know freedom of the press as a vital need. For them it is a matter of the head, in which the heart plays no part. For them it is an 'exotic' plant, to which they are attached by mere sentiment. Goethe once said that the painter succeeds only with a type of feminine beauty which he has loved in at least one living being. Freedom of the press, too, has its beauty – if not exactly a feminine one – which one must have loved to be able to defend it. If I truly love something, I feel that its existence is essential, that it is something which I need, without which my nature can have no full, satisfied, complete existence. The above-mentioned defenders of freedom of the press seem to enjoy a complete existence even in the absence of any freedom of the press'.[7]

Freedom must instead be embodied in the soul of the people, so that from an awareness of their present conditions they can form a new consciousness; the future must arise from the present, a free and spontaneous creation of the people themselves. In this way Good can come from Evil through that dialectical process that Marx had not yet developed into a theory of history but in accordance with which he was already beginning to see the emergence of events. 'It is precisely the advantage of the new trend that we do not dogmatically anticipate the world, but only want to find the new world through criticism of the old one … But, if constructing the future and settling everything for all times are not our affair, it is all the more clear what we have to accomplish at present: I am referring to *ruthless criticism of all that exists*, ruthless both in the sense of not being afraid of the results it arrives at and in the sense of being just as little afraid of conflict with the powers that be. Therefore, I am not in favour of raising any dogmatic banner. On the contrary, we must try to help the dogmatists to clarify their propositions for themselves. Thus, communism, in particular, is a dogmatic abstraction … Hence, nothing prevents us from making criticism of politics, participation in politics, and therefore *real* struggles, the

---

7 Marx *Rheinische Zeitung* No. 128, May 8, 1842, Supplement, in MECW 1, p. 132.

starting point of our criticism, and from identifying our criticism with them. In that case we do not confront the world in a doctrinaire way with a new principle: Here is the truth, kneel down before it! We develop new principles for the world out of the world's own principles. We do not say to the world: Cease your struggles, they are foolish; we will give you the true slogan of struggle. We merely show the world what it is really fighting for, and consciousness is something that it has to acquire, even if it does not want to'.[8]

Here, in these few lines, is Karl Marx, the real Marx, the great preacher of intransigence, Teacher and Educator of proletarian consciousness. In vain economists have dissected the corpse and cut it up into tiny parts to find a microbe of an error, not realising that by doing this they were preventing themselves from penetrating its Spirit.

---

8 Marx to Ruge, September 1843, MECW 3, pp. 142–3.

CHAPTER 3

The Reformation and European Thought: Marx

I think the strange fate that befell Marx, having his ideas systematically distorted by his disciples, is unlikely to happen to any other thinker; even Engels, who should have been Marx's best interpreter because of their long spiritual communion, is guilty of this.* The fact is that Marx, a thinker far ahead of his time, fixed his gaze too far ahead of his time, which was the time of a bourgeoisie that was still uncertain of its power and of a proletariat that had been discouraged by its first unsuccessful revolutionary attempts, and wishing only to assure itself of a quiet place in the sun while remaining on good terms with their neighbours. Thus his ideas were completely misrepresented: the indolent character of his contemporaries meant they were incapable of grasping the redeeming beauty of his revolutionary activities ('permanent revolution'), could not understand socialism as creation, class as consciousness. The actualisation of the new order could wait, delayed into a distant future; class was seen as something positive reflecting a disparity in economic interests; socialism was also something positive that would come about mechanically through the effect of certain causes; and revolutionary activity was transformed into passive expectation. Process was replaced with things; the synthesis of self-consciousness was replaced with the object disconnected from the subject. The rising sun [*sole dell'avvenire*] was a caricature of this socialism. A doctrine that wished to solve all the objectifications or self-alienations of the human spirit was itself sadly fated to be misunderstood and objectified.

To understand Marx's original conception we must, therefore, first sort out these myths in the self-consciousness that is the unity of created and creator, which is creation. It is precisely this much-abused self-consciousness, abused even by Marx in *The Holy Family*, which can give us the key to his doctrine. Despite the volumes that have been written on *Capital*, on surplus value and increasing immiseration, the very essence of this doctrine can be found in a few lines of the *Theses on Feuerbach*. From these we can glimpse his mistake, the mistake made by the empirical Marx, the political Marx, though his own doctrine enables us to overcome it. His mistake was to believe that all human objectifications could be resolved in the process of self-consciousness. He believed it was enough to explain religious self-alienations with the contradictions of the valley of tears, with the contradictions of the real world in order to resolve and

---

* Prometeo Filodemo, 'La riforma e il pensiero europeo: Marx', 25 July 1925.

overcome those self-alienations. But he did not realise that the will to transcend oneself was a manifestation of the religiosity immanent to humanity. And that this determination to transcend oneself ends up as the exteriorisation of new self-alienations, in new objectifications.

The history of thought is the perennial tale of this process. The Reformation turned the objects of Scholasticism into human creations: in place of truth, in place of the Church as the depositary of truth, it elevated conscience to the rank of priest and judge of human works.

Promptly, though, there came the reverse process: so eighteenth century philosophy made the individual – which the Reformation had revealed – into an idol and prostrated itself before the natural rights of the individual; thus Kant created the ghost of the thing-in-itself and of absolute practical duty, making the categorical imperative shine in human consciousness. Hegel resolves this new objectification, explaining it as an empty identity of man himself, and asserts the Spirit as creation. However, in Hegel, who was contemplative by nature, we return to absolute transcendence and the absolute Spirit of the world puts paid to individuality. Soon the left comes to the defence of the individual, but it recreates its myths: Feuerbach's humanity, the Bauers' aristocratic individuality, before degenerating into Stirner's anarchism. Marx decisively addresses these contradictions and with his powerful critique pulls apart the Idea-State, which is the tyrannical Prussian police state. History, which had been divided into esoteric and exoteric history, is re-established as a single creative process and in it Humanity again regains its self-consciousness.

Marx paves the way for an understanding of all history as a human and divine history, as continuous fall from grace and continuous redemption. For him there is no principle higher than Humanity, there is no shadow of transcendence above it. Humanity, which is all history, is itself the absolute unity. But in every moment of history this contrast between immanence and transcendence, between subject and object, between Good and Evil is repeated. Marx impressively highlights the dialectical function of evil and thereby banishes any type of reformism or paternalism. This clarifies the true meaning of the Marxist revolution, which is to be understood as redemption, as a palingenetic striving, a will to overcome one's own contradictions, that is, to transcend oneself. The class struggle is the consciousness of this tragic conflict (what else could it mean but class consciousness?) reflected in everyone and translated into active faith, into a stubborn will to overcome oneself by overcoming the object in a religious struggle towards renewal and purification. This, and nothing else, is the eternal process of praxis that overturns itself.[1]

---

1 See editor's introduction, pp. 4 ff.

It is clear that such a conception could not spring from a soil that had not already been fertilised by the Protestant Reformation. It contradicts the Catholic spirit most obviously, postulating and asserting as it does the freedom of the individual, revealing the desperate consciousness of antitheses, the culture of struggle and the pride in an inflexible intransigence. Just as Marx was launching his *Manifesto*, where poverty is singled out as an evil that must stir the workers to rebellion in order to regain their human dignity, to be masters of themselves; in Catholic France, the Socinian socialist Louis Blanc was moved by proletarian poverty to call for state subsidies, thus stripping the workers of their dignity and turning them into servants.

CHAPTER 4

Socialism and Idealism

To summarise briefly what I said in the previous article,[*][1] the fundamental elements of Marxism are: first, concrete historical development takes the place of fixed categories. Thus morality, law, economics and every other aspect of human life are no longer seen *sub specie aeternitatis*, as a more or less successful incarnation of an eternal truth which must be accepted with certain modifications and corrections but are understood as the history of morality, of law, of economics, and so on. Then there is the dialectical conception of history understood as necessity and rationality, replacing the myth of inevitable progress, of the ineluctable evolution towards a state of reason yet to be realised. From here springs the notion of the immanence of the ideal to the real, the critique of all abstract critiques of society based on principles drawn from outside our present reality. In contrast, there is the proclamation of the interiority of conflict as a matter of consciousness and the legitimation of one single critique of society, namely that which society aims at itself. Finally, and as a corollary to the above, the refusal of any predetermined solution or panacea for present or future problems, but instead, adherence to one great and eternal value: the force of the will to seek a solution.

So where is the true reality of socialism? Perhaps in the scientific predictions of its inevitable triumph? Maybe in the laws of increasing immiseration, growing concentration and so on? Or in the harshness of economic conflicts that nevertheless remain? Or rather in the inevitability of progress that leads straight to the realisation of absolute Equality, perfect Justice? None of this. The reality of socialism is in the consciousness of the workers, who feel inside themselves the fundamental antithesis that divides society, who now embody the inherent tragedy of history, and who have the will to overcome this antithesis and rise further up. This will is an act of faith; it is the religiosity of socialism [...] But I do not want to be misunderstood. The socialists have always understood faith and religion as something very different. By faith, I do not mean a belief in some transcendent deity, nor the ascetic annihilation of earthly values. I said before that history for Marx is entirely human and earthly. It is for

---

* Prometeo Filodemo, 'Socialismo e idealismo' in *Il Quarto Stato*, 10 aprile 1926.
1 Prometeo Filodemo, 'Socialismo e idealismo' in *Il Quarto Stato*, 3 aprile 1926.

this very reason, precisely because he does not admit the existence of anything completely perfected in history – or outside it, that is, outside of us there is nothing – it is obvious that history is an activity of perpetual realisation, a never-ending battle to overcome the antinomy within it. Now this activity of men who – placed between the two terms of this antinomy – decide to work in a particular direction to achieve a particular end, can only be moved by faith. The alleged scientific laws of economic determinism explain nothing. As I said before, the replacement of the system with the problem, means that the will to solve it is an act of faith.

Marxist faith is, therefore, an active faith that aims at each moment to overcome our finitude, to transcend the limits of our determination, to free men from the contradiction that haunts them, while knowing that this contradiction will return because it is inseparable from our very nature, that of finite beings. This constant striving for liberation, this gradual conquest of a greater dignity is the sign of our immanence to God, and at the same time the norms of our ethical actions.

In this way Marx's ethics reach the celestial heights that our good positivists could not even dream of. Its immense value lies in that it is formally absolute whereas its content is historically determined, thus definitively clearing Kant's hurdle. If it is a case of overcoming concrete historical contradictions, as they actually and necessarily exist, Marxist morality too falls under the historical dialectic. 'A moral that is above the struggle cannot serve as a weapon in the struggle', as Mondolfo admirably puts it.[2] So it is no longer an ideal that is opposed to the real, not anti-history against history but a necessary moment – even if a negative one – in the historical process; which is to say an ideal in the sense not commonly attributed to that word. Thus Marx definitively banished all the idle talk of the preachers of morality, all the dreams of the utopians who wished to impose an arbitrary direction to history, all the absolute truths preached by false priests to the proletariat as their aim in life.

The socialist revolution must be conducted in the name of the present situation, in the name of the antithesis it contains. The consciousness of antitheses: this is the true consciousness of the revolutionary, one who interprets the situation according to changes and changes according to the interpretations. To understand is to overcome. And for this very reason Labriola wrote that 'understanding history became from that point on the main concern of communist theorists. And how could one ever again oppose the fantasies even of the most

---

[2] EN: unfortunately it has not been possible to trace this quote.

perfect ideal to the harsh reality of history?'[3] Similarly, Marx said: 'They [the working class] have no ideals to realize, but to set free the elements of the new society with which old collapsing bourgeois society itself is pregnant'.[4]

What I have been illustrating clarifies the meaning that I, in agreement with far more authoritative writers, attach to Marx's violent invectives against those who establish moral maxims a priori for the proletarian revolution or to heal social ills. 'He who loves hates', writes Croce, 'and especially hates the falsification of the things he loves. Hence the criticism and satire of moralism to be found in Hegel and in his faithful pupil Marx'. He could not but despise the moralistic sermons which to him seemed like vulgar and irreverent caricatures of the ethical heights reached by so-called historical materialism, which in its greatest exponents – from Marx to Sorel – established a culture 'of austere and serious morals, stripped of emphasis and idle chatter, combative morals, designed to keep alive the forces that drive history and prevent it from stagnating and becoming corrupt'.[5] Therefore all those who speak of Marxist amorality are off track, as are all those who, either before or after Croce, like Malon and Chiappelli, looked for moral ideas in socialism not realising that the moral idea was socialism itself, the determination to overcome the present reality.[6]

And so I have returned to where I started, and what I had decided to prove: that socialism is the consciousness of the antithesis that is tearing this society apart and the will to triumph over it. And nothing more. Only if understood in this sense will socialism cease to be a nice idea thought up by philanthropists who want to help the poor, as it was for the utopians, and be seen as the workers' struggle to help themselves. Only if understood like this will socialism give the lie to the blatant hypocrisy of bourgeois charity and proclaim its first moral triumph as the achievement of human dignity. Only if understood in this way will socialism be an instrument of spiritual elevation for the masses, transform-

---

3 A. Labriola, *Saggi intorno alla concezione materialistica della storia. In memoria del Manifesto dei comunisti*, Loescher, Roma, 1895, p. 33.
4 Marx, 'The Civil War in France' in MECW 22, p. 335.
5 Croce 1907, *Lettera a Sorel* (EN: unfortunately it has not been possible to trace this quote).
6 EN: A. Chiappelli (1857–1931) was the author of *Il socialismo e il pensiero moderno*, Le Monnier, Firenze, 1897. In this period he was close to the revisionist line of Eduard Bernstein in stressing the ethical nature of Marxism. For him the workers' movement was ethical and its ideals ultimately coincide with those of Christianity. For this reason he advanced the notion of a conciliation of Christianity with socialism. In the years following the First World War, Chiappelli endorsed Fascism, which he believed could synthesise liberalism and socialism. B. Malon was the author of *Il socialismo. Suo passato, suo presente, suo avvenire*, La Plebe, 1875. Malon was a French writer and politician who was an important figure in the Paris Commune and the French socialist movement.

ing them from brutes into men, because it will instil in them the divine breath of faith [...] This does not mean that economic laws are without importance for our understanding of things or that the study of economic conditions is inessential for all socialist movements. If battle is to be waged against this society with its own weapons, it is necessary to study them and understand them, so as not to get lost in inane, fruitless, aimless and half-baked attempts. But Marx's work on this terrain does not overcome these limits. Baratono states this well: 'he gives us a forceful and realistic outline of society and the iron laws that govern it, giving us a plain picture of the battlefield and the best weapons to win'.[7] And it would be a mistake to confuse the weapons with the reasons for the struggle and to seek the reality of socialism outside the class-consciousness of the proletariat, outside the desire for emancipation.

Collectivism, communism, socialisation and all other forms of future organisation, which as we have seen Marx describes as demagogic abstractions, only have a value as criticism, as attitudes that are in opposition to this society – but they have no practical constructive value. It is to be hoped that the time is forever gone when there were serious discussions about whether a socialist regime should use money or labour vouchers, or when it was thought that socialism would inevitably come about through the laws of fate. Of course the laws of increasing immiseration, centralisation, and the disappearance of the middle classes are of great value as long as they are framed in the dialectic of history understood as the self-conscious process that I have outlined here. As the workers acquire dignity through struggle, they will increasingly feel the weight of their own oppression and will dramatise it through the irreducible and intransigent opposition of two classes and two principles, with no middle way.

Still today, against an accommodating democracy, against amorphous universalism, against compromising reformism, against evolutionary positivism, against the embraces of non-interventionists [*panciafichisti*], we assert today, as Marxists, that what we badly need is a ritual of class struggle, the acute sense of conflict, of a tragic conception of life, and of the exacerbation of antinomies.

I think I have, however briefly, provided an idealist interpretation of the socialist doctrine, although this is a strong and virile type of idealism that has nothing in common with humanitarian lamentations, with sentimental weaknesses, with the ideals of goodness and justice of demo-masonic and positivist

---

7   EN: A. Baratono (1875–1947) was a philosopher and politician, playing an important role in the PSI in the inter-war period. He was also author, amongst other writings, of *Le due facce del marxismo italiano*, Società editrice Avanti, Milan 1922, and *Fatica senza fatica*, Problemi moderni, Genoa-Turin 1923.

socialism that made the mistake of hypostatising the canons of bourgeois morality and projecting them onto the heights of the absolute. The myth of *The Holy Family* is repeated.

Since we are a long way from this way of thinking, we shall be careful not to deny any value to the positivist period. It was a response to the time when the proletariat, which had to assure itself of its conditions of existence and lacking the strength to act alone, needed to depend on a part of the bourgeoisie and its ideologies. The phenomenon was inevitable, and was not solely Italian. By taking the bourgeois principles to their extreme consequence, it served to reveal their real value – that of mythical self-alienation. This we can admit, but we cannot accept that this demo-masonic socialism can still be identified with Marxism, 'which is very much opposed to the masons and its tendencies, since it is grounded in Hegelian philosophy, armed with historical reality, violent, sarcastic, opposed to any sentimentalism and any brotherhoods'.[8]

Marxism stands in such contrast to it that it provides us with the tools to theoretically criticise those mythical self-alienations and to overthrow them in practice. This is precisely what our task is. Today the bourgeoisie has been forced to shed its mask. And the proletariat is faced with the dilemma: accept dictatorship or entirely reject the present order.

---

8 B. Croce, *Cultura e vita morale. Intermezzi polemici*, Laterza, Bari 1914, p. 172.

PART 2

Marxism and the History of Italy

∴

CHAPTER 5

The Working Class in the Social Republic

The problem of the working class in the [Italian] state is the problem of establishing a democracy in Italy.* It would be fair to say that democracy has never existed in Italy, not even in the traditional bourgeois sense of the word; but perhaps it is less clear to many that such a democracy cannot exist in Italy.

Since the end of the eighteenth century, democracy has assumed different forms in its historical development, and the democracy of free colonial peoples is not the same as that of industrial countries with large population densities. So too, social democracy is not the same as liberal democracy.[1]

Nevertheless, it may be generally said that democracy has been the political expression of the middle classes, who aim to base their political power on numbers rather than on economic strength or social importance. In this vision of democracy, the working class merely have to go to the ballot box for the benefit of the intellectuals. Such a democracy cannot take root among us. Democracy in all walks of life, democracy as an everyday experience, in the place of work and production, in all aspects of communal life, democracy as the political instrument of the working class – this type of democracy has not yet been envisaged by theorists in the classical sense of the word.

As in the years after the First World War, the problem facing Europe today is how to include the working class in the life of the state, ideally without violent rebellion and without the civil wars that till this moment have been caused by the reaction against this unstoppable historical development.

The problem is even more acute now than in 1919. A devastated civilisation such as that of Europe today, cannot be rebuilt without everyone contributing and making sacrifices in the best interests of the collective. This sacrifice cannot be made except within a regime where the working class can finally express itself as the central element in the life of the state. In an

---

* L. Basso, '*La classe lavoratrice nella Repubblica Sociale*', Istituto di studi Socialisti-Libreria Editrice Avanti!, Rome-Milan 1944–5, now in M. Salvati, C. Giorgi (eds.) 2003. L'espressione Repubblica sociale non ha nulla a che vedere con l'esperienza storica e nazifascista della Repubblica sociale italiana (RSI), ma allude alla nascita di un sistema democratico fondato sulla partecipazione e sulla direzione delle classi lavoratrici.
1 'Nell'accezione originaria della dizione, 'democrazia sociale' denota una 'democratizzazione fondamentale', una società i cui membri vanno trattati come socialmente eguali', Leone 1923 (Ed.: unfortunately it has not been possible to trace this quote).

impoverished Europe, with few prospects of greater wealth, bourgeois democracy would be unable to exist.

Bourgeois democracy can only remain the prerogative of powers like England and America, where there are sufficiently high incomes as a result of the great wealth they have accumulated and the worldwide exploitation of the work of others.

In 1919 this problem was addressed across Europe on a political terrain that was feeling the effects of the recent Russian Revolution and that of the reformist tradition of European socialist parties. On the one hand maximalist demands were made from outside the state in opposition to the particularistic, corporative ones of the state. On the other hand, the inclusion of the working class in the state was conceived in reformist terms, as a series of measures to be taken by the state for the benefit of the working class. It was not understood that this would not lead to the renewal of the bourgeois state. Sorel's proposition still rang true: '*Réformer dans la société bourgeoise c'est affirmer la société bourgeoise*' [to reform in bourgeois society is to affirm bourgeois society].[2]

The process had not been understood dialectically, such that the state could become an expression of the working class only by overthrowing the reactionary oligarchy that had dominated Italy for decades; only, that is, if all the forces of labour mobilised around the working class to achieve an effective democracy.

While it is true that the reformist stance of requesting the bourgeois state resolve the problems of the working class justified the Marxist critique, it must also be admitted that equally unrealistic was the opposite concept, that of a maximalist and catastrophic vision in which the working class would, from outside, in revolutionary fashion, found a new social order by attacking the state itself.

Today, no responsible revolutionary could subscribe to the words spoken in 1920 by Palmiro Togliatti about workers' control in *Ordine Nuovo*, in which he opposed the conscious section of workers not only to all class enemies but also to the timid, the uncertain and the fearful, advocating a clean break between revolutionary organisations and the bourgeois state, rejecting any state recognition of factory councils and workers' control.

The working class uprising of the post-War years failed due to these internal contradictions, a consequence of its immaturity, and the reactionary classes were able to reaffirm their dictatorial powers across Europe. There were to be

---

2 CG: The sentence should actually read: '*Réformer dans la société bourgeoise, c'est affirmer la propriété privée*' [to reform bourgeois society is to affirm private property], in *Introduction à l'économie modern*, Paris, 1903.

two further attempts at broad social reform later, new solutions aimed at advancing the position of the working class: Roosevelt's New Deal and the social experiment of the French Popular Front. Both cases set out from backward social legislation, which had already in part addressed other European countries (recognition of trade unions, collective agreements, paid holidays, etc.). In both cases the initial bold innovations were first halted and in large part the achievements were reversed.

We can draw few lessons, and essentially negative ones, from previous experiences. In the following section I shall draw some general outlines for reforms to establish a true workers' democracy in Italy [...]

Democracy, however, is not founded only on legislation: no law, no political institution can guarantee democracy if it is not founded on the firm democratic consciousness of its citizens, and there can be no strong democratic consciousness without an awareness of the rights of the person, which is itself founded upon economic security.

Therefore, to examine the problem in all its aspects we have to consider the worker as a whole, from his basic economic needs to his higher spiritual needs, from his factory life to his trade union life.

In my opinion, there are four key moments for the foundation of a true democracy: guaranteeing economic security for all workers; breaking the bourgeois monopoly on culture; bringing democracy to the workplace; eliminating the excessive power of the plutocratic oligarchy.

Thus in the first place we shall briefly deal with the material existence of the worker. It is not worth troubling the old theories which first arose in the French Revolution and which were suffocated in the blood of the Paris workers in June 1848. It is not a question of society guaranteeing workers the 'right to work' but of guaranteeing them the 'right to exist'.

Certainly, the right to exist means firstly the right to work if and where this is possible, the right to receive assistance when work is not possible or where it does not produce an income that is sufficient for life's needs. This aspect of the problem also involves taking the necessary steps to police the allocation of employment and ensure that workers get a fair wage.

Policing labour means safeguarding the jobs market from the arbitrary powers of the boss; it means creating and strengthening employment centres, which should become a sort of labour registry, providing assistance and oversight in all phases of a worker's technical and moral development, so that he may acquire confidence and understanding.

It is important, though, for these employment centres to be run directly by the working-class trade unions and it must be compulsory for employers to hire workers from them.

Equitable remuneration means earning a wage that covers the individual needs of each member of a worker's family, and which is adjusted to the cost of living by means of a sliding scale.

The unions should manage the technical aspects regarding the running of the employment centres, of family remuneration and of the sliding scale, although the guiding principles belong to the sphere of politics. In applying the principles to practice, account should always be taken of the exceptional circumstances of the time as well as of the sacrifices that the *working class as well* makes in the task of reconstructing the country.

But in a comprehensive plan of reforms adapting the conditions of the working class to the needs of modern civilisation, the sacrifices that may be required must be accompanied by guaranteed political gains, as set out below. These must give the working class the consciousness of participating effectively in the democratic life of the country through the organs of control and management that prepare them for self-government.

The reforms of social services should be more extensive and radical. Our social services are not homogenous, having arisen at different times in order to respond to a variety of needs. Today they constitute a rather disharmonious whole, both in terms of content, because they fail to provide support in many cases of real need, and in terms of legal institutions, since they lack coordination, often overlapping and are without a unitary existence.

[...]

Once the worker's material existence is assured, the worker must also be guaranteed access to spiritual goods. The primary need here is for educational reform, although I shall not dwell on this aspect because it will be the subject of another paper. I would like instead to briefly underline the points that are of real interest to the working class.

Besides creating more primary and vocational schools and making them readily accessible to all workers, in addition to the vocational schools within firms, the principle must be established that the most able working-class children shall have the right to higher education without being a financial burden on their families. This should be guaranteed not only by offering them a completely free education but also by providing a reasonable allowance to the families of workers, farmers or employees whose child goes to school, to compensate for the entire salary that the child might have earned by going out to work.

But school alone does not entirely fulfil man's spiritual needs: it merely prepares one for them. Workers must be provided with the most favourable conditions for spiritual development throughout their lives. In this regard there is the problem of working hours. In a half-destroyed country, where a huge productive effort is required to rebuild even the bare minimum for survival, it may seem out of place to speak of a reduction in working hours. In effect, until emergency conditions remain in place, sacrifices will have to be made by the working class. Equally, that a worker should be able to aspire to a working week of no more than 40 hours, which was already enacted in its time by the French Popular Front, cannot be passed over in silence within a general discussion of the problems of the working class.

Today the system of paid holidays patently privileges office workers over factory workers. It is essential that the system of paid holidays is maintained and extended in order to guarantee the spiritual life of workers.

Time off work and paid vacations must be directed at promoting culture, broadening horizons, and providing a more complete spiritual life.

[…]

Cultural clubs, libraries and schools in firms; cinemas and theatres for the working class; hotels and institutions requisitioned to guarantee, as far as possible, holidays that are spent away from the workplace; greatly reduced fares during holiday periods; organised tourism. All these issues must be addressed and resolved in this direction.

[…]

The issue of trade unions is one of the oldest and most debated issues.

Free or compulsory trade unions? One union or many unions? It is this writer's opinion that a compulsory union would respond better to the needs of working class unity and solidarity. We must wean the workers off the system used in the past, when they joined trade unions only in times of social conflict to then lose interest in them when things calmed down.

[…]

Where we need radical institutional change is in the democratisation of factories and businesses. Long struggles have been needed to limit, slightly, the all-powerful boss's right to set wages inside the factory. In all other aspects of factory life (hiring, layoffs and especially production methods, policy, sales price, etc.), the boss has a more or less free hand. One of the most patent contradictions in all bourgeois democracies, even where universal suffrage is truly sovereign, is that democracy can come to a halt at the gates of factories, banks, and businesses in general, wherever we find the magic words: private property.

It is the task of a new democracy to assert and put into practice the principle that, wherever there is a need to address and resolve problems that affect the community, that touch the interests of large social groups, no door shall remain closed to democratic control.

How should this control be exercised? After the First World War, workers' councils were set up in nearly all European countries. In Germany, where they were most widespread, they failed because of an irreconcilable conflict between the revolutionary vision, which saw in the workers' councils an organ for overturning particular social relations, and social-democracy, which saw them as subordinate to the trade unions. The social democratic approach prevailed and workers' councils, deprived of all their life force, ended up becoming anaemic and died off within a few years.

In Italy, too, as in most countries of Europe, there was a conflict between the political conceptions of workers' councils defended by the Communists and the beliefs of the leaders of the trade union confederations, who saw them as a dangerous competitor. For the communists it was essentially a case of shifting the heart of working-class activity from the office to the factory, from the union bureaucracy to the workplace, which is where the [working] class finds its most genuine expression. The councils were also a way of getting the unorganised masses, i.e. non-union members, mobilised and involved in the struggle.

There is no doubt that the communist conception represented a step forward in the march towards achieving political maturity and self-government. However, since it was based solely on working-class action and was cut off from specific proposals for government, it too foundered in the cataclysm that swept over the entire working class. Now the question has returned to the fore in Italy with the institution of Management Committees [*Consigli di gestione*]. Having to adhere as much as possible to concrete realities, and since political reform cannot be based on abstract ideologies, there is no doubt that any action taken to democratise factory life must be based on the existing institution of Management Committees [*Consigli di gestione*]. Action must also be structured in ways that can best satisfy the needs of the times, which prevent rash disputes and the wasting of energy; but these require a constant, concrete and harmonious action so as to include the working class in all levels of state affairs, to effectively destroy reactionary oligarchies and found a new democracy that is deeply rooted in daily democratic practice, in the active consciousness of the working world – not just in some articles of law or in some institutions divorced from the real life of the masses [...]

The Management Committees [*Consigli di gestione*] originated from a decree issued in 1943 and instituted by the CLNAI on 17 April 1945.[3] In practice it

---

3   EN: CLNAI, or *Comitato di Liberazione nazionale Alta Italia* (National Liberation Committee for Northern Italy) was part of the CLN, or *Comitato di Liberazione Nazionale* (Committee for National Liberation), that is the union of the political parties and movements that directed and coordinated the Resistance and out of which the first governments were formed after the liberation. The CLN emerged spontaneously from the anti-German and anti-Fascist struggle

was a case of realising some of the postulates of so-called fascist socialisation, starting with the assumption that the fascist law, too, had been imposed on Mussolini's government in the hope of attracting the sympathies of the masses who were hostile to him. It was, therefore, the result of the strength and fighting spirit of the working masses who had proved their great political maturity by boycotting the fascist law and refusing its benefits, and thereby demonstrating that they actually deserved to get those benefits. Thus, the CLNAI decree instituted Management Committees [*Consigli di gestione*] in companies socialised by the fascists, and gave orders that workers' representatives were to be elected in the three months following liberation, pending a new general regulation of the matter by legislation by the national government. The decree has yet to be generally implemented, probably because no legislative act by the Rome government has ensued.

However, a mass mobilisation calling for the establishment of Management Committees [*Consigli di gestione*] is gathering pace and is bringing concrete results every day: the spread of these bodies in an ever growing number of companies and the masses' increasing interest in the life of the factory and in the problems of production by virtue of their participation, albeit indirectly, in management.

Therefore, today, any attempt to suppress or change the nature of this institution would be a supremely impolitic act, one that would clash with the strong opposition of the masses and would involve taking a step backwards in the historical process. For this institution represents the outlet for the masses' efforts of self-education and self-discipline during the underground struggle led by company CLNs.

The problem today is, therefore, to legalise these institutions, strengthen them, link them more closely to the life of the masses, at the one end, and to the essential problems of national life (socialisation, planning, etc.), at the other.

The action of the masses needs to shift their focus from purely trade union demands for wage increases to conscious participation in the management of production; from the struggle for the distribution of company profits (wage rises at the expense of capitalist profits) to the struggle for the transformation of the production process itself; and from the defence of immediate interests

---

following the 8th September 1943. The central organ was formed in Rome and was composed of six parties (the Party of Action, the Communist Party, the Christian Democrats, Democratic Labour Party, the Liberals and the Socialists). In particular in the north, the CLNAI played a decisive role, where the partisan divisions carried out military operations leading to the national insurrection of 25 April 1945. This resulted in the first post-liberation government: the Parri Government (June–November 1945).

to the training of a new leadership to carry out the future tasks that socialisation will impose on the working class.

It is a case then of achieving new forms of Management Committees [*Consigli di gestione*], like the ones which after the First World War the workers' movement attempted to establish in the form of workers' committees and workers' control [...]

Working-class participation could take place on this basis:

a) Management Committees [*Consigli di gestione*] that deal with the internal management of the company, separate from the board of directors that would remain responsible for capital management;

b) joint composition of Management Committees [*Consigli di gestione*], plus a chairman appointed by the board of directors;

c) the right of workers to monitor all board activities, possibly having an advisory role;

d) the right of workers to appoint a member of the supervisory board.

This system would avert the danger of getting workers to take on responsibilities involving capital and, for this very reason, forestall the risk of collusion between individual workers and the capitalist management of the company. Given their minority representation on the management committees [*consigli di gestione*] and the supervisory board, the function of the workers would be essentially advisory and supervisory. Control would be exercised not from outside but from within the governing bodies and thus be more effective. It would provide a greater sense of responsibility and represent good preparation for self-government.

A school of self-government: this is the principal function of the management committees, the task of which is to prepare the cadres for future socialisation. But for this very reason they cannot be autonomous from working-class demands. It is important to maintain contacts between the workers' representatives in the committees and the workers themselves. This can be achieved, on the one hand, by giving each worker the right to ask his representative to appeal against any decision that appears unjustified (as regards company management, given that the internal commissions and the usual union organs will continue to take care of the union functions), which must be brought up for discussion by the workers' representatives in the committees where appropriate; on the other hand, and most importantly, [contacts will be maintained] by frequent and regular workers' assemblies where the management committee representatives account for what they have done and discuss the best way to exercise their mandate.

Moreover links should also be established among the various management committees, leading to the institution of federal organs by geographical area (provinces or regions) and by industrial sector. At the highest rung there would be a national organisation where the experiences of all management committees can be shared and that could become one of the fundamental institutions of economic planning.

It is through this constant cycle of activity from top to bottom and from bottom to top that the masses will learn democratic control. They will also acquire technical skills to match the consciousness and maturity they have already gained in the political arena and which are an indispensable prerequisite for socialisation.

This is not the place to talk of socialisation because it is the subject of another talk. Here we shall mention just one more problem, which is linked to that of worker control and which was the subject of the CLNAI decree establishing the management committees: the problem of limiting the dividend in non-nationalised companies. It seems to me that these provisions should be maintained so that dividends on excess industrial profit can be paid, at least in part, into a national social welfare fund or other body of the working class, while excluding any direct participation of individual workers in company profits.

CHAPTER 6

Training Cadres. Problems of the Party

Cadre Training*

The most serious and worrying problem for the socialist party at this time is undoubtedly the problem of cadres.

In August 1943, when the party emerged from hiding to which it had to quickly return, it was badly in need of cadres. Except for those comrades who – in most cases – returned from abroad having had a wide experience of party life but knowing absolutely nothing of the environment and psychological aspects of Italian life, were slow to integrate into local situations; and for those few comrades who had participated in clandestine activities and had experienced prison or exile in the *ventennio*,[1] the party did not have the men to carry out the tough duties awaiting them.

The men of the past, the old leaders who had kept to themselves while preserving their faith in the ideal, could in many cases act as the moral flag bearers but not as real leaders. The young people who flocked to the party were mostly entirely bereft of theoretical and organisational ability. It must be recognised that at the time the best, most active, most combative, and most capable preferred the Communist Party, which had a greater tradition of struggle behind it and benefited from the growing prestige of the victorious Soviet armies.

It was a period in which the party was fighting for its life. The tasks before it were enormous. It had to prove to the masses that it had broken with its old reformism and all the shortcomings of social democracy; that it could adapt to the tasks required of the new situation and again become the centre of attraction for the revolutionary energies of the young; it had to overcome particular local situations and personal positions, remove the encrustations and hesitancy so as to give the movement the ideological homogeneity and solidity necessary for a truly combative organisation; and it had to sweep away the vacillation that had undeniably nestled in our ranks so as to decisively take up position on the field of battle.

At the time the party cadres did not seem up to the immensity of the tasks, and their inadequacy caused organisational problems that in turn reflected on

---

* L. Basso, 'Formare dei quadri. I problemi del partito' in *Unità proletaria*, 15 April 1945.
1 TN: this refers to the twenty years of fascism.

the party as a whole, leaving it exposed to the forces of reaction. Many, too many comrades fell in that period, the work of which would have been valuable, all the more so today. Twice here in Northern Italy, the party even appeared leaderless.

And yet the party overcame this ordeal thanks especially to the heroism of little known militants who held the flag high; thanks to the energy of the new leaders who arose in the heat of the struggle; and thanks to the tenacity of a few leaders who patiently got on with the job that had been repeatedly disrupted. When it will be possible to document this great effort in full – and these pages aim to testify to the work – one will see socialism's great power of attraction, its admirable energy and vitality in triumphing over so many adversities.

From these hardships there at last emerged a renewed party, renewed in respect to its ideas, its methods, and its men. This is not to renege on the socialist tradition. On the contrary, this tradition had produced the faith that filled so many heroic comrades; it is merely to say that that tradition has been updated and adapted to the tasks of the moment. But much remains to be done in every sense: as regards a complete renewal of ideas and methods, and, above all, of greater ideological and organisational cohesion. Both of these issues are on the agenda and great efforts are being made in this direction, but as we have said, at the heart of these there lies, as with all the party's problems, the problem of training cadres.

It is only to the extent that the cadres work that an army, like a party, is able to march and fight. No ideological effort, no shrewd tactic can really be effective without an instrument in the party that is capable of implementing that tactic. That is why the training of cadres should be pursued with great care, despite the rapid succession of events, despite the urgent, the immediate tasks of the moment.

However, although this lack of cadres is undoubtedly a serious deficiency, it does have its positive side that also needs to be highlighted.

Today all parties feel the need for renewal, because the problems we are facing are new. We need to break with the narrowness of certain ideological positions and tactics that led to defeat 25 years ago and adapt to the new situation that is emerging.

This review of positions; this ideological and strategic renewal; this general rejuvenation of men, ideas and methods, cannot take place without difficulty. Each constituted party organ is linked to its past and its traditions, and this inevitably constitutes an obstacle, if only by force of inertia, to the attainment of this goal. This resistance is to be found even in the bosom of our party, in those who have remained anchored to the past, to the dead weight rather than the living force of tradition.

However, precisely because our party has fewer trained cadres than other fellow parties, precisely because there is a greater urgency for new party cadres, the obstacles, hesitations, impediments to the renewal of the party are not as numerous as elsewhere, where there are many more and stronger positions to be defended.

In this sense, our party, which has often been accused of being old and outdated, is today undoubtedly the most open to young people and offers them the richest opportunities. Since it is the most open to the young, the one with the newest cadres, it is also, at least potentially, the least tied to old schemas and formulas, the most agile, and the closest to the concrete situations of the present time. Officials formed in the heat of battle understand problems of the struggle better than others.

It would be a mistake, however, both anti-historical and anti-artistic, to interpret these considerations as a complete break with the past, as a fascistic apologia for youth, to which it might be said all would be permitted.

Youth has possibilities that the experience of others must be able to harness and guide. Fortunately, our party still has men of political and revolutionary experience, men educated in the school of Marxism-Leninism who can prepare the young, coach them, guide them. I would say that the strength of our party, which gives us the best hope for the future, is precisely the balance we have between tradition and youth, between old and new, a balance that allows the party to maintain its policies, even in the presence of the most adverse circumstances and, at the same time, to renew everything in it that is old and out-dated.

Indeed, the great vitality demonstrated by the party in these recent months of bitter and intense struggle, in which it has emerged stronger each time it has suffered police repression, is due to this balance and its great potential.

It is worth remembering, however, that for this potential to become reality and not just remain a vain hope, the party and all its members, not as an abstract and aloof entity, but each of us, must do all we can to realise this potential.

The party needs to attract masses of young people who will find a party that is responsive to their aspirations, that welcomes them eagerly, and that is able to put their abilities to good use. The older, experienced comrades should do whatever they can to instruct these young people, and prepare them for tasks of responsibility.

Events do not stop for anyone and if we find ourselves again unprepared and without party executives, we shall have wasted a great opportunity and shall only have ourselves to blame.

The problem of proselytising, like that of the preparation and training of cadres, should be on the agenda of every federation. But we shall speak of proselytising on another occasion. Here our aim is highlight the extreme importance of having trained party cadres. The task that the party has today – which is to lead the masses in secrecy – is certainly tough, difficult and requires great organisational skill, courage and initiative.

And yet, the tasks facing the party in the future, when it comes to guiding millions and millions of workers in the struggle to establish the republic and the triumph of socialism, not, as some would have it, by adopting the abstract schemas of the Russian Revolution that took place in very different economic, political and social circumstances, but by responding decisively to a situation as complex and difficult as we have in Italy, a defeated country, occupied and humiliated; the tasks of tomorrow, then, will be all the more difficult and complex, and will require greater talents as well as a profound political experience. The errors of today may cost the lives of several comrades, but those of tomorrow could bring about another defeat for the proletariat, a new fascist triumph over another generation, a new world war.

Is the party prepared for these tasks? Evidently not. Despite the favourable opportunities mentioned above, it is clear that very little has been achieved so far. This is due in part to superficial assessments of the problem; and in part because all our energies have been focused on immediate tasks. This has undoubtedly been a mistake, and it is our duty to remedy it however limited the opportunities and however small the results. To forget about this problem until tomorrow would be an unforgivable error.

So, what should be done to prepare the cadres of tomorrow or, rather, to start the preparation, given that effective preparation takes a long time?

First, a selection of cadres who might develop leadership or organisational qualities, in political and trade union terms, should be made. Unfortunately the airtight compartments we are forced to live in by our clandestine condition complicate this selection process. Nonetheless every effort should be made to identify candidates among the mass of members. Party leaders in the provinces who cannot, of course, be acquainted with all the comrades, should seek help in this work from trustworthy members in factories, towns, districts, workers' associations, inviting them to suggest any comrades with the ability and willingness to engage in party activities. To this end, comrades who have direct contact with the grassroots should call and arrange meetings with all grassroots comrades so as to acquire all that is needed for an assessment and then refer back to party officials.

The comrades selected in this way will then need careful training, and this should be done both through party schools and through experience, i.e. by entrusting them with responsibilities. The words 'Party School' should not be understood as something complex and difficult. We should not look at the example of the party schools in Russia and elsewhere, and conclude that anything similar would be impossible in occupied Italy. We have to see what can be accomplished today and do it as best we can.

For example, it is almost always possible for an older, more experienced, better prepared man to gather around him three or four young comrades to discuss general policy, party directives, or some topical political issue. There could be joint readings of party newspapers, or, if none are available, even fascist newspapers will do, because inspiration can always be drawn from them for discussion and instruction. All the better if some of the participants have books by Marx or Lenin or some other book or pamphlet that can prove useful for reading and discussing together. And if three or four companions are unavailable at a time, even one will do. Wherever a young socialist can be found next to a more experienced one, or even just two fellow socialists, a party school can be established.

In cities – or wherever there are greatest opportunities – this work should be done methodically: so in addition to joint readings, actual courses or just simple conversations can be arranged. In these cases, young comrades should try to express their views on the issues discussed, keeping in mind that political skills are not acquired through a set of notions learnt by heart, but by sharpening one's critical capacity, by dissecting issues, by teaching not what to think but how to think, as Labriola said. Comrades should also get used to plain reasoning, the precise framing of a problem, removing all rhetorical frills and all vacuous generalities. To this end, they should be encouraged to set down their own points of view on paper, keep records, write summaries of topics discussed and reports on what to discuss next. Writing leads to precision and a sense of responsibility.

Obviously party schools are not enough. Politics, like all the arts, is not to be learned in books but in practice. Party cadres learn through political experience. So young comrades that seem likely to succeed, that show sufficient ability and sense of responsibility, should certainly be included in party cadres without undue concern. They will make up for their shortcomings with their spirit of enterprise and the courage typical of youth. At first they should be assigned collegial tasks, introducing them to the various committees (organisational committee, political committee, press office, etc., depending on their particular aptitudes – the assessment of particular aptitudes is of the utmost importance for an organiser so as to get the best out of everyone), where they work in conjunction with more experienced comrades.

In this regard we can never stress enough the need to work collegially as much as possible. Individual work has – among other things – the serious disadvantage of often leaving other party positions, even prominent ones, empty in case of arrests. Collegial work produces comrades that are used to discussing, to expressing their thoughts clearly, to analysing and evaluating criticism from others, and to expressing their thoughts in a logical order, topic by topic, following an agenda that must be set beforehand.

Minutes should be taken for each session. This will get comrades used to acting as secretaries, to distinguishing minor points from essential ones in discussions, and to reporting accurately the topics discussed.

We know that many, perhaps most of these things said here may seem superfluous or even pedantic to many comrades; but we know from experience the enormous difficulties that we encountered every time we asked our colleagues for a report, for the minutes of a meeting, or the agenda of a session.

Nevertheless, we shall never tire of insisting and recommending that our comrades carefully consider these apparently pedantic suggestions, because their value goes beyond the formalism of the written word. It can be found in a slow and methodical approach to precision, the disdain of generic platitudes, seriousness and a sense of responsibility.

Without this slow and methodical education, we will not be able to train political and organisational cadres: what we shall get at most is a good speaker at rallies.

But the socialism that we want to build is first and foremost a school of seriousness, a complete rejection of any rhetoric and improvisation.

CHAPTER 7

Democracy and Legalism

Since the very first days of the re-emergence of the illegal socialist movement in Italy in 1941, I have always said, first in simple propaganda leaflets and policy statements circulated in the underground press, and then in programmatic Party declarations, and later in lectures, congresses and articles, that the current Italian crisis has only two possible solutions: either the reconstitution of the old structures of the bourgeois state, which would inevitably lead – for the same historical reasons as before – to new dictatorships and wars; or a decisive move towards bold structural reform which – by finally including the working class in the economic and political life of the community and making it the leading player – will open the road to a genuine socialist democracy.*

Given the historical conditions of our country, I have always discarded the possibility of a third, centrist solution, because it would have no vitality. I have always combatted every form of centrism, because I believe it can only lead to political instability followed by reactionary governments, which inevitably seize the opportunities offered by centrist uncertainties.

So, in the months preceding the insurrection in the North, I promoted an initiative within the Party to establish an agreement among the forces of the left on a common programme, an agreement that was – after the liberation – to replace the purely formal accord among the parties of the CLN. For this reason I have always worked for a unified policy with both communists and Catholics that was designed to achieve a common platform for all workers. Hence after 2 June, against the superficiality of [Giuseppe] Saragat and those of his ilk[1] who sang the praises of a political democracy that had finally been achieved, I argued that it was true that the Republic had marked the defeat of

---

* L. Basso, 'Democrazia e legalitarismo' in *Avanti!*, 23 February 1947.
1 EN: 2 June 1946 is the historic date of the birth of the Italian Republic and of the elections, taking place according to universal suffrage, of the Constituent Assembly whose principal task was to draft the Italian constitution. This was the first election in which women had the vote in Italy. Giuseppe Saragat (1898–88) was the leader of the *Partito socialista dei lavoratori italiani* (Socialist Party of the Italian Workers, PSLI), which was born of the split within the *Partito socialista* (in 1947). Because of his moderate standpoints, he was one of the principal targets of Basso's polemics, who accuses him for his petty bourgeois socialism and for creating a party made up only of middle-class elements.

the more overtly reactionary and monarchist classes, but it had made no substantial changes to the structures of society.

This is evident today. With the final illusion that the Constituent Assembly could solve the fundamental problems of bread and work dissipating, a more mature class consciousness is beginning to develop amongst the workers: through the pact of united action and the union of all the forces of the left, the workers are attempting to create a vast popular bloc that will clear a democratic path to power. Today more than ever a centrist politics that ignores the left means backing the Italian bourgeoisie and thus the forces of reaction [...]

... for the likes of Saragat and [Umberto] Calosso,[2] that is the petty bourgeoisie, democracy is essentially a formal adherence to legalism or to a quiet life, such that the existence of formal democratic laws and the respect of these laws is in itself sufficient to achieve democracy; for we socialists democracy is something more substantial. It is the conscious and effective participation of the workers in the running of the political and economic life of the country. This means the masses have to reach adulthood, namely the conquest, through struggle, of a higher material and intellectual level of life. While the Italian proletariat is forced to fight unemployment, poverty, hunger and disease every day of its existence, democracy is an illusion, whatever the law [...]

Whereas for the sake of a quiet life the petty bourgeois are opposed to unrest and avoid any form of illegality, we, while deploring lawlessness, believe that a much more substantial contribution to democracy is made by the mass of peasants who, breaking the chains of centuries-old slavery, fight for more humane living conditions. It is in this struggle that they acquire the true dignity of citizens, not in the formal and orthodox compliance with every law.

---

2   EN: Umberto Calosso (1895–1959) was a journalist and socialist politician. He left the *Partito socialista di unità proletaria* (Socialist Party of Proletarian Unity) along with Saragat in 1947, to join the PSLI.

3   EN: the framework for these reflections is that of Italy as it emerges from war and fascism, which according to Basso leaves space for only two solutions: either a reconstruction of the old structures of the bourgeois state, which would lead to new dictatorships and to new wars; or to decisively and courageously begin to reform the structures of Italian society. Reforms that by inserting the working class into the economic and political existence of Italian society, effectively make it the protagonist and open the path to an authentically socialist democracy. Against Saragat, Basso insists that Italy cannot take a middle path, which might result in the formation of reactionary governments with consequent political instability. The accusation directed at Saragat and his followers is against their identification of democracy with formal legality – and vice versa. Basso lays claim – as a socialist – to a substantive conception of

In other words, democracy for us is, above all, a movement that rises from below; it is the development of a consciousness among the workers that they have a role to play: that they are to become the new ruling class; it is the realisation of this consciousness through the increasingly effective participation leagues, cooperatives, management committees, mass organisations, mass organs, local administrations, right up to the political government of the country[3] [...]

---

democracy, understood as effective and conscious participation by the workers in the running of the political and economic life of the nation.

PART 3

*The Interpretation of Marxism
After Rosa Luxemburg*

CHAPTER 8

Rosa Luxemburg

The German Social Democratic Party was – especially after the abolition of the anti-socialist laws – the most typical party of the Second International.* Having developed at a time without revolutionary possibilities in Europe, with the exception of Russia, German social-democracy accepted the existence of the imperial state and of capitalist social organisation as irrevocable fact, whereas socialist revolution disappeared in the nebulous distance of the future. Like the entire Second International, German social-democracy considered its principal task to be the safeguarding and improvement of the material lot of the working class within the framework of the bourgeois state. In this field, the old social-democracy, above all thanks to the independent Trade Unions that were allied with it, achieved splendid results up to 1914. On the other hand, for the German Socialists, as for the entire Second International, Marxism served only as a means to separate ideologically their own movement from the bourgeoisie; and the formal radicalism of the Second International exhausted itself in a continuous, bitter polemic against the bourgeois state and its organs, against feudalism and the dynasties. All co-operation with the government or with the bourgeois parties was refused; the Party would vote against the budget and the government's military and foreign policy opposed; but the Social Democrats never considered the real processes through which the existing state could be transformed.

Thus, pre-War Social-Democracy, whose representative was August Bebel, combined extensive politico-social activity with a formal and passive radicalism in all other spheres of public life. The average Social Democratic Party functionary had no real interest in problems of foreign policy and the military, of schools and justice, not even broad economic problems, and especially not agrarian ones. He never realised that the day might come when the Social Democrat would be called upon to decide on all these matters. His interest was concentrated solely upon everything that concerned the technical interests of the industrial working class in the narrow sense of the term. In this sphere he was both well informed and active. Beyond this he was perhaps interested above all else in the question of suffrage ... The Reichstag elections were the barometer that showed the condition of the Social Democratic movement and

---

* L. Basso, *Il Quarto Stato*, 15 January 1949.

the highest honour that could be conferred upon a local socialist organisation was to win a seat in the Reichstag [...]

'A tiny group composing the extreme left rejected the notion that stable economic and political conditions must be reckoned with for a long time to come. Instead, this group prophesied a great war in the immediate future and arising out of it vast revolutionary shocks. They demanded that social democracy should adjust its policy in line with these predictions, thereby preparing the working class for revolutionary struggles and the seizure of power'.[1]

For about twenty years, the heart and mind of this far left was Rosa Luxemburg, who always upheld the traditions of a living Marxism, which she defended against any form of deviation, opportunism and betrayal. And just as official social-democratic policy, which was founded on the separation of the maximalist revolutionary programme from practical reformist activity, would logically lead to the capitulation of 4 August 1914 and the revolutionary impotence of 9 November 1918, so Rosa Luxemburg's persistent and relentless polemics against party policy were to lead her to an open fight against this capitulation and this impotence, which she effectively saw as a betrayal. And just as she suffered more than three years in prison during the war for her opposition to official party policy, so too on 15 January 1919 she paid with her death for her opposition to the social-democratic government's policy of bourgeois restoration.

It is impossible in such a short space to provide an adequate analysis of the thought and actions of one of the greatest Marxist spirits; so I will confine myself to mentioning only a few elements of her arguments ... She devoted a large number of her writings and speeches in congresses, journals and newspapers to the struggle against revisionism, especially with regard to the German and Polish workers' movements. In the pamphlet she wrote in opposition to Bernstein, *Reform or Revolution*, published in 1899, she shows that it is impossible to realise socialism simply through industrial and parliamentary action, since these actions can only be accomplished within the framework of bourgeois society. In opposition to these unilateral visions that conceive of history as an indefinite line of development at the end of which socialism appears as a distant goal and thus lacking all practical interest, she places the dialectical conception of the totality of the historical process that proceeds by contrasts and antinomies. On the one hand, capitalism develops production processes that respond ever more closely to collective needs, while conversely exacerbating anarchy and conflict in class relations. On the other, the proletariat fights

---

1 Rosenberg 1936, pp. 12–15.

an industrial and parliamentary battle to achieve better living conditions in the present society; but in this fight it acquires the consciousness that the solution to its problems, namely its real emancipation, lies in destroying and replacing current social relations. Thus socialism progresses day by day: objectively, through the crisis of the capitalist world, where conditions gradually deteriorate, leading to increasingly serious phenomena (economic crises and wars) which will herald its final collapse; and subjectively through the development of the consciousness and organisation of the proletariat as the new ruling class.

Equipped like few other Marxists with a lively sense of the totality of reality and the inextricable interconnection of all phenomena, Rosa Luxemburg analysed different aspects of the march to socialism. Her study of the objective aspects makes her one of the leading scholars of the era of imperialism. Although many of her conclusions are unacceptable, her seminal work on the accumulation of capital (which appeared in 1913) is still a valuable contribution to the study of imperialist policy, especially with regard to colonial policy. Georg Lukács considers this work and Lenin's *State and Revolution* as 'the two fundamental studies which inaugurate the theoretical rebirth of Marxism'.[2] However, she not only devoted her time to the study of economic imperialism, about which she was particularly knowledgeable and which she also taught in party schools (her lessons were published posthumously), but also the key aspect of military imperialism. She was a constant and stubborn opponent of Prussian militarism, for which she was arrested, tried and sent to one year's imprisonment. She did not denounce militarism as an isolated phenomenon that could be eliminated from society together with all other economic and political problems, but as an intrinsic part of a policy that would necessarily lead to imperialist war.

She saw the outbreak of the imperialist war as the climax of the crisis of capitalism and a herald of proletarian rule. At the Paris Congress of the Second International in 1900, as rapporteur for Commission IV on the problem of war, she asserted the need to abandon old stereotypes and pronounced a speech in which she said, among other things, that: 'The policy of militarism has become generalised and more widespread as imperialism's world policy. It no longer just involves armament in preparation for a possible war between two or three neighbouring states, but a type of militarism in which all the major powers of the world are constantly fixated on new colonial conquests ... Bourgeois society has truly entered a new phase of its evolution. The capitalist world is gaining new momentum as it develops, but in the end it will fade and precipitate fatally

---

[2] 'The Marxism of Rosa Luxemburg', in Lukács 1971, p. 34.

into a state of collapse ... When the socialist movement began, it was generally thought that a huge economic crisis would mark the beginning of the end, the great defeat of capitalism. Now, this supposition has lost much of its credibility. Instead, it looks increasingly likely that a vast global political crisis will sound capitalism's death knell'.[3] Later, at the 1907 Stuttgart Congress, in full agreement with Lenin, she developed the practical consequences of this standpoint. It was in fact Lenin who wanted Rosa Luxemburg among the delegates and gave her a seat amongst the Bolshevik Party delegation. And it was Rosa Luxemburg who, on behalf of the Russian and the Polish delegations, was responsible for the famous amendment that bore not only her signature but also that of Lenin, which was then also approved by [August] Bebel and the Congress. The value of this amendment lies in the fact that, after discussing the need to combat the danger of war in Bebel's resolution, the possibility was examined that war would break out anyway, despite the proletariat's opposition to it; and that the practical rules for action should focus on this eventuality, should use the crisis created by war to mobilise the masses and accelerate the fall of capitalist class domination.

To obtain the consent of Congress, Rosa Luxemburg drew especially on the experiences of the Russian Revolution, which had already provided her with material for a heated exchange with Bebel at the German Social Democrat Congress of Jena (1906), and especially for a major study, *The Mass Strike, the Political Party, and the Trade Unions*. This study provides a particularly vivid example of Rosa Luxemburg's take on the unity and concreteness of the historical process, and the political and revolutionary actions within it, one which does not submit to any organisational schemes and is not imposed from the outside. It can never be abstracted from the totality of the social situation from which it is born, in which it unfolds and which it then modifies in a continuous dialectic where every moment is inseparable from the other, objective and subjective elements, organisation and class consciousness, economic and political aspects, leaders and masses. It has wrongly been claimed that Rosa Luxemburg was a supporter of the 'spontaneity' of the masses, but she was simply pointing out that, in Marxist fashion, revolutions and strikes in general cannot be improvised at will; because they are phenomena that concern the broad mass of the population and that can only be set in motion when the right conditions have matured. She knew, however, that this action can only bear fruit if it is consciously guided by a revolutionary doctrine and supported by party organisation. Indeed, her entire opposition to Bernstein was precisely a rigor-

---

3   EN: it has not been possible to trace this quotation.

ous defence of Marxist theory as a guide to proletarian action; this is in clear contrast to any theory of spontaneity. However, she did feel the need for the wholehearted participation of the masses and the need for class consciousness to develop at the same pace as, or even in advance of, the development of the objective factors on the way to socialism.

As Lukács observes, this concept reflects the Marxist unity of theory and practice (which was ever-present in Luxemburg's thought), in which the Party is assigned the grandiose role of *'bearer of the class consciousness of the proletariat and the consciousness of its historical vocation'*, in which doctrine merges with the conscious will of the masses, and through which 'knowledge becomes action, theory becomes battle slogan, the masses act in accordance with the slogans and join the ranks of the organised vanguard more consciously ... Class consciousness is the "ethics" of the proletariat, the unity of its theory and its practice, the point at which the economic necessity of its struggle for liberation changes dialectically into freedom. By realising that the party is the historical embodiment and the active incarnation of class consciousness, we see that it is also the incarnation of the ethics of the fighting proletariat. This must determine its politics'.[4]

Given her conception of the dialectical development of capitalist society towards its ultimate crisis and the proletariat towards its revolutionary consciousness, her practical attitudes could not but be in favour of a constant and increasingly widespread struggle of the working class against the politics of imperialism, both in peace and – even more so – in war. Rosa Luxemburg was one of the strongest critics of the capitulation of social democracy, which – on 4 August 1914 – voted the war credits that it had always refused in peace. With Franz Mehring she founded the journal *Die Internationale*, of which only the first issue was published, and that contained an article by Luxemburg on the need for a new International. Having been arrested for an earlier conviction, she developed her thoughts in gaol, outlining the approach that the International group (which included herself, Mehring, Liebknecht, Clara Zetkin, and Ernst Meyer) should have adopted in its actions in Germany and in Zimmerwald. Finally, to advance this position she wrote the famous pamphlet on *The Crisis of Social Democracy*, published in Switzerland under the pseudonym Junius and distributed illegally in Germany. It is known that this pamphlet, which normally goes by the name of *Juniusbroschüre* [*The Junius Pamphlet*], was warmly welcomed by Lenin, who dedicated a study to it (republished in *Gegen den Strom*, 1921, pp. 415 ff.), where he points out a number of errors in

---

4 'The Marxism of Rosa Luxemburg', in Lukács 1971, pp. 41–2.

Luxemburg's writings – as a contribution to self-critique – but also underlines its profoundly Marxist character and the great importance that the pamphlet had and was to have in the fight against capitulatory opportunism and for the transition to revolutionary action. Despite the fact that Rosa Luxemburg spent almost all the war years in prison, she participated enthusiastically in the activities of the group and collaborated in the *Spartacus Letters*, which illegally spread her ideas and those of her friends. It was mainly thanks to the extraordinary organisational skills and the iron will of Leo Jogisches, Rosa Luxemburg's life-long companion, that the Spartacus League became an organisation of active militants that influenced ever-broader strata of the proletariat. On 8 November 1918, the Spartacus group, the old group of the International, launched a revolutionary proclamation to workers and soldiers, inviting them to assume power.

As we know, things did not go her way: social democratic traditionalists stopped the revolutionary impetus in its tracks, with power ending up not in the hands of the workers and soldiers but in those of the old Social Democratic leaders, [Friedrich] Ebert and [Philipp] Scheidemann, whose main concern was to avoid a break with bourgeois legality; for whether or not they were aware of it, without breaking the power of bourgeois legality, capitalist power would inevitably be restored and all the aspects of old society reconstituted. Rosa Luxemburg and Karl Liebknecht fought against this solution with all their might. They were convinced that by continuing the struggle class consciousness would be awakened in a few months and the immense reserves of the German proletariat mobilised; but they had none of the facile illusions of the utopians that the course of the revolution could be changed with a few *coups de main*.

Rosa Luxemburg's writings and speeches in the last two months of her life are among the most vivid in revolutionary literature: the programme of the Spartacus League (*Was will der Spartakusbund?*), the speech at the League's Congress, where it changed its name to the German Communist Party (December 29–31 1918), and the articles in *Die Rote Fahne*. Rosa Luxemburg, who in prison during the war had written some notes on the Russian revolution in which – amongst other things – she criticised the Bolsheviks for dissolving the Constituent Assembly, recognised – in the course of the German revolution – that inexorable historical forces had forced the Bolsheviks to choose between the power of the revolutionary councils, which represented the new proletarian regime, and the Constituent Assembly which was the expression of a formal bourgeois democracy. She herself took a stand in Germany against bourgeois power, i.e. the National Assembly, and in favour of revolutionary power, i.e. the councils. She laid bare before the consciousness of the German workers' movement the inescapable dilemma: either it had to advance the socialist revolution in accordance with its own needs and without lingering over the past, or fall once again victim to a restoration of a fatally reactionary capitalist power.

All the defenders of the old order, from the ex-officials of the Kaiser to the Social Democratic government, immediately saw that Rosa Luxemburg and Karl Liebknecht were the only major obstacles in their way. Incitement to hatred and murder against these two great leaders of the working class grew day by day. Newspapers, posters, speeches, all the instruments of propaganda were mobilised to publicly denounce the leaders of the Spartacus League as those responsible for the tragedy of the German people. During the Spartacus riots in Berlin, which neither Rosa Luxemburg nor Karl Liebknecht planned not initiated, [Gustav] Noske called in the Imperial troops against the workers and the hunt for Spartacist leaders was ruthlessly organised. Rosa Luxemburg refused to flee. Was this a trace of romanticism in one who Franz Mehring thought was the greatest living Marxist intellect – according to the historian [Arthur] Rosenberg? Or [is this evidence of] the unity of theory and practice of her actions, which prevented her till the very end from detaching herself from the masses whose consciousness she wanted to contribute to forming, as Lukács believed?

On 15 January, Rosa Luxemburg and Karl Liebknecht were arrested and immediately assassinated. A few days later, Leo Jogisches was arrested and assassinated. Franz Mehring, the historian of the German workers' movement, the author of the best biography of Marx, could not stand the pain of losing his great friends and died soon after.

Thus, the German proletariat lost its best leaders at a time of great difficulty. Reaction had identified its target well.

CHAPTER 9

The Contribution of Rosa Luxemburg to Marxist Thought

[...] In this introduction to the debate, I shall attempt to indicate which points seem to me the worthiest of further examination – which I hope will be undertaken by the other speakers and in the discussions that follow.* For the sake of convenience, I shall group these points into three sections, which are all closely connected. The first relates to the Marxist method, the second to the revolutionary process, and the third to the goals of socialist revolution. For each of these three fundamental areas, I shall necessarily have to refer to Marx's thinking, as interpreted by myself and so certainly not one shared by all those here today. However, my aim is to encourage constructive criticism from those present and whose cooperation is essential to achieve the progress that we expect from our conference. However, I shall try to avoid continuous comparison with the contemporary thinking of Lenin, though this would be quite natural not only for specific discussions in other sessions but also because, personally, I see the work of the two revolutionaries as complementary, despite the contrasts and their disagreements.

As for the method, I am among those who believe that the central concept of Marx's dialectics is that of concrete totality. Because it is only through the totality that we can understand the real relationships between things; discover the hidden substrate (*verborgene Hintergrund*) behind the appearance of phenomenal forms (*Erscheinungsform*); identify the relations between men that in science and everyday understanding are presented as things; cast off the mystic veil that produces fetishes everywhere; show the historical and transitory nature of all social formations, especially that of capitalism; and in short put back on its feet a world overturned by bourgeois ideology. This will enable the producer to become master of his product once again and – in particular – to become master of the production processes, which today are alien to him, and stand before him as enemy and ruler.

It is on this basis that I judge Rosa Luxemburg's contribution to be important. She should be credited with being the first to have restored these concepts

----

* 'Il contributo di Rosa Luxemburg allo sviluppo del pensiero di Marx', in Basso 1976a. This lecture was delivered at a conference on Marxist studies at the Lelio and Lisli Basso-Issoco Foundation, 18–22 September 1973.

to their rightful place and to have used the weapon of dialectics and, in particular, the concept of totality to combat the crude Marxism of German Social Democracy. This includes not only the revisionism of Bernstein but through Bernstein also the current interpretations found in official party policy. A comparison of her polemic against Bernstein with Kautsky's arguments reveals a fundamental difference, which is also at the root of Luxemburg's future polemic against Kautsky and the top echelons of Social Democracy. For Kautsky, Bernstein's position was the mistaken position of a social democrat, while for Luxemburg 'it is much worse than false: it is the total negation of what is social democratic. It is not a mistaken opinion of a social democrat', but 'the right thoughts of a bourgeois democrat, who mistakenly believes he is social democrat'.[1]

Therefore, the Bernstein debate does not represent a dispute between socialists but a polemic against the penetration of bourgeois conceptions into the social democratic movement. By calling for the expulsion of Bernstein from the party, to which both Bebel and Kautsky were opposed, she wished to safeguard the party's class character and eradicate, at the outset, the seeds of the process of social democracy's integration into the capitalist system, which was to be given the green light in the following years under the protective aegis of Kautsky's do-nothing strategy. In her critique of Bernstein, we find in a nutshell all the future arguments that would lead Rosa Luxemburg to fight against official social democratic policy, up to the resounding defeat of 4 August 1914, and perhaps even up to the tragic days of January 1919. Not by chance, many of Luxemburg's most lucid and inspiring positions of her later years were first formulated in this first battle. This can be easily seen if we interpret, as I do, Luxemburg's fight against the official positions of her party not only as a battle of the left against the right and the centre or for or against certain tactical positions, but as a theoretical clash between a dialectical and a non-dialectical interpretation of Marxism.

Since my aim in this introduction is principally to draw attention to what seem to me to be the key elements in Luxemburg's interpretation of Marxism, I will not burden you with quotes to buttress my opinions. Suffice it to say that the concept of 'totality' can be found in her polemic against Bernstein, with which she more or less started her activities as a German social democrat, as well as in her polemic against the Social Democratic Party position in favour of the war that in practice concludes them. In essence her critique of Bernstein is that 'when he abandoned scientific socialism he lost the axis of intellectual

---

1 R 'Nachbetrachtungen zum Parteitag', in Luxemburg 1970, p. 253.

crystallization around which isolated facts group themselves in the organic whole of a coherent conception of the world';[2] and that 'Bernstein's theory does not seize these manifestations of contemporary economic life as they appear in their organic relationship with the whole of capitalist development, with the complete economic mechanism of capitalism. His theory pulls these details out of their living economic context. It treats them as *disjecta membra* ... of a lifeless machine'.[3] Against the support given for the war on the grounds that it was purely defensive, Luxemburg notes that this claim is based on a 'lack of understanding of the whole war and its world relations',[4] separating the problem of 'victory or defeat' from the totality of the historical process, which remains even in time of war the history of class struggle; in contrast, German social democracy decided to suspend the struggle during the war. In both cases, the concept of totality presides over her analysis of the historical process. It is on this same basis that she also examines the phenomenon of capitalist accumulation. Leaving aside any examination of the merits or otherwise of Luxemburg's ideas on accumulation, which we shall discuss in the coming sessions, from the methodological point of view her aim was to investigate 'capitalist accumulation as a whole'[5] within the totality of the historical process, where two aspects of accumulation emerge: one hidden under the illusory guise of 'exchange of equivalents' and the other whose 'arena is the world stage' and whose 'methods are colonial policy, an international loan system – a policy of spheres of interest – and war'.[6] Both are tightly connected, indeed inseparable, so that imperialism emerges as a necessary manifestation of capitalism and not – as its opponents would have it – a pathological form that can be eliminated.

Of course, these remarks have little or no importance for those who do not see the concept of totality as essential to Marxian dialectics, but those who instead share it should also agree on the need to study Rosa Luxemburg's use of it in all her theoretico-practical activities.

On the level of thought, the notion of totality is needed – as it was for Marx – to see the reality behind the appearance of phenomena. In the above quote from *The Accumulation of Capital*, it is significant that, after mentioning the two aspects of accumulation, Luxemburg says that Marx's incisive dialectics of Marx's scientific analysis revealed the real social relations and economic laws that were hidden behind the notion of exchange of equivalents; so now it was

---

2 *Reform or revolution*, in Luxemburg 2008, p. 98.
3 *Reform or revolution*, in Luxemburg 2008, p. 70.
4 Luxemburg 1919, p. 100.
5 Luxemburg 2003, p. 22.
6 Luxemburg 2003, p. 432.

the task of social democracy 'to discover within this tangle of political violence and contests of power the stern laws of the economic process'.[7] It is no easy task to use the weapon of dialectics as Marx did, to discover the mysterious and hidden connections behind immediate appearances. She points out that 'as much as we would all like to think dialectically, we are, in our immediate conditions of consciousness, incorrigible metaphysicians who cling to the immutability of things'. And yet, immediately after writing these words on the sudden outbreak of the revolution in 1905, she adds that one must 'clarify the internal historical sense ... of the movement',[8] to understand the logic of history, which is the objective logic of the social process, because 'from the beginning the revolutionary seed was in the events'. The workers' movement cannot become revolutionary if this logic is not understood, if the nut within the shell is not grasped, if metaphysics is not abandoned for dialectics, ideology for reality. It is only through the method of totality that this can be done. Rosa Luxemburg must be credited for repeatedly stressing its fundamental importance for the purposes of practical revolutionary action.

In practical terms, the method of totality led Luxemburg to demonstrate the meaning and primary importance for the strategy of the working-class movement of the inseparable unity of the daily struggle for partial goals and for the final goal, where the final goal refers precisely to the totality. Without this reference, individual struggles, trade union campaigns or parliamentary action, goals, even partial gains lose their specific characteristic of being moments in a revolutionary process. On the contrary, they become moments in the process of working class integration into the system. 'The movement in itself, without any relation to the final goal, the movement as an end in itself is nothing for the working class. The final goal is everything', she said in a speech at the Social Democratic Congress in Stuttgart in 1898.[9]

Lukács underlined the importance of the ultimate goal being 'rather that *relation to the totality* (to the whole of society seen as a process), through which every aspect of the struggle acquires its revolutionary significance',[10] and many authors have subsequently stressed this. We could probably say that today no one would challenge the theoretical validity and practical importance of Luxemburg's argument, though we can hardly say that it is indeed applied in the

---

7   Ibid.
8   'Nach dem ersten Akt, in Gesammelte Werke', in Luxemburg 1972a, p. 487; *Die Revolution in Russland*, in Luxemburg 1972a, p. 509.
9   'Parteitag der Sozialdemokratischen Partei Deutschlands', vom 3. bis 8. October 1898 in Luxemburg 1970, p. 241.
10 Lukács 1971, p. 22.

movement's everyday praxis. On the contrary, as in the past we still see today disputes between those that Marx would have called the 'alchemists of the revolution'[11] and the 'practical politicians', the *realpolitikers*. The former see the ultimate goal as the immediate seizure of power, and all partial goals despised as 'reformist'. For reformists, the 'ultimate goal' has either been abandoned or is considered to be impractical, unconnected to daily action. Single gains are seen as having value in themselves, without any real reference to the general context of the process of social transformation. In this way we again gradually lose the 'power of seeing the larger connections and of taking a survey of the whole position'.[12] This was the criticism she made of the separation of economic struggle and political struggle, and of the supposed neutrality of the trade unions that tended to deprive the mass 'of the knowledge of the ... contradictions of the existing order and the complicated character of its development'[13] essential to social democratic political action. We can thus sum up her position as follows: first, in this total vision, the economic struggle and the political-parliamentary struggle, which at that time took up almost all the energies of the movement, are understood to be two distinct but not separate aspects of class struggle; they are two sides of the same activity whose totalising aspect is the political aspect. Therefore neither trade unions nor parliamentary groups can manage without the party or claim to exercise an equal or even superior role to the party. This means that although unions are independent in their specific field of activity, and are not a mere transmission belt, they must see this field as a place for general proletarian action for which the party acts as interpreter and unifier. Similarly, parliamentary groups, whose usefulness are not disputed, must be seen only as an instrument of party action and cannot claim any monopoly over political action or any hegemony over the party. Rosa Luxemburg's opposition to the formula '*nur Parlamentarismus*' (which more or less corresponds to the present-day 'parliamentary road to socialism'), is the continuation of Marx's fight against 'parliamentary cretinism'. She rightly points out that the key factor is not the parliamentary strength of the party, not the number of seats won in an election, but the party's real strength in the country, namely its consensus among the working masses and their capacity to fight.

To develop consistently these ideas today would lead to a critique of the political action of the majority of labour parties now operating in Western Europe, and perhaps even to the development of an alternative strategy that

---

11   EN: For the phrase, 'alchemists of the revolution', see MECW Volume 10, p. 318.
12   *The Mass Strike*, in Luxemburg 2008, p. 177.
13   *The Mass Strike*, in Luxemburg 2008, p. 179.

would guide the conscious intervention of the workers' movement within the heart of the social process and its various dimensions, giving it a clearly revolutionary direction.

I have thus reached the second aspect I wish to discuss: Rosa Luxemburg's thoughts on the modalities of the revolutionary process. Here too, though, I think it necessary to summarise briefly my interpretation of Marx's ideas of the revolutionary process, because only through such a comparison can we see whether Luxemburg made a contribution to the development of Marxist thought. Of course, I am obliged to simplify and so, inevitably, to give only a brief outline and for this I apologise to my authoritative listeners. It is clear that Marx presents the contradiction between the social development of the forces of production and the private character of the relations of production as the fundamental contradiction, and that he argues that this contradiction generates a self-destructive process within the system that unfolds with the necessity of a natural process. And yet this objective process would never lead to socialism without the conscious intervention of the working class. In a rarely quoted passage of *Herr Vogt*, Marx defines revolutionary action precisely as the 'conscious participation in the historical process revolutionising society before our very eyes'.[14] What Marx never clearly states is what would happen if the workers' movement did not enter into this conscious participation that must direct the objective processes of capitalist society towards the goal of socialism. As I understand it – and I apologise once again for presenting a rather personal interpretation of Marx's doctrine – the fact that capitalist society is a concrete totality means that a totalising force acts within it, one that is commonly called the logic of the system and on which the structuralist interpretation of Marx is based. This totalising force, this logic of the system, acts continuously to unify the different aspects, to restore a balance that has been upset, 'subordinating all elements of society to itself', as Marx puts it. Thus not only is there a self-destructive force acting within capitalist society stemming from the fundamental contradiction, but also a rebalancing force that is part of the very nature of the system. Thus, two antagonistic forces operate, or, if we prefer, two antagonistic logics: the logic of the forces of production and the logic of the current system. The first, as a result of coming into conflict with the relations of production, exerts a force that pushes towards a new mode of production and new socialist relations. The second, the logic of capitalist relations of production, or the logic of the current system, tends to reproduce the same relations of production, to try continuously to restore the system's disturbed balance, to

---

14   Marx, MECW 17, p. 79.

bend all forces of disturbance towards its needs, to try and iron out the contradictions, albeit provisionally, which will then return with a vengeance. It will try, in a word, to rationalise the entire social formation, to make it functional to the needs of profit, even to the extent of attempting to include the antagonistic class and mercilessly marginalising anyone who does not agree. What Marx describes as the conflict between the forces of production and the relations of production is the conflict between these two antagonistic logics. One of them, the forces of production, is decisive at the diachronic level, to use a term currently in fashion (i.e. at the historical level, which is what interests Marxism). The other, the relations of production, may be stronger, unless effectively countered, at the synchronic level.

We must admit that, despite having always insisted on this being the fundamental contradiction, Marx never clearly explained it. He repeated till the end that the development of the forces of production would lead to the overthrow of the current relations of production. However, he himself probably did not sufficiently gauge the level of resistance offered by the logic of the system, namely the inner coherence of the economic configuration of society understood as a totality. We only discover here and there an occasional note on the logic of the system that is said to deploy ideology to mask the reality of social relations and overturn producer-product relations, so that, ultimately, the workers will themselves come to accept capitalist relations as 'natural'; in other words, it determines a process that is today known as the 'integration' of the working class into the system. Moreover, we know from the above-cited passage of *Herr Vogt* that to prevent this process of integration and replace it with a revolutionary process, the mere subjective will of the movement is insufficient. The movement needs to 'participate consciously' in the objective revolutionary processes that develop within capitalist society. This, the passage goes on to say, is based on 'the scientific study of the economic structure of bourgeois society as the only tenable theoretical foundation'.[15]

Clearly I cannot claim to have summed up Marx's revolutionary design in these few lines, but I think I have highlighted its central point, a point missed by those who interpret Marx in a deterministic-evolutionary sense, based primarily on the 'Preface' to *The Critique of Political Economy*, and also by those who see Marxism in terms of voluntaristic subjectivism, in which the fundamental contradiction is the clash between classes, relegating to the background, or even ignoring, the scientific analysis of bourgeois society and the self-destructive processes that develop inside it. Nor would I subscribe to

---

15   Ibid.

the view of those who identify the contradiction between the forces of production and the relations of production with the class struggle. Marx distinguishes them clearly, but creates a synthesis in the way I shall now describe. He links the conscious participation of the proletariat to the objective processes taking place in the actual movement. Thus, the logic of the socialisation of the forces of production, which stems from capitalist development, can be used as the basis for a new mode of production that can lay new economic foundations for society. If this dialectical interaction between objective processes and subjective intervention does not take place, we do not get the true revolutionary praxis which Marx spoke of in the third thesis on Feuerbach, and society will not advance towards socialist revolution. The thesis expressed by Marx in *The Holy Family* – later taken-up by Lukács – that the working class is historically required to assume this true class consciousness and cannot escape its historical revolutionary mission, seems to me more metaphysical than dialectical, and I do not think there is a basis for it in Marx's mature writings.

In any event, it seems to me that Luxemburg made an original and valuable contribution in this regard too. Indeed, I would be very pleased if this conference could help clarify the matter. I will not spend too much time refuting the argument of those who attribute a deterministic or fatalistic interpretation of Marx to Luxemburg, making her a proponent of the theory of collapse. It is likely that will be done by others during the debate, and I do not have time in an introduction that is meant to be a quick review of the main issue. Moreover, the excerpts I am about to quote and the interpretation I am about to give, point to the opposite of a determinist perspective. In the controversy as to whether capitalism possessed an indefinite vitality and an indefinite adaptability, the practical result of which would mean either renouncing socialism or reducing it to a mere ethical aspiration, she took the contrary view, highlighting the contradictions of capitalism and self-destructive processes produced by these contradictions. In this she was merely following Marx, and to some extent extending his analysis in analysing the phenomena of imperialism, discovering there other contradictions, all derived from the fundamental contradiction, and other self-destructive processes that the workers' movement needs to grasp so as to intervene in them in their revolutionary activities. The fact that she uses expressions like 'historical necessity' or 'iron law' is in no way an indication of fatalism or determinism. Marx himself had used similar or even more extreme expressions and so did Kautsky and, after him, Lenin. And certainly no one would think of Lenin as a determinist.

Neither was Rosa Luxemburg. Not only does she explain that historical laws are always tendencies that clash with other laws or tendencies, but also, and above all, she does not see these laws as separate from social struggles. She does not conceive the proletariat as a spectator waiting for the inevitable crash, as Kautsky does. She sees the proletariat as the protagonist whose task, as Marx indicated, was to intervene in ongoing processes whose causes and governing laws must be identified.

'Here, as elsewhere in history, theory is performing its duty if it shows us the *tendency* of development, the logical conclusion to which it is objectively heading. There is as little chance of this conclusion being reached as there was for any other previous period of social development to unfold itself completely. The *need* for it to be reached becomes less as social consciousness, embodied this time in the socialist proletariat, becomes more involved as an active factor in the blind game of forces. In this case, too, a correct conception of Marx's theory offers the most fruitful suggestions and the most powerful stimulus for this consciousness'.[16]

There exists, therefore, a 'logical conclusion' towards which the tendency of development is heading, and this logical conclusion coincides with the ultimate goal of the workers' movement. However, the fact that they coincide at the end, for both Rosa and Marx, does not mean they coincide at the beginning, because the objective historical processes must be discovered behind the veil of ideology, inside the shell that conceals the kernel, behind the phenomenal form that conceals the substrate. So Rosa warns us that the 'logic of the objective historical process precedes the logic of its protagonists', and it is only through struggle, experience, mistakes, and self-criticism that the proletariat can become aware of these processes and historical laws, and can learn to use them in its revolutionary praxis.

Since Rosa never wrote a handbook of revolutionary strategy, we must look to all her writings to identify and follow the main points of this strategy. However, it seems clear that it is a development of Marx's conscious participation of the proletariat in objective processes. When she says that 'The proletariat is not all-powerful ... its power all lies in the realization of the revolutionary side of the tendencies of capitalist development',[17] she is stressing the revolutionary side of the development tendencies, thus implying that there also exists a non-revolutionary side, which seems to be a reference to the two antagonistic logics we talked about and to which we shall return. However, it must be clear that the fact that the proletariat must exploit an objective

---

16   Luxemburg 1972b, pp. 146–7.
17   Luxemburg, 'Nacjonalizm a socjaldemokracja rosyjska i polska: 1. Socjalpatriotyczna robinsonada', in *Przegląd Socjaldemokratyczny*, no. 10, 1903.

tendency that is immanent in capitalist development does not mean that the proletariat should not develop all its revolutionary energy.

'Far from blunting or sapping our revolutionary fervour, a sensitivity to the objective movement of history tempers the will and pushes us to action by showing us ways to drive the wheel of social progress effectively forward and by sparing us from impotently and fruitlessly knocking our heads against the wall, which sooner or later inevitably brings disappointment, despair, and quietism; through this knowledge we are protected as well from mistaking, as revolutionary activity, aspirations that have long since been transformed by the forces of social evolution into their reactionary opposites'.[18]

Thus, the proletariat has an active task that permanently requires all its capacity for creative initiative and struggle. In Rosa Luxemburg, this capacity of the masses for initiative and struggle has often been criticised as 'spontaneity', while it is none other than the *geschichtliche Selbsttätigkeit* of the working class mentioned by Marx. To be clear, the activities are conscious because the first task of the proletariat is to discern the 'revolutionary side of the tendency of capitalist development' within the ambiguity of the historical process.

This concept of the ambiguity of the historical process, to which Rosa returns on several occasions, develops the notion of the two antagonistic logics operating in capitalist development; these, as we saw, were only hinted at in Marx. 'World politics', writes Rosa, using an expression that was then equivalent to what later became known as imperialism, 'and the workers' movement. Each is only a different aspect of the present phase of capitalist development'.[19] This in her Anti-Bernstein. In *Juniusbroschüre*, written during the war, she reiterates this with even greater clarity:

> Historic development moves in contradictions, and for every necessity puts its opposite into the world as well. The capitalist state of society is doubtless a historic necessity, but so also is the revolt of the working class against it. Capital is a historic necessity, but in the same measure is its grave digger, the Socialist proletariat. The world rule of imperialism is a historic necessity, but likewise its overthrow by the proletarian international. Side by side the two historic necessities exist, in constant conflict with each other.[20]

---

18   Luxemburg 1976, p. 94.
19   *Reform or revolution*, in Luxemburg 2008, p. 87.
20   Luxemburg 1919, p. 123.

This explicit recognition of an ambiguity of history and the coexistence of two logics, two contradictory historical necessities, is the clearest condemnation of any fatalism or determinism. It is a direct appeal to the conscious action of the proletariat, which Rosa epitomised during the war in her rallying call of 'socialism or barbarism'.

> Scientific Socialism has taught us to recognise the objective laws of historical development. Man does not make history of his own volition, but he makes history nevertheless. The proletariat is dependent in its actions upon the degree of righteousness to which social evolution has advanced. But again, social evolution is not a thing apart from the proletariat; it is in the same measure its driving force and its cause as well as its product and its effect. And though we can no more skip a period in our historical development than a man can jump over his shadow, it lies within our power to accelerate or to retard it. Socialism is the first popular movement in the world that has set itself a goal and has established in the social life of man a conscious thought, a definite plan, the free will of mankind … Socialism will not fall as manna from heaven … Friedrich Engels once said: 'Capitalist society faces a dilemma, either an advance to Socialism or a reversion to barbarism'. … Thus we stand today, as Friedrich Engels prophesied more than a generation ago, before the awful proposition: Either the triumph of imperialism and the destruction of all culture, and, as in ancient Rome, depopulation, desolation, degeneration, a vast cemetery; or, the victory of Socialism, that is, the conscious struggle of the international proletariat against imperialism, against its methods, against war. This is the dilemma of world history, its inevitable choice, whose scales are trembling in the balance, awaiting the decision of the proletariat. Upon it depends the future of culture and humanity.[21]

Which of these two alternatives will win? In the dark period in which she wrote the *Juniusbroschüre*, she saw with clear foresight where social democracy's renunciation of its revolutionary role would lead: since socialism cannot win without the conscious intervention of the proletariat, it will be barbarism that triumphs, namely the Nazi fascist dominion of Europe and the Second World War.

---

21   Ibid.

new, feverish armaments in all nations, defeated Germany, of course, at the head, and it would introduce an era of undivided rule for militarism and reaction all over Europe, with a new war as its final goal.[22]

In her last few weeks of life, after being released from prison, she would repeat her cry of 'socialism or a reversion to barbarism'.[23] Finally, in the keynote speech at the founding congress of the Communist Party, she would repeat that 'if the proletariat fails to fulfil its class duties, if it fails to realize socialism, we shall crash down together to a common doom'.[24] I hope I have made clear why I attach importance to her concept of the ambiguity of history. If what Marx says is right, that two antagonistic logics co-exist in this society, one expressed by the relations of production, which strengthens the system (logic of integration), and the other expressed by the forces of production, which tends to destroy it (logic of revolution), and if it is true that revolution can only happen when the proletariat becomes conscious of the processes set in motion by the revolutionary logic of the forces of production and takes an active part, then Luxemburg takes us forward along this path, because she shows us that the two antagonistic logics are both present, as contradictory historical necessities, at all times, even though the forces driving are not always equal.

'Our necessity receives its justification with the moment when the capitalist class ceases to be the bearer of historic progress, when it becomes a hindrance, a danger, to the future development of society':[25] this is the objective element that can determine the success of the revolution if subjective intervention is ready to grasp it.

But the subjective element, i.e. working class action, is faced with the abovementioned ambiguity: the two antagonistic historical necessities. And this takes us back to the problem of totality, the problem of the link between everyday struggle and the ultimate goal, because the historical necessity of capitalism, the logic of the system pushes for integration and, therefore, can encourage and facilitate the attainment of partial objectives on condition that they are separated from the ultimate goal; whereas the antagonistic logic, that of the forces of production, shows the revolutionary side of social processes and indicates the lines of development that the proletariat must follow to mediate between the existing situation and the final goal. If the proletariat separates the partial objectives from the final goal, it will not find the road to revolution

---

22   Ibid.
23   Luxemburg 1919, p. 18.
24   'Our Program and the Political Situation', 31 December 1918, in Luxemburg 2004, p. 364.
25   Luxemburg 1919, p. 123.

and fall into opportunism; that is, it will submit to the process of integration, to the logic of the system. However, the danger of falling into opportunism is not only a danger for the labour aristocracies but to the entire movement, because it is immanent to the contradictory nature of development, to the ambiguity of the process on which we have placed such emphasis.

> Marxist doctrine cannot only refute opportunism theoretically. It alone can explain opportunism as a historic phenomenon in the development of the party. The forward march of the proletariat, on a world-historic scale, to its final victory is not, indeed, 'so simple a thing'. The peculiar character of this movement resides precisely in the fact that here, for the first time in history, the popular masses themselves, *in opposition* to the ruling classes, are to impose their will, but they must effect this outside of the present society, beyond the existing society. The *will* the masses can only form in a constant struggle against the existing order. The union of the broad popular masses with an aim reaching beyond the existing social order, the union of the daily struggle with the great world transformation, that is the task of the social democratic movement, which must logically grope on its road of development between the following two reefs: abandoning the mass character of the party or abandoning its final aim, falling into sectarianism or bourgeois reformism, anarchism or opportunism.[26]

It is clear from this passage, which Luxemburg considered to be so important as to repeat it verbatim in two of her writings many years later, that opportunism is a characteristic of the whole workers' movement whenever it sets itself only partial goals, outside the context of the global transformation of society. That is, whenever it fails to see things from the standpoint of the totality and fails to choose the road of active intervention in the objective revolutionary process, which paves the way for the other logic, the other historical necessity, that of integration. This was the road followed by German social democracy and by every workers' movement that followed its example, despite gaining, like German social democracy, impressive electoral successes and even managing to become part of the government of the country.

But just as opportunism is immanent, so too is the revolution immanent to the historical process of development. Rosa Luxemburg did not conceive the revolution as an event that is completed in a single stroke, in a specific

---

26   *Reform or revolution*, in Luxemburg 2008, pp. 102–3.

moment, with the seizure of power. For her, it was a long historical process – as described by Marx in the Preface to *The Critique of Political Economy* – during which revolutionary praxis will transform both men and society. Rosa says that to conceive the revolution only as a violent confrontation is to have a thriller-like vision of the revolution, with recognising that the struggle for power is a long struggle, part of a vast process where the final blow, the catastrophe is but a culminating moment. 'Catastrophes', she warns, 'do not conflict with development, but represent a moment, a phase of development'. Rosa Luxemburg, therefore, never had in mind a purely objective catastrophe that would occur when capitalism had exhausted its capacity to subject new non-capitalist areas or sectors to its will, finding itself, therefore, unable to survive economically. This moment is a 'theoretical fiction, precisely because capital accumulation is not just an economic but also a political process'.[27] 'The objective tendency of capitalist development in this direction is much sooner sufficient to produce such a social and political sharpening of contradictions in society, that they must terminate the dominant system'.[28] It is the same reasoning that Lenin uses to reject Kautsky's ultra-imperialism.

I can, therefore, conclude this section by making it clear that for Rosa Luxemburg the contradictory logic of capitalist development always includes contradictory historical necessities. This places the workers' movement before the difficult choice of aiming either for totality and the ultimate goal, or mere reformist empiricism and submitting to the system's integrating logic. Either choice – revolution or opportunism, class consciousness or mystified consciousness – are immanent to every moment of the historical process and it is the duty of labour parties to always keep the tension high and direct it towards the ultimate goal, to never submit to the temptation of piecemeal reformism, because, whatever the good intentions, this means objectively strengthening capitalism.

It would certainly be interesting to analyse the specific content of Marx and Luxemburg's strategy of permanent attack that was aimed not at the immediate seizure of power but at reaching a set of partial goals that globally would constitute a nascent future society that would emerge from the bosom of the old at the end of a process of gestation. However, neither of them gave us detailed programmes, although the Spartacus programme is a good illustration of this strategy. Both of them did provide us with a frame of reference that can be valuably used by workers' movements now operating in advanced capitalist countries, where the system is so complex and variously structured that a

---

27   Luxemburg 1972b, p. 146.
28   Luxemburg 1972b, p. 258.

sudden violent break would seem a difficult proposition, whereas conscious everyday action may be able to leverage the social development of the forces of production, so as to increasingly drive capitalist relations of production into crisis.

And yet, even this permanent interaction between objective revolutionary processes and conscious proletarian intervention would not lead to socialism unless, at a certain point, a revolutionary crisis were to arise, which, as we have seen, cannot simply fall from the skies but is an intensification of existing contradictions. Here, too, it seems to me that Rosa Luxemburg made an important original contribution. Marx, as we know, saw the revolution as a consequence of an economic crisis. However, at the end of the century, after a long depression that had begun in 1873, and after the vigorous capitalist recovery that culminated in a new imperialist phase, this possibility seemed remote. Bernstein was to use it as a basis for his revisionism. Luxemburg was, to my knowledge, the first to argue that Marx's statement about the economic crisis should not be taken literally, because what mattered was that the contradictions of capitalism should become so evident that they would lead to sedition. She advanced the thesis that what was not generated by the economic crises could be produced by political crises, i.e. by wars, to which imperialism necessarily led. So it was that at the party congress in Mainz in 1900 she spoke of a new era that was dawning for capitalism. The same year, speaking of militarism in the International Congress of Paris, she clearly stated her thesis with these words:

> Citizens, at the beginning of the socialist movement, it was generally supposed that the beginning of the end would be marked by a huge economic crisis, the great capitalist debacle. This has now become much less likely. But what is becoming more and more likely is that the death knell of capitalism will, instead, be sounded by a vast global political crisis. So, citizens, if the capitalist Marlborough has left for war, perhaps never destined to return, if world politics generates conflict and unexpected, incalculable, events, we have to be prepared for the great role which, sooner or later, we shall be called on to fulfil.[29]

The great role was the revolution, the revolution that could have arisen from war (and which, in fact, did arise from the Russo-Japanese War, the First World War and then the Second World War) but could come about only if the pro-

---

29 Unofficial stenographic record of the French version of the Fifth International Socialist Congress held in Paris from 23–7 September 1900, Paris, 1901, pp. 181–5.

letariat had previously begun, in time of peace, its struggle against militarism, imperialism and war. Seven years later, at the International Congress of Stuttgart, these considerations originated the famous amendment she submitted, signed also by Lenin and Martov, which can be considered the first draft of the formulation of the Leninist strategy for transforming imperialist war into revolution, and which the Third International recognised as a cornerstone of the revolutionary Marxism of the Second International.

German social democracy always tended to ignore the danger of imperialism and militarism, which the opportunist wing of the party presented as deviations from the normal development of democratic capitalism. It was Luxemburg who was the first to show that militarism was essential to capitalist development: as well as playing a role in foreign policy and internal repression, they also had an economic aim, functioning as a subsidiary market to create the demand needed to prevent the profit mechanism from getting stuck. Today, after the post-war experience of the United States has shown that the primary function that rearmament has had in the American mechanism of accumulation (from World War II to the Korean War and Indochina War), this statement of Rosa Luxemburg, which dates back to exactly 75 years ago, demonstrates the acuteness of her analysis and the valuable contribution she made to Marxist studies.

To conclude, we shall now turn to the third topic I wished to speak of, namely the nature of the socialism that Luxemburg would have liked to build through this revolutionary process. However, my introductory speech has already been too long. So I shall not discuss the questions of the relationship between socialism and democracy, a topic to which Rosa Luxemburg made a contribution that in my opinion is of inestimable value. It might perhaps serve as a topic for discussion in the next sittings. (In any event, I intend to return to the issue in the final sessions of the conference). Not only did she conceive socialism in the Marxian sense, not as a mere socialisation of the means of production, but as a reversal of the relationship that exists today between the product that dominates and the producer who is dominated, so that workers gain full control over collective social processes, but she directed her whole conception of the relationship between masses and party, spontaneity and consciousness, movement and organisation towards this goal. Of course, due to the disputes and controversies that accompanied her activities within the party, she may have sometimes used expressions that lend themselves to criticism and sometimes made mistakes by failing to give proper consideration to a number of non-capitalist factors, such as the role played by agriculture or nationalism. She also focused more on strategy than tactics, as was right, though she perhaps sacrificed too much, since the importance of tactics lies in the precise knowledge of all the particulars on the ground on which one operates. Yet, as Lenin wrote, despite the mistakes, she was and remains an eagle, an eagle from which we still have much to learn because her spiritual heritage has not yet been fully studied and remains, unfortunately, not fully known.

CHAPTER 10

The Dialectical Nature of the State According to Marx

The workers' movement in the West is in the middle of a serious theoretical crisis that is inevitably also affecting the development of appropriate strategies for the socialist transformation of society.* We are convinced that Marx, in his studies of the laws of the development of capitalist society, anticipated its development to such an extent that it was difficult for the workers' movement, which was confronted with the immediate pressures of the time, to grasp the spirit of his thinking. Over the course of a century or so it has undergone a series of reductive interpretations that have gradually rendered it schematic and dogmatic. Marx's original vision has been replaced by that of his followers, who interpreted him according to the immediate requirements of their own struggles and translated it into formulas that are ill suited to the developed capitalist societies in which we live today.

However, it seems that precisely the extraordinary development of the forces of production triggered by capitalist society and the socialising impetus that erupts from it, in radical contrast to the capitalist relations of production, have made Marx's true ideas much more topical today than those of his followers. Indeed, perhaps only now are we going through a historical experience that can allow us to fully grasp Marx's significance. The time seems to have come, to use the expression of a communist comrade who teaches philosophy at the University of Florence, to interpret Marx according to Marx, that is, by re-reading his works, stripping them of any commentaries except for the reality around us and thereby drawing lessons valid for the times in which we live. This seems to be a need that is widely shared by many Marx scholars, the purpose of whose studies is precisely to re-read Marx, especially in the key points of his thought, so as to understand with the aid of the instruments he provided not so much the reality in which he worked as the reality in which we now live, which has changed profoundly in many ways. However, these changes have taken place precisely in the direction he had indicated, so that we can now understand their meaning more clearly. Perhaps the time has come when the workers' movement will be able to uncover the hidden kernel of reality that

---

* 'La natura dialettica dello Stato secondo Marx' in Basso, Carandini et al. 1977.

lies behind the phenomenal form of capitalist relations, demystify fetishes, put back on its feet the reality of the social relations that now stand on their head, gain consciousness of the historical and transient character of the current social formation and thus pave the way to higher social relations, ones that are more consistent with the immense possibilities created by technical development.

In this context, what seems to us most important is not so much a discussion of Marx's conception of the state, the relationship between his youthful and more mature writings on this issue, the concordances and discordances in statements made by Marx, Engels and Lenin, but a study, employing the Marxist method, of today's state whose functions are so different from that of Marx's time, and even from that of 1917. It seemed to us that we cannot seriously address the problem of overcoming capitalist society and winning political power without a detailed analysis of the state and of power in today's advanced capitalist countries. Clearly this analysis is impossible without first taking a look at Marx's method; which is why we will preface the concrete analysis of the phenomena within today's capitalist states with a discussion of Marx's conception of the state.

I shall restrict myself to the aspects that I believe deserve further analysis, expressing in this regard also my personal views.

The first point concerns the relations between the state and society, often seen in a light that does not seem to me to correspond to Marx's ideas. I am referring especially to the arguments of those who uphold the autonomy of the state, based especially on some partial allusions by Marx, forgetting that Marx himself had promised to deepen this theme, which he then did not have the time to write. It is precisely this lacuna that, in my opinion at least, forces us to seek the fundamentals of Marx's doctrine of the state not so much in scattered explicit references, as in his general conception of society and its historical development, of which the state is but an aspect and which cannot be conceived of separately, however important it may be. On this basis we can reach two conclusions. First, the state is always an expression of existing social relations, from which it can never be independent. Secondly, since these social relations are characterised by dialectical contradictions, these contradictions, these lacerating antagonisms, cannot fail to be reflected within the state itself. Therefore I believe it is wrong to consider the bourgeois state as a monolithic power block rather than as the seat of permanent struggles for power between contrasting tendencies.

The first statement is not only confirmed in many of Marx's works but, more importantly, it responds to his conception of history as a global social process, held together by dialectical relations and where the structural aspect conditions the entire process. In this global social process, the state certainly plays a specific role, but this role is directly connected to the needs that emerge from relations of the base and, in particular, with the need to reproduce the capitalist relations of production. However, the way in which the state fulfils this role varies in accordance with the conditions accompanying the reproduction of capitalist relations of production, and especially with the need to overcome resistance and contradictions.

Marx affirmed his view of the dependence of the state on society as early as 1844. That year, Engels says in 'On the History of the Communist League', Marx had come to the conclusion that it was not the state which conditions and regulates civil society, but civil society which conditions and regulates the state.[1] In *The German Ideology* Marx writes: 'The material life of individuals ... their mode of production and form of relations that are mutually dependent are the real foundation of the State ... These real relationships are not created by the power of the state: they are rather the power that creates it'.[2] Similarly, in *The Holy Family*: 'Only *political superstition* still imagines today that civil life must be held together by the state, whereas in reality, on the contrary, the state is held together by civil life'.[3] And in *The Poverty of Philosophy*, 'the sovereigns who in all ages have been subject to economic conditions, but they have never dictated laws to them. Legislation, whether political or civil, never does more than proclaim, express in words, the will of economic relations'.[4] I could go on forever with these quotes because, until the end of his life, Marx remained true to this concept, which is also part of his materialist interpretation of history. Let us then conclude here with a quote from the *Critique of the Gotha Programme*, where he says that 'the German Workers' party ... in that, instead of treating existing society (and this holds good for any future one) as the *basis* of the existing *state* (or of the future state in the case of future society), it treats the state rather as an independent entity that possesses its own "intellectual, ethical, and libertarian bases"'.[5]

But what is the specific role of the state in its dialectical relation with the material basis of society? For a long time Marxists, following Engels' interpretation rather Marx's, placed the emphasis almost exclusively on the repressive function. They saw the state almost exclusively as a tool of repression in the hands of the ruling class. Yet already in the famous definition of the *Manifesto*,

---

1 F. Engels, 'On the History of the Communist League', in Marx and Engels 1970, p. 178.
2 Marx, *The German Ideology*, in MECW 5, p. 329.
3 Marx, *The Holy Family*, in MECW 4, p. 121.
4 Marx, *The Poverty of Philosophy*, MECW 6, p. 147.
5 Marx, *Critique of the Gotha Programme*, MECW 24, p. 94.

Marx's view of the state is much broader: 'The executive of the modern State is but a committee for managing the common affairs of the whole bourgeoisie'.[6] We can make two observations in this regard. First, the state is seen primarily as an 'administrator of business', that is as an organiser of economic life in the interests of the ruling class. Second, the state has the task of mediating between the conflicting interests of the various factions of the bourgeoisie in order to administer the common interest of the entire class. In other words, the state pursues the goal of aiding the reproduction of relations of production not only by resorting to violence to suppress any rebellion against the established order but also by organising economic life, and by unifying disparate interests in one common interest.

Although the organisational functions of the economy were very limited at the time, it would be wrong to think they were entirely absent. Capitalism has always needed state intervention of various kinds to make the profit mechanism work, to guarantee a workforce, to expand markets, to help beat foreign competition, to procure necessary infrastructure, to enact laws and rules of coexistence deemed necessary or useful. Even though old style capitalism argued that, in the words of Lord Melbourne, 'the whole duty of government is to prevent crime and preserve contracts', in reality its aim was to avoid state interventions that could limit its freedom, while calling for and promoting all measures that could help establish, maintain or develop capitalist relations and facilitate the process of accumulation. In fact, it was government measures that forced large masses of British workers to enter the market to sell their labour-power to the capitalists. And it was with other government measures, such as the abolition of duty on wheat, that the English bourgeoisie finally gained the upper hand over the old aristocracy.

While this was happening in England, in other countries, like France and Germany, and even more so in countries where capitalism developed later, the state played a key role in starting the process of accumulation.

Simplifying, we could say that from the moment the development of the forces of production made capitalist society possible, government intervention has been required above all not to break the old relations of production but to establish new relations, corresponding to the new level of the forces of production so as to remove any kind of obstacle which could hinder the natural course of this process. These obstacles could arise from the persistence of pre-capitalist forces and relations, or as a result of internal conflicts in different sectors of the capitalist world, or the resistance and rebellion of the exploited

---

6 Marx, *Manifesto of the Communist Party*, in MECW 6, p. 486.

classes, or the contradictions inherent in development. It was the state's task to find an answer to the problems posed by each of these obstacles.

One could go so far as to say that if it were possible to imagine a society without conflicts, if the relations of production could be reproduced unhindered, if the development of the forces of production did not at some point come into conflict with the relations of production, society would be less dependent on state mechanisms. Therefore, we can imagine the relationship of society to the state as one that increases or decreases according to whether the contradictions and discrepancies within society itself makes its survival more or less easy.

To the extent that we accept Marx's conception of the state as the 'official expression of antagonism in civil society',[7] in the words of his *The Poverty of Philosophy*, we may deduce that the appropriation of political power by the working class cannot be, according to Marx, the premise for building socialism, but that political power can be gained only if the conditions for the appropriation of power have already matured within society as a result of the spread of social contradictions. Marx explicitly stated this several times. In 1847, in an article in the *Deutsche Brüsseler Zeitung*, he said 'If therefore the proletariat overthrows the political rule of the bourgeoisie, its victory will only be temporary, only an element in the service of the *bourgeois revolution* itself, as in the year 1794, as long as in the course of history, in its "movement", the material conditions have not yet been created which make necessary the abolition of the bourgeois mode of production and therefore also the definitive overthrow of the political rule of the bourgeoisie'.[8] In his magnum opus, *Capital*, he said: 'But the historical development of the antagonisms, immanent in a given form of production, is the only way in which that form of production can be dissolved and a new form established. This is the secret of the historical movement that doctrinaires, optimists or socialists, do not want to understand'.[9] Again towards the end of his life, in a letter to Domela Nieuwenhuis, dated 22 February 1881, he writes: 'Of one thing you may be sure – a socialist government will not come to the helm in a country unless things have reached a stage at which it can, before all else, take such measures [as will so intimidate the mass of the bourgeoisie as to achieve the first desideratum – time for effective action]'.[10]

---

7   Marx, *The Poverty of Philosophy*, MECW 6, p. 212.
8   Marx, 'Moralising Criticism and Critical Morality', MECW 6, p. 319.
9   Marx, *Capital* vol. 1, MECW 35, p. 491.
10   Marx to Ferdinand Domela Nieuwenhuis, London, 22 February 1881, MECW 46, p. 66. [TN: it is unclear why Basso excludes the rest of the sentence, here presented in square brackets. This might be an editorial oversight].

Of course this correspondence between the social structure and the state should not be understood as a completely mechanical, almost automatic congruence: the global historical process, to which I referred at the beginning, includes all aspects of social life operating as a totality, influencing one another so any change in any part of the process affects all the others. If we accept that the state and the law are the expression of social antagonisms, they in turn can contribute to accentuating, mediating or overcoming these antagonisms. What must be underlined is that we cannot conceive of independent historical processes, of separate evolutions such that modifications in political-legal relations take place without corresponding changes in social relations; and, reciprocally, social relationships cannot change profoundly without affecting the structure of the state.

A further consequence of this process is that the capitalist state, like capitalist society, must be conceived dialectically; it should not be seen as a monolithic expression of class power, but as a permanent site of class struggle. A common view of Marxism is that it tends to present the state and the law as instruments of bourgeois domination, so any attempt to change class relations by means of the law would be in vain. Any reform would be reformist, in the worst meaning of the word. Since the legal system is by definition directed entirely and exclusively at protecting the bourgeois social order, anything introduced into it can only result in a defence of the established order. In other words, laws form a condensed body, without gaps or contradictions, entirely subject to the will of the ruling class, and finalised towards the defence of its own interests.

In no way does this correspond to reality and is the complete antithesis of Marx's thought. It is true that the second observation on the correspondence with Marx's thought would lose its importance if the reality were different: *amicus Carolus, sed magis amica veritas*.[11] However, we must not forget that our primary institutional task is to verify Marx's authentic ideas and then compare them with reality. It seems indisputable that the dialectical nature of the global social process, as illustrated by Marx, means that each of its moments are dialectical moments, which is to say contradictory moments composed of antagonisms and struggles; so why should the state be exempt from this characteristic. It seems to me that this is one of the key points that must be clarified if we are to establish a viable political strategy for the workers' movement. I think this is all the more important because most of those who studied Marx's theory

---

11   TN: Karl is my friend, but a better friend is truth. This is a modified version of Aristotle's phrase: 'while both are dear, piety requires us to honour truth above our friends' (*Nicomachean Ethics*, *The Complete Works of Aristotle*, vol. 2, Princeton University Press, New Jersey 1985, 1096a15, p. 1732).

of the state have, in my opinion, neglected and underestimated the importance of its dialectical character. They have failed to see that, according to Marx's concept, two contradictory and antagonistic aspects coexist in every moment of the historical process (whether structural or superstructural), and hence in every institution, and especially in the state. For the purpose of analysis, we must understand the incidence of each of these aspects, and for the purposes of strategy (i.e. political praxis) we need to know how to use the one and the other to achieve the desired goals.

But not only is this dialectical conception of the state plainly visible in Marx's general view, it is also set out in numerous writings, beginning with a passage in the aforementioned *The Poverty of Philosophy* where the state is referred to as 'the official expression of antagonism in civil society'.[12] A little later, in an article in the 'NRZ' [*Neue Rheinische Zeitung*] of 29 October 1848, Marx wrote: 'For Friedrich Hecker social questions are consequences of political struggles, for the *Neue Rheinische Zeitung* political struggles are merely the manifestations of social collisions'.[13] Social conflicts are the very fabric of class struggle, which Marx rightly considers a struggle for power. It is, therefore, class struggle that is reflected in the institutions of bourgeois society and, being an integral part of it, it penetrates the legal and political framework of capitalist society.

No one can certainly have forgotten the importance that Marx attached to English factory laws, which he sees as working-class successes at the heart of capitalist economy. He also attaches similar importance to universal suffrage in England. He wrote in an article in *New York Daily Tribune* of 25 August 1852 that 'Universal Suffrage is the equivalent of political power for the working class of England, where the proletariat forms the large majority of the population, where, in a long, though underground civil war, it has gained a clear consciousness of its position as a class ... The carrying of Universal Suffrage in England would, therefore, be a far more socialistic measure than anything which has been honoured with that name on the Continent. Its inevitable result, here, is the political supremacy of the working class'.[14] Marx remained largely faithful to this conception of universal suffrage throughout his life, as evidenced by the commitment with which he fought for it and got the International to fight for the extension of suffrage, which was finally achieved in 1867. However, he did not attribute any miraculous value to universal suffrage. He

---

12   MECW 6, p. 212.
13   Marx, 'Public prosecutor "Hecker" and *The Neue Rheinische Zeitung*', MECW 7, p. 488.
14   Marx, 'The Chartists', MECW 11, p. 335. [EN: The article is dated August 2, 1852 but it was only published on August 25, 1882].

distinguished the suffrage bestowed by Bismarck on a country under a military-bureaucratic regime from the suffrage achieved in England by a class-conscious proletariat. It was not a legal-formal problem but one of substance. Suffrage can be a weapon in the struggle for power if it is accompanied by real power and a developed class-consciousness.

Similar views are expressed in many other texts of Marx's, a point we do not need to press: he reiterates the call for the International to press for new laws to benefit the working class, and for these laws to have a revolutionary value, as well as listing the measures that represented steps in the 'process of subversion, spontaneously developed in modern industry'.[15] Among these measures he also included vocational schools, which may perhaps surprise us today; however it confirms that he did not share the view of them as monolithic and exclusively bourgeois, because he saw them as a continuous opportunity to introduce antagonistic elements in the legal-political system expressed by the bourgeois state.

We can now look at things a little more closely to get a better understanding of this dialectical process that also involves the state, to then draw out some practical guidelines for socialist strategy in advanced capitalist countries. I shall make use of a concept that I have illustrated many times and which is none other than a summary of Marx's famous 1859 'Preface'.[16] At a certain point in the development of modern industry and mechanisation in a capitalist society, there comes a time when the correspondence between the forces of production and the relations of production breaks down. The former are driven to ever more social forms by the very need for capitalist development, while the latter tend to perpetually reproduce a society based on private profit. Marx describes this process as the real self-destructive process of capitalist society and does not hesitate to say that machines are the real revolutionary forces, more than any Blanqui, Barbès or Raspail.

I believe that the history of capitalism from Marx onwards has provided a clear confirmation of this analysis. The development of the forces of production has been continuous and unstoppable, upsetting the old capitalist relations while never completely subverting them. How can we explain this? I believe that grasping the true nature of this process is the key to understanding the role of the state and to defining a strategy for the working class. It is clear that a society wherein there are two contrasting processes, the socialisation process advanced by the forces of production and the privatising process

---

15   EN: no reference is provided for this quotation.
16   EN: 'Preface' to *A Contribution to the Critique of Political Economy*, in Marx 1969, pp. 502–6.

advanced by the relations of production, is a society that is in permanent tension; one where new equilibriums must be continuously sought in order to adapt the defence of privatising relations, i.e. those of private profit, to the advancing social needs of productive development. The state, the public power, legislation and administration are the principle sites within which takes place the struggle to adapt and overcome imbalances between one or the other of the antagonistic tendencies, to find a platform for compromise that may be provisional but which will keep alive the fundamental aspect of capitalism, the private appropriation of surplus value. The increasing intervention of the state in economic and social life, especially since the American New Deal, the nationalisation of whole sectors of the economy, state programmes or plans, compulsory price control, the redistribution of income and the so-called welfare state are steps in this process. Thanks to these state actions, the private relations of production are safeguarded from any crisis and new compromises may be found, despite the growing socialisation process imposed by the development of the forces of production. This succession of imbalances and unstable equilibriums, of breaches and compromises, of tensions and adjustments was outlined by Engels with these words: 'to a great extent the course of the "development of right" consists only, first, in the attempt to do away with the contradictions arising from the direct translation of economic relations into legal principles, and to establish a harmonious system of law, and then in the repeated breaches made in this system by the influence and compulsion of further economic development, which involves it in further contradictions'.[17]

Can the working class intervene effectively in this process to continually change the relations of power? Engels believed this intervention was taking place in the historical process, as evidenced by his assertion that the bourgeois legal system, embodied by the Napoleonic Code, was forced daily to be weakened in all manner of ways owing to the rising power of the proletariat. Marx went even further because he pointed to this intervention as the principal path to revolution. We have already seen that, according to Marx, the only way to overcome a social formation is to exacerbate the contradictions within it. These contradictions arise spontaneously within capitalist society and set in motion self-destructive processes 'before our own eyes'.[18] However, these processes can lead to a socialist society only by means of the conscious intervention of the working class. The more the proletariat's objectives coincide

---

17   Engels to Conrad Schmidt, October 29, 1890, in Marx and Engels 1968, p. 687.
18   Marx, *Manifesto of the Communist Party*, MECW 6, p. 516.

with the concrete opportunities offered by the development of objective contradictions, the more its struggle against capitalism becomes a class struggle for power. For Marx, only with the conscious participation of the workers' movement in these spontaneous processes and only in the presence of both subjective action and objective tendencies can true revolutionary action take place, according to a statement contained in *Herr Vogt*, which has always seemed to me to be of paramount importance. In it, Marx defines the revolutionary action as 'conscious participation in the historical process revolutionising society before our very eyes'.[19]

If this actually happens, if the proletariat's conscious intervention not only becomes part of the real movement of history but also takes the lead, then the growing development of the forces of production, their socialising nature, the irreconcilable contradictions with capitalist relations will increase until all the elements of the new society created by this action gradually form an organic unity, until the foundations of a new mode of production are finally created and new relations established. No doubt this process will also include partial objectives and provisional compromises; but the unstable nature of these compromises, their inability to solve the underlying problems of capitalist society will become increasingly evident. Then the pace of history towards new social forms will increase at the same rate as the contradictions develop, and the awareness of these contradictions will becomes clearer to the working class freed from bourgeois mystification. The final goal will then become clearer: the definitive acquisition of power and the establishment of socialist relations. The fundamental contradiction of capitalist society, which contains in its dynamic development – that Marx viewed as a global social process – the seeds of destruction of the old society and the creation of new one, will only in this way be able to fully unfold its potential.

If, however, the proletariat's conscious action does not come together with the real development of the objective contradictions, this could lead to dangerous stasis; not only because capitalism will be able to arrive at a series of provisional solutions, adaptations and ever-new compromises through the increasing interpenetration of political power and economic structures. It will also be able to prolong unnaturally the life of these subsequent reincarnations, which will now bear within them the permanent seeds of fascism and prolong in unnatural fashion the reproduction of capitalist relations. In other words, whereas on the diachronic plane the explosive force arising from the development of the forces of production is certainly more powerful than the

---

19   Marx, *Herr Vogt*, in MECW 17, p. 79.

conservative force that stems from the tendency of the relations of production to reproduce themselves, the fact that the workers' movement does not take conscious lead of the process and does not direct it towards the goal of destroying the old and building the new, allows capitalism to exploit to the maximum the system's capacity for re-establishing equilibrium. On the synchronic plane, the system operates as a whole to which the parts are subordinated, so that the inherent contradictions and the antagonistic forces resulting from them become mere forces of disturbance that can be reabsorbed, thanks especially to the use of all the state instruments available to the ruling class. These contribute, on the one hand, to rendering increasingly complex the articulated interweaving of the political, economic, social and cultural, which constitute the historic bloc and superstructure; on the other hand they tend to anchor political power in the very structures of society, making it much more complex, and thus also more difficult for the workers' movement to control the revolutionary process necessary to seize it.

I think this is a key to understanding what I judge to be a crisis in the workers' movement strategy in advanced capitalist countries. The roadmap outlined by Marx provided for conscious involvement in the objective self-destructive processes that take place before our eyes; but for this to take place requires a non-mystified consciousness, while capitalist relations constantly reproduce not only themselves but also the mystification of consciousness. It is this mystified consciousness that fails to critically understand the society in which it lives and therefore does not grasp its dynamics of development. Some responsibility for this also falls on the leaders of the workers' movement. Whether they be social democratic leaders who offer partial and reformist objectives, isolated from a global perspective of revolution and who provide no lasting alternative; or whether it be others who continue to believe that the revolution, even in the capitalist world today, can be achieved by the militant vanguard seizing power and building socialism from scratch and from above – both contrast with the lengthy revolutionary process outlined by Marx in the third thesis on Feuerbach, where the objective conditions change as men change until society as a whole is transformed.

It is this situation, in which capitalism makes careful use of the logic of the relations of production and of a workers' movement not yet able to take full advantage of the antagonistic logic of the forces of production, that breeds the phenomenon of working-class integration into the system, and not only of its vanguards, in accordance with a process described by Marx in *Capital*. 'The advance of capitalist production develops a working class, which by education, tradition, habit, looks upon the conditions of that mode of production as self-evident laws of Nature ... The dull compulsion of economic relations completes the subjection of the labourer to the capitalist'.[20] What Marx calls the 'silent compulsion of economic relations', which makes the working class accept a world stood on its head as natural, a world where the product dominates the producer, where dead labour dominates living labour, is precisely the mystifying logic that is naturally inherent in the relations of production.

But if this ideological mystification, which we might in fact describe as natural, were not sufficient, if the silent compulsion of economic relations were not to appear to safeguard a system capable of containing the development of class consciousness and struggle, the state would intervene, not just as the regulator of the economy or the guarantor of profit and accumulation, nor only as a repressive force *a posteriori*, but as a preventive force of ideological mystification, using the vast resources at its disposal, beginning with education, to induce a less natural form of integration. But I am personally convinced that induced mystification by itself would not be sufficient were the mechanisms we have talked about not in place and were the proletariat's answer not the one outlined by Marx in the aforementioned thesis on Feuerbach and passage in the *Herr Vogt*.

It seems to me, then, that the underlying reason for the survival of capitalism is that the objective process does not coincide with subjective action. Capitalism has today reached a stage where the internal contradictions are so strong and tensions so high that the process of decline and revolution should be much more advanced. Instead we see the continuation and consolidation of ambiguous situations of compromise, which increase mystification because of their 'advanced' and almost 'socialising' appearance, while in reality they represent trenches for the resistance of the old social and political relations.

For example, universal suffrage, which Marx thought could lead, under certain conditions, to an effective socialisation of power and so to the advent of working-class power, is negated not only by the mystified consciousness that is unable to turn it to revolutionary use, in Marx's sense. But this is even truer of parliamentary power, which is increasingly dominated by the executive that in turn works in close connection with capitalist forces and with the bureaucratic-military apparatus. Thus the decision-making power that universal suffrage should have bequeathed to the people is there only in appearance, while in reality parliament is short-circuited by alien powers, sometimes even occult powers that it merely registers the will of.

So higher salaries, which were won by workers only after hard struggles, promote the development of consumerism, support capitalist development,

---

20   K. Marx, *Capital*, Vol. 1, MECW 35, p. 726.

and expand the process of accumulation. Similarly, even though nationalisations are contrary to the original logic of capitalism, which is that of private capitalism, they promote the adaptation of private relations of production to the social needs arising from the development of the forces of production.

I could continue, but I think that these few examples are enough to clarify one aspect of the dialectical nature of the state I mentioned at the beginning. Its actions are always accompanied by a certain ambiguity: a negative sign of capitalist conservation and a positive sign of progress towards the creation of elements of a new society. Ultimately, one or the other of these signs will prevail, depending on the general context of the historical process in which they occur. In this sense, we may question the validity of Lenin's assertion that state capitalism is the antechamber of socialism. I believe that if the expression 'antechamber of socialism' has the entirely positive meaning of development towards socialism, the expression is inadequate and does not reflect reality. If, rather, this expression connotes an aggravation of the contradictions; the increasingly complex and difficult efforts to ensure the survival of the system against the logic of the historical process; an escalation of tensions which might lead to changes to higher forms of production, then state capitalism can be considered to be the antechamber of socialism; albeit a very long antechamber to traverse, and indeed one that society has been traversing for several decades. It is in this light that we can interpret Rosa Luxemburg's assertion about increasing state intervention in economic and social affairs: 'In this sense, capitalist development prepares little by little the future fusion of the state to society. It prepares, so to say, the return of the function of the state to society ... it is undoubtedly what Marx had in mind when he referred to labour legislation as the first conscious intervention of "society" in the vital social process'.[21]

In conclusion, I believe that we can consider Marx's statement as valid, as are those of Lenin and Rosa Luxemburg, provided we never lose sight of its dialectical meaning, the ambivalence of every single act of this process and the process as a whole. Marx gave us an example of this dialectical interpretation when he welcomed the abolition of duty on wheat, though he thought that it would harm the working class in the short term. Today this process has become so complex, intricate and contradictory, that it cannot be given just a cursory glance. So I hope that valid collective work can help the workers' movement to improve its understanding of the reality of the situation in which it has

---

21 Luxemburg 2008, p. 61.

to operate. In any event, I would sum up this analysis by saying that the more developed state capitalism is, the more developed the contradiction and the crisis it faces.

Let me add some brief final observations, which would certainly deserve more extensive treatment. The first relates to an assertion that I have already made, namely that there is an implicit tendency towards fascism in the current phase of capitalist development. The word 'fascism' is used here inappropriately if it is understood as referring to the historical experience of Italian and German fascism, which were both the consequences of a crisis (in 1921 for the former and the Great Depression of the '30s for the latter), which had jammed the workings of capitalist mechanisms and required an energetic response. Instead today we are facing a more serious threat; because the crisis, the dysfunction of the system, the contradictions it exhibits, the expansion of the forces of production and the spread of a generalised non-acceptance of the system (which does not necessarily express itself in immediate rebellion but works underground like Marx's 'mole'), encourages the system to adopt authoritarian regimes out of the inevitable necessity of defence that threatens to engulf the entire world.

Another observation concerns the difficulty of isolating the problem of the state from the international context, where today we find advanced capitalist states, socialist states, dependent states and underdeveloped states; and even within each of these three groupings, there are particular differentiations. However, I think it is important to underline briefly the need to avoid the risk of focusing on the state alone; forgetting that the life of every state, especially the most developed, is closely connected to the world market and international relations; for the future of the state will also be affected by the future development of these international relations.

The third and last observation refers to the workers' movement's strategy to win power. It seems clear that, if what I say is true, the workers' movement has to find a suitable strategy, through the experience of struggle and reflection on this experience, something I do not see today in any of the major parties. If it is true that the political-economic-social-cultural mix that we outlined leads to power being increasingly anchored in social structures, then it is at the level of these structures that the fight must take place (not only in factories but in all the various structures and institutions which make up society, because this complex mix can be seen in each of them). If it is true that mystified consciousness represents a major weakness in the workers' movement, then the demystification of consciousness, which involves a real cultural revolution, should not follow but must precede the acquisition of power and accompany the long revolutionary process of structural and institutional transformation. If it is true that these have a dialectical nature, a double possibility, the struggle within them should not be rejected a priori as leading to integration. Of course, the danger of integration is always present in every battle fought within the institutions, but it will be the greatest proof of the strength of the workers' movement to be able to lead this struggle from within whilst retaining its revolutionary consciousness. This must be present at all times and in every act, which should all be placed in the general context of the revolutionary process. Because this is the only way to avoid falling into the trap of reformism and integration.

But of course it is not just a question of taking the fight to bourgeois institutions and powers, but also of creating autonomous and alternative counter-powers for the collective management of specific social functions. This is an especially interesting problem, which I cannot examine in this short contribution. What is needed is a militant of a new kind, a new man, in the sense that Marx himself used this expression. In short, a new way of life is required.

CHAPTER 11

Society and State in the Thought of Marx

When confronting the issue of the relationship between state and society in Marx's thought, one is always obliged to concede that Marx did not leave us any specific work on the problem.* Nevertheless, it played an important part in his thinking and, as we discover from his notes, he wished to dedicate a systematic study to it – one which he unfortunately was never able to find the time to write. The few notes he left which set out the main points of this future work clarify neither the basis nor the general outline of his thoughts.[1] To establish this outline we are, therefore, obliged to draw from a fairly large number of passages in writings that touch on the problem, and from which, in our view, a position emerges that is not only clear but also theoretically coherent. It is coherent not only in relation to the whole systematic reconstruction of his notion of the state, but also with his doctrine as a whole; and thus also with the implications that may be derived from it for praxis. It is to this organic reconstruction, albeit brief for reasons of time, that we shall dedicate ourselves in this paper.

First, we shall state the criteria adopted in composing these pages. We refused to consider Lenin's *State and Revolution* as an organic exposition of Marx's ideas.[2] We have said many times, also in an earlier talk in Santiago, that we consider the idea that Leninism is the Marxism of the contemporary age, the Marxism of the era of imperialism, to be a Stalinist residue of Marxism-Leninism deriving from Stalin himself. We have repeatedly said that we consider this argument to be highly reductive not only as regards the immense wealth of Marxian thought, still full of unexploited potential for the workers' movement, but as regards Lenin himself. Lenin was not a mere interpreter of Marxism but was above all an incomparable strategist and tactician

---

* Basso 1973a, pp. 13–14.

1 In the notes written at the end of 1857, Marx wrote: 'the State. – State and bourgeois society. – Taxes, or the existence of the unproductive classes. – The state debt. – Population. – The state externally: colonies. External trade. Rate of exchange. Money as international coin. – Finally the world market. Encroachment of bourgeois society over the state. Crises. Dissolution of the mode of production and form of society based on exchange value. Real positing of individual labour as social and vice versa' (Marx 1993, p. 264).

2 See, for example, Girardin 1972, which discusses Marx's concept via Lenin's *State and Revolution*, even though he writes that in this book 'the political militant goes beyond the theorist, due to the urgency of the situation'.

of the revolution, possessing a creative capacity that would be very difficult to encompass in the framework of a doctrine.

This does not mean that we cannot learn any theoretical lessons from Lenin. We owe to him the lessons on how to analyse concrete situations and find an answer to each, an answer that may be only provisional and perhaps improvised in difficult situations but one aimed straight at resolving the main problem, leaving out, if necessary, those that can be put off till later. Another lesson we learn is that for every occasion we need the right tools. Among these tools are also his writings. The teachings of Lenin are valuable for the workers' movement provided that they are understood as a theory of the state to which Lenin adds nothing essential; indeed he synthesises Marx's ideas and, in a way, simplifies them.[3]

This is why we reject Stalin's formula, which Lenin would not have accepted if he had lived and which was disputed by the comrades closest to Lenin in exile. Lenin did not adapt Marxism to the era of imperialism: on the one hand he did much more, because he taught us how a revolution can triumph in conditions other than those envisaged by Marx; but on the other, in order to focus on the preparation of the revolution in Russia he had to neglect many aspects of Marx's thought which did not specifically concern the concrete situation in which Lenin found himself.[4] We can summarise the difference between them as follows: Marx always thought of the socialist revolution as capitalism's highest point of development, and so at the centre of capitalism itself (even though he predicted revolutions in the periphery); Lenin developed the theory of the weakest link and, therefore, focused mostly and successfully on the use of pre-capitalist forces (peasants and colonial peoples).[5]

For different reasons, of course, we shall not base our analysis on Marx's youthful writings, not even his 'Critique of Hegel's *Philosophy of Right*', in which he addressed the problems of the state. Many authors consider this to be a basic text, marking, according to some, a break with the culture of his time and thus also with Marx's previous cultural education. We are inclined to think that the importance of Marx's early writings – which we do not deny – has been exaggerated. If we may make a consideration that seems to be precisely

---

3 See Basso 1968, pp. 34 ff. In the introduction to his work Lenin himself states that his work is practical and not theoretical.
4 'Every theoretical novelty Lenin introduced into Marxism stems from a precise and concrete evaluation of the political situation in Russia, rather than from a Marxian text. His originality, and his genius, derive from a shrewd intuition encapsulated in a phrase, which although it saved the system it speeded up the achievement of the set goal' (Zilli 1970, p. 400).
5 See Basso 1971, pp. 28 ff.

of a Marxist nature, ideas, as Antonio Labriola said, do not fall from the sky, but can arise only on the terrain of historical practice. Now Marxism, in whose permanent validity we profoundly believe, is the criticism of capitalist society and its dynamics, and this criticism – i.e. true Marxism – could not have arisen in either Germany or France but only in the one truly capitalist country of the time, England. Therefore, whatever the epistemological breaks represented by this text, or, according to others, by *The German Ideology*, we continue to believe that Marx's thought, as a scientific analysis of reality and as a guide to practical action, must be sought primarily in his mature writings, those of the years after 1850. We can of course find many beginnings, especially as regards methodology, in prior writings to which we too shall refer, since they can help us to reconstruct his thinking process and clarify any ambiguities of interpretation.

Our analysis, like those conducted by other scholars of Marx's thought on the state, will cover a whole series of writings. We, however, shall not cling to the belief that all Marx's writings constitute the invariably consistent exposition of a systematic doctrine. Marx, like Lenin, frequently wrote for polemical purposes, and a serious interpreter of either one or the other can never disregard the circumstances in which a writing was published to appreciate its real meaning. However, even if we bear in mind these necessary precautions, it seems to us that Marx's ideas on the relations between state and society emerge clearly and organically from this analysis.

It is especially important to follow his line of thought from *The 18th Brumaire of Louis Bonaparte* to *The Civil War in France*, in which Marx writes about the current developments of the French State, and studied the relationship between state and society in the light of the materialist conception of history that he was working on. Of particular importance is the *18th Brumaire*, because this is one of only a few works Marx wrote which he edited personally, a second edition being published exactly seventeen years after the first (1852 and 1869, respectively), introducing some changes, some of which were very significant. This allows us to confirm that the entire non-revised parts of the second edition mean that his ideas had remained faithful to his previous analysis. Moreover, a comparison of the texts clearly shows that he was thinking of his *18th Brumaire* when he began writing *The Civil War in France*, especially the first draft of this book, which not only uses the same concepts but often even the same words. In these two writings there is a continuity of thought during Marx's most fruitful decades, in which we can see the clear outline of his conception of the state and its relationship with society.

Finally, as regards Engels, we shall refer to his writings only when the ideas expressed in them correlate to Marx's. Our conviction is that this is not always the case and, indeed, on some points, especially after the death of Marx, Engels paved the way for distorted interpretations of Marxist thought.

It is commonly held that in vulgar Marxism the state is simply an instrument of repressive violence to curb the pretensions of the exploited classes. The common view of Marxism interprets the famous words of the *Manifesto*, 'the political power of the modern state is but a committee, which administers the common affairs of the whole bourgeoisie',[6] in the almost mechanical sense of a state receiving and applying the orders of the bourgeoisie. As we shall try to demonstrate, these interpretations, unfortunately still common today, have little to do with Marx's brand of Marxism. The state is certainly an organ of the classes, but one that not only represses but 'oppresses' the exploited classes (the concept of oppression is much broader and, indeed, fundamentally different from that of repression). It also mediates between the different and often conflicting interests of the various factions of the ruling class. In this second sense, as regards the above quote from the *Manifesto*, the accent should be placed on the words 'the common affairs of the whole bourgeoisie'.[7] As for the first sense, in the *Civil War* political power is defined as 'a public force organized for social enslavement'.[8] Social enslavement is something far more complex than simple police repression.

However, to fully understand Marx's concept of the state and to thereby derive practical indications from it, we must go back to its origins. The state is a historical construction, and an explanation of the reason for its genesis can help us understand its function. Long before Engels wrote his book *The Origins of the Family, Private Property and the State*, Marx had already addressed this issue in *The German Ideology*. For Marx, every community, large or small, faces a series of common problems (defence from natural disasters such as droughts, floods, epidemics, and etc., and also defence from aggression or invasion by other tribes or peoples). These common interests can be jointly addressed by the community itself, but may (and if the community is a certain size, must) be entrusted to specialised groups such as priests or augurs, soldiers, bureaucrats, etc., depending on the circumstances and the problems to be resolved. But what usually happens in all collective organisations, what also happened throughout history in the Catholic Church, and what often happens before our eyes in parties or trade unions, is that due to the need for special qual-

---

6   Marx, *Manifesto of the Communist Party*, in MECW 6, p. 486.
7   In his review of E. De Girardin: *Le socialisme et l'impôt*, Marx states that the 'bourgeois state is nothing more than the mutual insurance of the bourgeois class against its individual members, as well as again the exploited class' (MECW 10, p. 333).
8   Marx, *The Civil War in France*, in MECW 22, p. 329.

ifications to carry out different tasks, certain people are invested with certain functions and relative powers. These tend to form an autonomous power group, and what was entrusted to them in the service of the community becomes for them a personal attribute, and they tend to legitimise their own interests as collective interests. In other words, the organisation becomes an end in itself. Bureaucracy (civil, military, priestly) ceases to be a subordinate institution and becomes a separate body, estranged from the community, imposed on the community and, at the same time, opposed to it. Thus, state organisation arose from primitive communities.

Out of this very contradiction between the particular and the common interests, the common interest assumes an independent form as the *state*, which is divorced from the real individual and collective interests, and at the same time as an illusory community, always based, however, on the real ties existing in every family conglomeration and tribal conglomeration – such as flesh and blood, language, division of labour on a larger scale, and other interests – and especially, as we shall show later, on the classes, already implied by the division of labour, which in every such mass of men separate out, and one of which dominates all the others.[9]

> ... in the Orient where civilization was too low and the territorial extent too vast to call into life voluntary association, the interference of the centralizing power of Government. Hence an economical function devolved upon all Asiatic Governments, the function of providing public works.[10]

But, as we said, in addition to fulfilling functions that really affect the community, like the regulation of water, the groups who exercise power tend to present their own interests as common interests, and they give themselves the power to regulate common interests, or supposedly common interests, for their own benefit, as if they were private interests.[11] As regards the situation in France, Marx writes in the *18th Brumaire*:

---

9   Marx, *The German Ideology*, in MECW 5, p. 46.
10 Marx, 'British Rule in India', *New York Daily Tribune*, 25 June 1853, in MECW 12, p. 127.
11 Engels reiterated this concept on numerous occasions, for example in *Antidühring* (MECW 25, pp. 166–7). 'In each such community there were from the beginning certain common interests the safeguarding of which had to be handed over to individuals, true, under the control of the community as a whole: adjudication of disputes; repression of abuse of authority by individuals; control of water supplies, especially in hot countries; and finally when conditions were still absolutely primitive, religious functions. Such offices are found in aboriginal communities of every period – in the oldest German marks and even today in India. They are naturally endowed with a certain measure of author-

Every common interest was immediately severed from society, countered by a higher general snatched from the activities of society's members themselves and made an object of government activity – from a bridge a schoolhouse, and the communal property of a village community, to the railroads, the national wealth, and the national University of France.[12]

The same concept is repeated, in almost the exact same words, in the first draft of *The Civil War in France*, where the state authorities who usurp this function are called 'priests of state power'.[13]

Hence the process through which a certain social situation originates gives rise to a certain form of state can be summarised as a process of division of labour, of estrangement, usurpation and class oppression. The division of labour arises from the tendency or the need to assign certain functions of collective interest to certain persons who are, or appear to be, the most qualified, be they civil, military or religious functions. Estrangement arises when the holders of these functions form a separate body, endowed with special powers.

---

ity and are the beginnings of state power ... These organs which, if only because they represent the common interests of the whole group, hold a special position in relation to each individual community – in certain circumstances even one of opposition – soon make themselves still independent, partly through heredity of functions, which comes about almost as a matter of course in a world where everything occurs spontaneously, and partly because they become increasingly indispensable owing to the growing number of conflicts with other groups. It is not necessary for us to examine here how this independence of social functions in relation to society increased with time until it developed into domination over society ... Here we are only concerned with establishing the fact that the exercise of a social function was everywhere the basis of political supremacy; and further that political supremacy has existed for any length of time only when it discharged its social functions. However great the number of despotisms which rose and fell in Persia and India, each was fully aware that above all it was the entrepreneur responsible for the collective maintenance of irrigation throughout the river valleys, without which no agriculture was possible there'. And in the Preface to *The Civil War in France*: 'What had been the characteristic attribute of the former state? Society had created its own organs to look after its common interests, originally through simple division of labour. But these organs, at whose head was the state power, had in the course of time, in pursuance of their own special interests, transformed themselves from the servants of society into the masters of society' (in MECW 27, p. 189). [TN: rather than a Preface, in MECW this is termed an 'Introduction' and was published along with the third edition of *The Civil War in France* by the *Vorwärts* newspaper in 1891].

12   Marx, *The 18th Brumaire of Louis Bonaparte*, in MECW 11, p. 186.
13   [TN: the closest remark similar in Marx's First Draft of *The Civil War in France*, is the reference to 'Holy State Power', MECW 22, p. 488.] Previously, in *Critique of Hegel's Philosophy of Right*, Marx had said that bureaucracy tended to transform the purposes of the state in accordance with bureaucratic purposes, or purposes into bureaucratic state purposes.

They will of course continue to use the contribution of the whole community for the performance of their duties (wars, public works: such as water regulation, roads, bridges, etc.), both in the form of personal activity and in that of the extraction of surplus labour through taxes, fees, tolls, labour services, etc. But in the long run, they end up by appearing in the eyes of the community itself as placed above it, and sometimes also endowed with sacral attributes by virtue of the authority of tradition or weight of social structures that have been created around them, so that the community is no longer able to perceive that these social structures and the relative state forms are ultimately their creation.

> The social power, i.e., the multiplied productive force, which arises through the co-operation of different individuals as it is determined by the division of labour, appears to these individuals, since their co-operation is not voluntary but has come about naturally [i.e. not decided by the community, but existing before the birth of individuals who accept it as a natural fact], not as their own united power, but as an alien force existing outside them, of the origin and goal of which they are ignorant, which they thus cannot control, which on the contrary passes through a peculiar series of phases and stages independent of the will and the action of man, nay even being the prime governor of these.[14]

In the process of usurpation, those who hold political power always tend to say they represent the public interest, thus justifying their supremacy and power.[15] In reality, however, in addition to the functions of general interest that are at the origin – logically or even chronologically – of this power, they transform private interests into general interests until they coalesce into material (economic) and political power structures, to then become the ruling class that uses political power to consolidate and organise its political dominion. It is this coalescing of class interests which perpetuates the state institution. If it were only a question of managing real common interests, they could be collectively managed directly by the community, especially since the progress of technology and culture no longer makes it necessary to carry out certain functions through a specific political power and, even less so, through a certain ownership structure. It is true that the state also carries out functions required

---

14   Marx, *The German Ideology*, in MECW 5, p. 48.
15   'The state was the official representative of society as a whole; the gathering of it together into a visible embodiment. But it was this only in so far as it was the state of that class which itself represented, for the time being, society as a whole' (*Anti-Dühring*, in MECW 25, p. 267).

by any organised community. But these can – and should in a conscious collective – be self-managed in the actual interest of the community. Whereas if they remain the attribute of a power that is above society, one endowed with sovereignty and organised into separate bodies, these functions too, starting with the administration of justice, will be moulded by the interests of a ruling class that is able to present the defence of the existing order – and hence, above all, of its own privileges – as a defence of collective interests. It is in this sense that Marx speaks of 'illusory "general" interest under the form of the state'.[16]

All this explains why Marx always speaks of the 'state' or 'political state' as a class state, destined to die out with society's re-appropriation of the power of self-government in the interests of the collective, no longer needing to entrust it to class domination. This class power that, in order to maintain itself, must attempt to prevent this re-appropriation by society, must attempt jealously to conserve its capacity for domination, perhaps by surrounding itself with mystery, as did the Church,[17] and that is why Marx puts state bureaucracy on a par with the Church, describing state officials as the 'priests of state power'. It is the defence of this class privilege that makes the state an instrument of oppression and not simply of repression. Oppression is based primarily on the perpetuation of social, economic and cultural inequalities, as well as the use of a number of mechanisms, including ideology, developed in the modern capitalist state with the aim of reproducing capitalist social relations.

In a necessarily brief paper, we cannot conduct a detailed examination of all the specific characteristics of the bourgeois state. We will focus only on those that seem essential to our discussion. First, in pre-capitalist societies the rule was that the classes with material and economic power also exercised political power (we stress the word rule because every socio-economic formation has its own specific and sometimes exceptional characteristics, and in history it is hard to find a system in its purest form). Capitalist society accentuated the distinction between economic power and political power, and we can say that the rule was and is to distinguish between those who hold economic power and those who exercise political power. Note the use of the word 'exercise'. To

---

16   Marx, *The German Ideology*, in MECW 5, p. 47.
17   'The whole sham of state mysteries and state pretensions was done away with by the Commune ... Making in one order the public functions, – military, administrative, political – *real workmen's functions*, instead of the hidden attributes of a trained caste', (First Draft of *The Civil War in France*, in MECW 22, pp. 488, 490).

exercise power is one thing, effective power is something else, but a study of who truly possesses effective political power would require us to digress too far.

The other distinction, linked to this one, is that in the course of its development capitalist society has needed to integrate workers into the system so as to institutionalise exploitation. This allowed it to give to all citizens the illusion of participating in power via universal suffrage in representative institutions. It of course protected itself against the danger that a democracy given free rein might subvert the existing order by means of repression, which in extreme cases lead to Nazi-Fascism and hence to the point of suppression of universal suffrage and all other democratic guarantees; or, in normal cases, by securing the majority's support of the social order. It is no coincidence that despite the freedom to vote in many capitalist countries, elections have never led to the system being overthrown, even though Marx himself thought it was possible. A unique case, perhaps, is Czechoslovakia after World War II, when elections brought a communist and socialist majority, which despite the defection of right-wing socialists, was sufficient to secure a parliamentary majority for the Gottwald government. However, the exceptional circumstances in which this occurred do not allow for generalisations. There was also a majority of socialists and communists in France after World War II, but the French socialists had become a party that had no desire to realise socialism, like the social-democratic majorities that govern many European countries today and carry out extensive social reforms while accepting the hegemony of the ruling class. The same is true of the majority of the popular fronts in France and Spain in the interwar years, which also included bourgeois parties. Chile is a unique case, where a president was elected under a programme for social transformation; but it was a minority government that – amongst other difficulties – was opposed by a parliamentary majority.

Enough has already been said of the methods used to obtain adherence to the system, which range from exploiting the ignorance of the masses to using religion to support the system, from the role of schools to that of the mass media. Although Marxist literature continues to emphasise repression (the police state), there is also serious Marxist literature on what we shall call 'induced adherence', which is obtained ex ante rather than imposed post facto with repressive methods. However, we believe there is another, and as yet largely unexplored, aspect we might call 'spontaneous adherence', the importance of which seems to have been undervalued by Marxist authors, although Marx did not fail to draw attention to it.

It is certainly difficult to draw a precise line of demarcation between what we call induced adherence and spontaneous adherence, although we think that the logical distinction is clear. In any event, without an element of spontaneity induced adherence would be more difficult. To a certain extent, then, it is the synthesis of both which causes the 'political socialisation' through which many of the exploited classes accept the system and act in a way that is contrary to what should be, if not class consciousness, at least class instinct.

What is this 'spontaneous adherence' based on? In our opinion, there is a 'systemic logic' that operates independently of the actions of any one specific will.[18] As we have mentioned on other occasions, Marx sees the system as a 'concrete totality': a totality with its own intrinsic logic that regulates the coexistence of different components and tends to correct deviations and discrepancies of all kinds, bringing them back within the system's.[19] Men born in a system like this are naturally inclined to accept this 'logic' as if it were *the* logic of society in all ages. They do not see the historical context and even less do they note the basic contradictions that appear to them only as temporary deviations or discrepancies. When Engels noted, in a letter to Marx, that British society wants bourgeois aristocrats and bourgeois workers, he was not simply stating a fact but he was seeing the logic of the system in action. The workers themselves, writes Marx, are led to believe their exploitation is 'natural', which is to say that society is divided into classes that is based upon this exploitation.[20] Although, it is certainly true that bourgeois society has many means of

---

18   'Liberal democracy has never dared face the fact that industrial capitalism is an intensely coercive form of organisation of society that cumulatively constrains men and all of their institutions to work the will of the minority who hold and wield economic power; and that this relentless warping of men's lives and forms of association becomes less and less the result of voluntary decisions by "bad" or "good" men and more and more an impersonal web of coercions dictated by the need to keep "the system" running' (Robert Lynd, Forward to R.A. Brady, *Business as a System of Power*, Columbia University Press, New York, 1943, p. xii, cited in Miliband 2009, p. 53).

19   'While in the completed bourgeois system every economic relation presupposes every other in its bourgeois economic form, and everything posited is thus also a presupposition, this is the case with every organic system. This organic system itself, as a totality, has its presuppositions, and its development to its totality consists precisely in subordinating all elements of society to itself, or in creating out of it the organs which it still lacks. This is historically how it becomes a totality. The process of becoming this totality forms a moment of its process, of its development' (Marx 1993, p. 278). Also, 'With its coming-together in the city, the commune possesses an economic existence as such; in the city's mere *presence*, as such, distinguishes it from a mere multiplicity of independent houses. The, here consists not merely of its parts' (Marx 1993, p. 483).

20   'The advance of capitalist production develops a working class, which by education, tradition, habit, looks upon the conditions of that mode of production as self-evident laws of Nature ... The dull compulsion of economic relations completes the subjection of the

psychological conditioning to socialise individuals politically in this direction, it is also true that these means of conditioning would not prove effective unless there were already a natural inclination towards this, which springs precisely from the system's intrinsic logic.

It is the relative autonomy of the political sphere, and the fact that all citizens can participate in it, that creates a split between man and citizen, as Marx describes to great effect in *On the Jewish Question*. Between man immersed in the selfish sphere of the private interests of social life and the abstract citizen gliding in the skies of apparent political equality.[21]

The relative autonomy of the political sphere has led to a series of debates, interpretations, and also, in our opinion, misunderstandings among Marx scholars, which we must now examine. These debates and misunderstandings can to some extent be explained because Marx did not address the subject systematically. Instead, we have to resort to odd references and allusions, written perhaps at different times and using different terminologies, sometimes improperly, all of which lend themselves to different interpretations. Let us then try to find our bearings on the terrain that we have so far uncovered, and then draw some practical lessons from our interpretation.

It is well known that Marx spoke of political power being independent of social classes and even of the ruling class, especially in connection with Napoleon III and his empire; and that Engels compared Bismarck's Prussia to the French empire. According to Marx this independence was due to a certain balance of forces in the class struggle: where the bourgeoisie was no longer able

---

labourer to the capitalist' (Marx, *Capital*, vol. 1, MECW 35, p. 726). The dull compulsion of economic relations is part of the logic of the system.

21   'Where the political state has attained its true development, man – not only in thought, in consciousness, but in reality, in life – leads a twofold life, a heavenly and an earthly life: life in the political community, in which he considers himself a communal being, and life in civil society, in which he acts as a private individual' ('On the Jewish Question', MECW 3, p. 154), which is a reflection of 'the universal secular contradiction between the political state and civil society' (MECW 3, pp. 159–60). Marx had noted this characteristic of bourgeois society, as compared to previous societies, in which each individual had a private and political sphere, since everyone had a position in political society due to them by way of their position in material life. 'The abstraction of the state as such belongs only to modern times because the abstraction of private life belongs only to modern times. The abstraction of the political state is a modern product. In the Middle Ages there was serf, feudal property, trade corporation, corporation of scholars, etc., that is, in the Middle Ages property, trade, society, man was political; the material content of the state was fixed by reason of its form; every private sphere had a political character or was a political sphere, or again, politics was also the character of the private spheres' (K. Marx, *Critique of Hegel's Philosophy of Right*, in MECW 3, p. 32).

to rule and the proletariat was as yet unable to do so.[22] But history has refuted this explanation of the situation in France at that time: the bourgeoisie, in fact, proved capable of governing. However, it is true that history may come up with other situations that involve a balance of forces in the class struggle, albeit relative and unstable, where political power can gain greater independence, as long as a situation of dual power does not arise. And yet, the independence of political power is actually always conditioned by social structures that it cannot violate; only structural transformation can bring about a radical transformation of power.

In this respect, we can even say that political power has greater independence in pre-capitalist societies than in capitalist ones, because the functioning of society was less complex, mechanisms were simpler, even elementary (village agricultural economy). This gave the central government greater freedom for manoeuvre. Let us not forget that, by definition, the state is a power that is in contrast to society and which places itself above it, despite the fact that it is an expression of its class contradictions and linked to its ruling class.[23] As we said, in pre-capitalist societies, the dominating class coincides with the class that exercises political power and, despite being placed above society, the power was exercised in the interests of the dominant class. But if we imagine that in exceptional circumstances, perhaps because of a war or a revolution, power falls into the hands of a dictatorship that is not of the dominant class, such a dictatorship – operating in a society based on simple relations – can use this power much more freely than can happen in a complex society like our own, where economic and social mechanisms are extremely delicate and any arbitrary interference, even by those who wield political power, would not be easy. One should not confuse two different problems: the autonomy of the political moment from the various sectors of the ruling class and its autonomy with respect to the system as a whole. As for the first aspect, the autonomy, or rather, the specificity of the political moment arises only in a capitalist society that assigns the management of political power to a specialised social group, while in pre-capitalist societies the people with political power also had economic power, and the problem of autonomy did not exist. As for the second aspect, namely the autonomy with respect to the functioning of the system,

---

22 EN: There reference is to *The Civil War in France*, in MECW 22, p. 330: 'In reality, it was the only form of government possible at a time when the bourgeoisie had already lost, and the working class had not yet acquired, the faculty of ruling the nation'.

23 '... this power, arisen out of society, but placing itself above it and increasingly alienating itself from it, is the state' (Engels, *The Origin of the Family Private Property and the State*, in MECW 26, p. 269).

this will diminish the more complex become the social mechanisms in which the state is inserted, as an element essential to their functioning, but on whose operation the state itself depends. It is clear that the chances of countering the logic of the system, which the state is required to serve, are minimal if not completely absent, except in the case of the development of an antagonistic power, of which we shall speak later.

For this reason we do not share Poulantzas's theoretical framework, founded on the autonomy of this political moment, from which a whole series of practical consequences in relation to the problem of seizing power, the revolutionary party and its function are supposed to follow. We do not believe that this thesis can be attributed to Marx. So what is the permitted degree of autonomy according to Marx – whose thought it is we are trying to clarify? First, as stated in the quote from the *Manifesto* and amply illustrated in his historical writings, political power is said to represent the interests of the whole ruling class.[24] If the various factions of the ruling class start fighting among themselves, the sphere of political autonomy widens because political power is forced to play a mediating role. Seen in these terms, the problem of autonomy does not emerge as 'another view of the state', albeit secondary, as recently stated by Miliband.[25] In our view, this fits perfectly into Marx's general theory.[26] Marx left no ambiguity in outlining the very narrow limits of the autonomy of political power, which cannot be in conflict for very long with the social structures that expressed it and that constitute a totality, which is endowed with a logic that the individual spheres of activity, including politics, must in the end obey; even if they

---

24 See also *The German Ideology*, MECW 5, p. 90: 'By the mere fact that it is a class and no longer an estate, the bourgeoisie is forced to organise itself no longer locally, but nationally, and to give a general form to its average interests'.

25 TN: Basso references the Italian translation of this article by R. Miliband published in the journal *Critica Marxista* in 1966. The article, 'Marx and the State', was first published in the *Socialist Register* in 1965. It has recently been reprinted in Miliband 2015, p. 9.

26 'Because the state arose from the need to hold class antagonisms in check, but because it arose, at the same time, in the midst of the conflict of these classes, it is, as a rule, the state of the most powerful, economically dominant class, which, through the medium of the state, becomes also the politically dominant class, and thus acquires new means of holding down and exploiting the oppressed class ... By way of exception, however, periods occur in which the warring classes balance each other so nearly that the state power, as ostensible mediator, acquires, for the moment, a certain degree of independence of both' (Engels, *The Origin of the Family*, MECW 26, pp. 270–1). Here Engels, fully in the spirit of Marx, greatly limits the possibilities of autonomy; it is a limited kind of autonomy, which only emerges exceptionally and momentarily. Because of its limited and transient nature, this exception confirms the rule that political power is closely connected to economic power.

often operate at a different temporal rhythm, so that in some cases, such as Italy today, the political sphere is one of the most backward, while as we have seen in others, it was a driving force (this in the past was the case for Italy too).

In his *History of the Communist League*, Engels says that as early as 1844 Marx had come to the conclusion that it was not the state that conditions and regulates civil society, but civil society which conditions and regulates the state,[27] that therefore, politics and its history must be explained on the basis of economic relations and not vice versa. This concept we find clearly expressed a few years later in *The German Ideology*:

> The material life of individuals, which by no means depends merely on their 'will', their mode of production and form of intercourse, which mutually determined each other – this is the real basis of the state, and remained so at all the stages at which division of labour and private property are still necessary, quite independently of the will of individuals. These actual relations are in no way created by the state power; on the contrary they are the power creating it.[28]

Soon afterwards, the concept is repeated in *The Holy Family*:

> It is therefore not the state that holds the atoms of civil society together ... Only political superstition today imagines that social life must be held together by the state, whereas in reality the state is held together by civil life.[29]

This is just as expressed just as directly in *The Poverty of Philosophy*:

> sovereigns who in all ages have been subject to economic conditions, but they have never dictated laws to them. Legislation, whether political or civil, never does more than proclaim, express in words, the will of economic relations.[30]

The same concept turns up again in the dispute with Bakunin. In a letter to Cuno, Engels writes that 'Bakunin maintains that the *state* has created capital,

---

27   Engels, 'On the History of the Communist League', in Marx and Engels 1977, vol. 3, p. 178.
28   Marx, *The German Ideology*, MECW 5, p. 329.
29   Marx, *The Holy Family*, MECW 4, p. 121.
30   Marx, *The Poverty of Philosophy*, MECW 6, p. 147.

that the capitalist has his capital only *by the grace of the state* ... We, on the contrary, say: Abolish capital, the appropriation of all the means of production by the few, and the state will fall of itself'.[31]

Four years later, in the *Critique of the Gotha Programme*, Marx again mentions the same concept:

> The German Workers' party ... shows that its socialist ideas are not even skin-deep; in that, instead of treating existing society (and this holds good for any future one) as the *basis* of the existing *state* (or of the future state in the case of future society), it treats the state rather as an independent entity that possesses its own '*intellectual, ethical, and libertarian bases*'.[32]

The state and politics, therefore, are not really independent from social structures. They were not independent yesterday, they are not today, nor will they be tomorrow. Even the bourgeoisie, despite what we have said about the distinction between the exercise of economic power and the exercise of political power, is no exception to the general rule. In fact, *The Manifesto* states that 'each step in the development of the bourgeoisie was accompanied by a corresponding political advance of that class'. Neither can the proletariat dissociate the conquest of political power from a change in social relations: 'The political rule of the producer cannot co-exist with the perpetuation of his social slavery', Marx says in the *Civil War in France*.[33]

In contrast to these insistent and repeated statements, which are logical expressions of Marx's general conception, clearly stated in the 'Preface' to *The Critique of Political Economy* are the references to the autonomy of Napoleon III's executive power, which should be seen in the context of the heated attacks Marx directed against him. In his eyes, Napoleon personified the suffocation of the long revolutionary tension that dominated France from 1789 to 1849, for which reason Marx had come to Paris in 1848 from exile in Belgium. But what are the limits of this autonomy? In the first draft of the *Civil War in France*, Marx writes:

---

31   Engels to T. Cuno, London, 24 January 1872, MECW 44, pp. 306–7. [TN: I have provided a more extensive quotation than Basso does, to clarify the meaning.]
32   Marx, 'Critique of the Gotha Programme', MECW 24, p. 94.
33   Marx, *The Communist Manifesto*, MECW 6, p. 486; *The Civil War in France*, MECW 22, p. 334.

> The governmental power with its standing army, its all directing bureaucracy, its stultifying clergy and its servile tribunal hierarchy had grown so independent of society itself, that a grotesquely mediocre adventurer with a hungry band of desperadoes behind him sufficed to wield it.[34]

These words could also be applied to Mussolini and Hitler. They too had a degree of autonomy in the exercise of political power (note that Marx speaks of exercise), but no one could think them to be really independent of the social structures. Moreover Marx had already written of Napoleon III in the *18th Brumaire* that 'As the executive authority which has made itself an independent power, Bonaparte feels it to be his mission to safeguard "bourgeois order"'.[35] Historically, not only did Napoleon III secure bourgeois order but also laid the foundations for French industrial development. Although he may have enjoyed greater autonomy from the ruling class than did other governments, it can in no way be said that he was able to act independently of the bourgeois social structures that he had, in fact, done much to strengthen.

In contrast to Poulantzas, then, we believe that Marx's true revolutionary ideas are expressed in the abovementioned 'Preface' to *The Critique of Political Economy*, which Poulantzas wrongly considers to be reformist. Of course, as regards this text and its claim to the dependence of political power on the general logic of the system, we are not saying that the state is purely a passive reflection of the social situation, which may be the impression given by some of Marx's phrases. It must not be forgotten that Marx was a polemicist who loved

---

34   Marx, 'First Draft of *The Civil War in France*', MECW 22, p. 485.
35   *The 18th Brumaire of Louis Bonaparte*, MECW 11, p. 194. The passage following the quote deserves careful reading. 'But the strength of this bourgeois order lies in the middle class [the term is used here in the sense of the English middle class, i.e. the bourgeoisie, LB]. He poses, therefore, as the representative of the middle class and issues decrees in this sense. Nevertheless, he is somebody solely because he has broken the power of that middle class, and keeps on breaking it daily. He poses, therefore, as the opponent of the political and literary power of the middle class. But by protecting its material power [i.e. economic power, LB], he revives its political power. Thus, the cause must be kept alive, but the effect, where it manifests itself, must be done away with. But this cannot happen without small confusions of cause and effect, since in their interaction both lose their distinguishing marks. New decrees obliterate the border line ... This contradictory task of the man explains the contradictions of his government'. As can be seen, therefore, Napoleon's political autonomy is also relative. He cannot continue opposing the economic power of the bourgeoisie for long. He must ultimately promote it and, consequently, increase its political power. This is what actually happened, until eventually the bourgeoisie managed to get rid of him. Marx's analysis was exact, but should not be forced beyond its true meaning (*The 18th Brumaire of Louis Bonaparte*, MECW 11, p. 194).

peremptory sentences, and so his statements should be placed in the general context of his thought, over and above the words that he may have used on certain occasions.

First, it should be pointed out that, for Marx, structure and superstructure are not related mechanically but dialectically. Engels stressed this point strongly in his final years, when historical materialism spread in a deterministic guise, as is clear from this passage in a letter to Mehring of 14 July 1893:

> Hand in hand with this goes the ideologists' fatuous conception that, because we deny independent historical development to the various ideological spheres which play a role in history, we also deny them any *historical efficacy*. Underlying this is the ordinary, undialectical conception of cause and effect as rigidly opposite poles, quite regardless of any interaction. The gentlemen forget, often almost deliberately, that an historical element, once it is ushered into the world by other, ultimately economic, causes, will react in its turn, and may exert a reciprocal influence on its environment and even upon its own causes.[36]

It is from this point of view that the relationship between state and society should be seen. The state emerged from the above-mentioned circumstances to guarantee and maintain a certain class structure, to exercise oppression. On the one hand, it is a mere parasitic product of society[37] that would dispense with it if it could manage things for itself (it must be admitted that the collective management of certain community functions was not historically possible in the past, as Marx himself acknowledged). On the other hand, the state actively performs its function as the bourgeoisie's instrument of proletarian oppression and of the reproduction of capitalist social relations. In this sense, Marx describes executive political power as a body that coils itself like a snake around society, crushing its lungs, exerting its power over the society that expressed it.[38]

---

36 Engels to Franz Mehring, London 14 July 1893, in MECW 50, p. 165.
37 'The unity of the nation was not to be broken, but, on the contrary, to be organized by Communal Constitution, and to become a reality by the destruction of the state power which claimed to be the embodiment of that unity independent of, and superior to, the nation itself, from which it was but a parasitic excrescence' (*The Civil War in France*, MECW 22, p. 332).
38 EN: Basso is probably thinking of passages from chapter three of *The Civil War in France*, MECW 22, more specifically perhaps, pp. 328–33.

We believe our interpretation of Marx to be correct when we say that the social system, as a totality, creates this state instrument that answers to the oppressive logic of the system itself and hence is not autonomous except to a very small degree. It is an active mechanism that keeps the system of social oppression active and guarantees not only its repressive functions but also many other functions, including the most important in our context: those of ideological manipulation and economic intervention, which today are of great importance.[39] These last two aspects have developed significantly since Marx's time, and it is obvious that they are not extensively discussed in his writings. Nevertheless both are problems that he was aware of: the ideological hegemony of the bourgeoisie has its theoretical basis in Marx's conception of ideology, which is an enduring element of the sociology of knowledge, which Marx refers to explicitly when he tells us that 'the ruling ideas' are 'the ideas of its ruling class',[40] ideas that the ruling class naturally manage to convey as absolute and eternal. In another work Marx mentions the 'stuntification by the priest',[41] even though he could not have predicted the yet more serious stultification by modern mass media techniques. On state intervention in the economy there are prescient statements in *Capital*; and the definition of the state as a collective capitalist, which we find later in Engels's *Anti-Dühring*, correctly forecast what would happen: the state now plays an indispensable role in advanced

---

39   As we said at the beginning, vulgar Marxism has always considered the state to be a mere organ of repression. Althusser has now added to it the ideological apparatus or apparatuses. But all scholars of Marx seem to ignore Marx's repeated references to the different functions of the state: in addition to the oppressive functions there are 'legitimate' or, as he calls them elsewhere, 'general' ones; that is to say, functions of the organisation and protection of social life. Certainly in a class society, these functions become 'political', that is to say classist and lose their 'general' and 'legitimate' character. However, the fact remains that they can be characterised neither as repressive nor as ideological. In his 'Conspectus of Bakunin's *Statism and Anarchy*', Marx writes that 'as soon as the functions have ceased to be political ones, there exists 1) no government function, 2) the distribution of the general functions has become a business matter, that gives no one domination, 3) election has nothing of its present political character' (MECW 24, p. 519). Despite the vagueness of the terms used ('political', 'government' or 'class', which are more or less equivalent, and 'administrative', 'general' or 'legitimate' mean the same thing), Marx makes a clear distinction between the two orders of functions, one of which must be removed and the other remain, but stripped of its class character. Therefore, to reduce the state to an organ of repression is clearly a non-Marxist notion, especially at a time when the state's ideological and organisational functions were becoming increasingly important.
40   *The Manifesto of the Communist Party*, MECW 6, p. 503.
41   TN: *The Civil War in France*, MECW 22, p. 337. In more recent translations, the word used is 'stultification' (see Marx 1996, p. 190).

capitalist countries as the motor of the profit mechanism, due to the flagging strength of much acclaimed private initiative.

The evermore secure interconnection between the economic and political sectors has had two effects. On the one hand it has widened the margins for autonomy, or the appearance of autonomy of political agents through the management of the public sector of the economy. On the other, it has tied public power more closely to the functioning of economic mechanisms, thus reducing its autonomy. Of course there is no denying that the state now plays a decisive role in the economy, both to maintain the growth rate in developed countries and to initiate processes of industrialisation in underdeveloped countries. In the last century, the state was the driving force behind the industrialisation of less developed countries like Germany and Japan, and so the state no longer just interprets the interests of the whole class against the particular interests of this or that fraction, but it also interprets the future interests of the dynamic of capitalist development. In other countries, like Mexico, it is political power that has given the country an institutional framework that conforms to the interests of the bourgeoisie. The political moment always has a unifying function and so the state promotes, coordinates, mediates, and rationalises the system; it also seeks to exclude harmful particularisms, to advance worker integration, and create institutions and mechanisms to help the system work, tackling the inevitable difficulties that keep arising. For this purpose it relies not only on its own political force but also on the very logic of the system that requires it to work in the common interest of the entire ruling class and, if necessary, against the interests of certain backward or marginal sectors. In this sense, under the appearance of autonomy the state merely responds to forces deriving from the dynamics of the system, and perhaps through the international channels of more advanced countries, thus becoming the real executive arm of the system's rationalising logic. Political power, then, is autonomous from individual groups of the bourgeoisie but is more than ever a tool that obeys the logic of capitalist development. This was true for Napoleon III, and for all states where the intervention of the central government was and is required to start a process of development to bridge the gap with more advanced countries.

One thing is certain: the political sector in the strict sense of the word has lost some of its autonomy, since it has become increasingly difficult to find a political power than can act freely in economic life. This is even truer today in advanced capitalist countries, where political power is increasingly less identifiable within a single person (Napoleon III, Tsar) or organ (government, parliament), because it is now increasingly rooted in and dependent on the social structures, of which it has increasingly become a mechanism necessary for the functioning of these structures but that is conditioned by their laws. This obviously affects that much-discussed question within the workers' movement, the winning of power. In fact if – like Poulantzas – we emphasise the autonomy of politics, we come to the conclusion that the first (but not final) goal of the proletariat has to be the winning of political power in order to then change the social structures. If, however, we see political power as being closely linked to the social structures, where it has its roots, the proletariat's main battle will have to be fought on the social terrain, because it is only through a modification of the base of the state that the proletariat can gain greater power. Far from being reformist, this thesis – which is Marx's own – is truly revolutionary, because it paves the way for the winning of political power, insofar as it weakens the basis of the opponent's power and accentuates the weight of the antagonistic class. Certainly, the political moment retains its function of unifying and, ultimately, resolving all the battles waged on the economic and social terrain; but precisely because it is the synthesis of these battles, it cannot be something that is expressed separately and a priori.

If the state rests on society and not vice versa, if political power is a creation of the ruling class and necessarily reflects a balance of power, it follows that the proletariat cannot hope to seize power only by changing this balance of power within society. If, as we believe, Marx made a mistake in his historical assessment, believing that a balance of power had been reached between the bourgeoisie and the proletariat under Napoleon III, we can nevertheless draw a lesson from this mistake. According to Marx, the proletariat can acquire the social power to counterbalance that of the bourgeoisie even under capitalism. If this happens suddenly, such as during a revolutionary crisis, we get an example of dual power (the Soviets and the Provisional Government in Russia in 1917); but if it happens in the course of a long process, as the result of daily struggle, we then have a proletariat that is an antagonistic force within the state institutions and an alternative legislation or an alternative interpretations of the laws will increasingly become the object of class struggle, as will the cultural and ideological values that vie for hegemony in society.

This brings us to the core theme of this seminar: that of state and society in a period of transformation, as in the case when the antagonistic forces balance out, and the proletariat can overturn the traditional balance of forces and initiate the construction of a socialist society. If the proletariat is also able to use some of the instruments of the state in this struggle, as today in Chile, it is not because political power is autonomous but precisely the opposite, because it is not autonomous and is subject to the pressures of the society that expresses it. But we cannot end here without first examining another connected problem concerning the nature of the socialist revolution. Does there really exist, as Poulantzas states, an 'all-important *difference* between the transition from feudalism to capitalism and that from capitalism to socialism',[42] in the oft-repeated sense that capitalism was able to develop within feudal society, whereas socialism cannot come about without first seizing power? The difference is clearly enormous because the transition from feudalism to capitalism means the transfer of power from one class to another, while the transition from capitalism to socialism means the end of class society. However, to achieve the definitive abolition of classes, we first need one class – the proletariat – to seize power and this is precisely the point: can the proletariat gain power in the same way as the middle class came to power? Since Marx believes that political power rests on social structures and not vice versa, it would be consistent with Marx's doctrine, even though Marx did not expressly state it many times, to imagine a dialectical process similar to the one that brought the bourgeoisie to power. That is to say, a process in which there is a struggle for the transformation of the structures, a struggle to gain cultural hegemony and another for political power, all happening at the same time and affecting each other, so that the elements of a new society begin to develop within the old. According to Marx, not even in the case of the proletariat can one separate off and prioritise the aim of acquiring political power, because then a socialist society would have to be constructed ex nihilo, and thus from above.

We shall provide here merely the summary of a thesis that we have developed elsewhere: in the *Manifesto* Marx explicitly stated that the process through which the proletariat transforms society is analogous to the one through which the bourgeoisie carried out its revolution, a process he describes as a gradual extension of economic power and the creation of elements of the future society from within the old. He stated on more than one occasion that revolutionary violence is merely the midwife of the new society that develops in the womb of the old. And on more than one occasion he indicated the elements of this future society emerging from within capitalist society. Here we would like to recall another little-known passage from Marx, little known because it belongs to the first draft of *The Civil War in France*, published posthumously:

> The working class know that they have to pass through different phases of class struggle. They know that the superseding of the economical conditions of the slavery of labour by the conditions of free and associated

---

42 Poulantzas 1973, p. 160.

labour can only be the progressive work of time. The economical transformation requires not only a change of distribution, but a new organization of production, or rather setting free the social forms of production in present organized labour (engendered by present industry) from the trammels of slavery, their present class character. These forms require harmonious national and international co-ordination. The working class know that this work of regeneration will be again and again slowed down and impeded by the resistance of vested interests and class egotisms. They know that the present 'spontaneous action of the natural laws of capital and landed property' can only be superseded by 'the spontaneous action of the laws of the social economy of free and associated labour' by a long process of development of new conditions, as was the 'spontaneous action of the economic laws of slavery' and the 'spontaneous action of the economical laws of serfdom'.[43]

Marx's ideas as stated here are clear: the transition from capitalism to socialism will take place just as the previous transitions did, through a long process that must allow the new social forms already present within the old to achieve a harmonious relationship in a new system. What we called the thesis of the two contradictory logics is practically the same. That thesis claims that within capitalist society, which is a contradictory society, there are two logics: the logic of the system (the logic of the relations of production and private profit) and the socialising logic of the forces of production, which, as it develops, triggers objective processes that tend to socialise the relations of production. Marx taught us that it is precisely by supporting itself on these objective processes and by taking up a place within them that the proletariat can build the elements of a new society around the antagonistic logic, changing the balance of power and the social structures, the laws and institutions, leading to a radical overthrow of the situation but only if preceded by this long process. This thesis we illustrated in an earlier symposium in Santiago[44] and we would like to reiterate it by recalling a passage from Marx that, despite referring to a different society from today's, describes the process of transition in the same way.

In a draft of the famous letter to Vera Zasulich, Marx notes that the 'agricultural commune' is a contradiction: property is in common but the farm house and the farmyard belong to the farmers. The cultivated land is in common but

---

43 Marx, *The Civil War in France* in MECW 22, p. 491.
44 This was published as 'Ancora sull'imperialismo', in *Problemi del socialismo*, no. 5/6, 1971.

periodically divided among the members of the farming community so that each cultivates the fields assigned to them for their own purposes and, most importantly, reaping the harvests.

'This is why the "agricultural commune" occurs everywhere as the *most recent type* of the archaic form of societies, and why in the historical development of Western Europe, ancient and modern, the period of the agricultural commune appears as a period of transition from communal property to private property, as a period of transition from the primary form to the secondary one. But does this mean that in all circumstances the development of the 'agricultural commune' must follow this path? Not at all. Its constitutive form allows this alternative: either the element of private property which it implies will gain the upper hand over the collective element, or the latter will gain the upper hand over the former. Both these solutions are *a priori* possible, but for either one to prevail over the other it is obvious that quite different historical surroundings are needed. All this depends on the historical surroundings in which it finds itself'.[45]

A society in transition is precisely a society where two opposing dynamics are present at the same time. The predominance of one over the other depends on the historical conditions. Specifically, the transition from capitalism to socialism depends primarily on whether the workers' movement can make use of favourable dynamics, i.e. the socialising logic of the development of the forces of production, to achieve final victory. Only through this long process can the proletariat finally seize political power, which is the final goal of class struggle (*Endzweck*), not the first – as Marx writes in a letter to Bolte.

A different solution would not be consistent with Marx's thinking as a whole. We have seen that class society requires the state to dominate society and usurp its functions; the socialist revolution must bring about a reversal of this situation.

In the first draft of *The Civil War*, Marx wrote:

> The Commune – the reabsorption of the state power by society as its own living forces instead of as forces controlling and subduing it, by the popular masses themselves, forming their own force instead of the organized force of their suppression.[46]

---

45 Marx, 'Drafts of the Letter to Vera Zasulich', MECW 24: 352. TN: the passage has been provided in full, whereas Basso only provided a truncated extract.
46 Marx, 'The Civil War in France (First Draft)', in *MECW* 22: 487.

And in the final version he writes:

> The old centralized government would in the provinces, too, have to give way to the self-government of the producers.[47]

This, then, is the terrain of class conflict: the struggle of the 'producers', i.e. of the working class in the broad sense, to win back control over its collective interests. This implies a progressive growth from below of the power of the masses, and the reassertion of their democratic initiative and capacity for self-government in all areas of social and economic life. It would be inconceivable for a politically mature working class to be administered from above by the political power it had won, since – on the contrary – it is this democratic maturity, the result of long dialectical processes transforming the social structures and men and women, that provides the foundation for the winning of political power. It is a revolutionary process involving unremitting daily struggle in the nerve centres of society, in the factory, schools, town councils, and the administration of justice and the state; with the firm and consistent antagonistic participation, accompanied by the creation of counter-powers that provide the exploited class with the opportunities and the capacity to assume its responsibilities; and at the same time using all the existing contradictions to impose a progressive extension of its capacity for self-government: the gradual re-appropriation of its public functions. To imagine that this process can be controlled from above, by the achieved state power, is to ignore the fact that socialism is first and foremost a desire for freedom from all alienation, from encrusted bureaucracy, from any residual traditional power. As Marx wrote in *The Critique of the Gotha Programme*, 'It is worthy of Lassalle's imagination that with state loans one can build a new society just as well as a new railway'.[48] Moreover, when asked in an interview for *The Chicago Tribune*, published on 5 January 1879, about the distinction he had made in his famous speech in Amsterdam in 1872 between countries in which the revolution could have been peaceful, and those, like Germany, Russia, Austria and Italy, where it would necessarily be violent, he added that also 'those revolutions will be made by the majority. No revolution can be made by a party, but by a nation'.[49] This seems to confirm that, even in places where violent revolution is necessary, it will be a revolution of the majority and of the entire nation against a small rul-

---

47   Marx, 'The Civil War in France (First Draft)', in MECW 22: 332.
48   Marx, 'The Critique of the Gotha Programme', MECW 24: 93.
49   Interview with Karl Marx, in *The Chicago Tribune*, published on 5 January 1879: https://www.marxists.org/archive/marx/bio/media/marx/79_01_05.htm.

ing class, thus guaranteeing the democratic nature of socialist society. And this will be possible only if, through the above process, the majority of the nation can acquire a capacity for self-government.

It is only when this process has progressed that the masses can hope to seize power totally and definitively so as to destroy it, not to replace it with another analogous power. Clearly, when Marx says that we should not simply take possession of the state machine but smash it, he does not mean that the bourgeois police and the bourgeois instruments of repression and oppression should be replaced by similar ones of the opposite sign, established by those loyal to the revolution. What Marx was saying, as is clear from the whole context, is that the entire system must be changed: the 'political' state must be replaced by self-government, not by repression or oppression.[50] Moreover, in the first draft of *The Civil War in France*, in reference to the Commune, Marx says:

> It was a revolution against the State itself, of this supernaturalist abortion of society, a resumption by the people for the people of its own social life.[51]

We know that Marx's extolling of the Commune contains a tinge of utopianism, due also to the need to support the revolution. However, Marx was clearly fully convinced that, in its general outlines, the Commune was 'the political form at last discovered under which to work out the economical emancipation of labour'.[52]

This of course does not mean that as long as the battle rages, the proletariat should not also use the tools of the old world – Marx states explicitly that it should; but they should rid themselves of them as soon as possible. There is no socialism outside of this re-appropriation by society of its functions. Marx clearly stated with regard to public function that the state had usurped them by subtracting them from society and moulding them to the service of the ruling class or classes. The revolution must overturn the situation. 'While the merely repressive organs of the old governmental power were to be amputated, its legitimate functions were to be wrested from an authority usurping pre-eminence over society itself, and restored to the respons-

---

50 In the introduction to his edition of *The Civil War in France*, Engels summarises Marx's thinking in this regard with the words 'the shattering [*Sprengung*] of the former state power and its replacement by a new and really democratic state' (1891 Introduction by F. Engels, on the 20th Anniversary of the Paris Commune, MECW 27: 190).
51 Marx, *The Civil War*, in MECW 22: 486.
52 Marx, *The Civil War in France*, in MECW 22: 334.

ible agents of society',[53] he said, again in the *Civil War in France*. Thus, the repressive functions must disappear, leaving only the 'legitimate functions', which are to be governed by society itself. Marx says, 'The few but important functions which would still remain for a central government' which 'were not to be suppressed ... but were to be discharged by Communal and thereafter responsible agents'.[54] Marx expresses this same idea again in the *Critique of the Gotha Programme*, when he says that 'Freedom consists in converting the state from an organ superimposed upon society into one completely subordinate to it'[55] – not one of his best dictums but justified given the polemical context. The same idea was differently expressed again in *The Civil War in France*, when he defined communism as 'united co-operative societies' that 'regulate national production upon a common plan, thus taking it under their own control'.[56] Engels expresses the same concept: the 'administration of things' replaced the 'political rule over persons',[57] an image borrowed from Saint-Simon. The 'administration of things' without authoritarian interventions means self-administration of social affairs, which again means socialism rising from the bottom up.

This is what Marx and Engels understand by the withering away of the state. It means that central government has lost its class character and lost its specifically oppressive functions. The legitimate functions, stripped of class deformation, are handed over to the community, which carries them out democratically. In his *Conspectus of Bakunin's Statism and Anarchy*, Marx states 'only if class rule has disappeared, and there is no state in the present political sense'.[58] In his article 'On Authority', Engels, again in dispute with Bakunin, takes up a phrase from Marx's anti-Bakunist pamphlet on the supposed splits in the International:

> All socialists are agreed that the political state, and with it political authority, will disappear as a result of the coming social revolution, that is, that public functions will lose their political character and be transformed into the simple administrative functions of watching over the true interests of society.[59]

---

53   Marx, *The Civil War in France*, in MECW 22: 332.
54   Ibid.
55   Marx, *Critique of the Gotha Programme*, in MECW 24: 94.
56   Marx, *The Civil War in France*, in MECW: 335.
57   Engels, *Anti-Dühring*, in MECW 25: 247.
58   Marx, 'Conspectus of Bakunin's Statism and Anarchy', in Marx 1992b, p. 336.
59   Engels 'On Authority' in MECW 23: 425.

We are not so utopian as to suppose that this can happen in a single day. For this very reason we think that it has to be a long process, which, as Marx wrote, can last an entire historical era, a long process of struggle during which workers must not only change the social structures, not only the balance of power, but also themselves. Capitalist society contains its own contradiction, a force that pushes in this direction: it is the logic of the growing socialisation of the forces of production that demands an increasingly social and collective management of the production process. Lenin's assertion that state capitalism is the antechamber of socialism may be a bit simplistic, but it does contain an element of truth. Capitalism itself is driven by this logic to accept, at least apparently, forms of collective management, even though it then manages to interfere in this collective management so that the opposite logic comes into operation, the logic of the relations of production, the logic of profit. Perhaps Rosa Luxemburg was closer to the truth when she wrote that, through the increasing intervention of the state in economic and social life

> capitalist development prepares little by little the fusion of state with society. It prepares, so to say, the function of the State to society ... and it is undoubtedly this that Marx had in mind when he referred to labor legislation as the first conscious intervention of 'society' in the vital social process.[60]

This is an allusion to Marx's famous claim in *Capital* that factory legislation is a necessary consequence of the process of socialisation of the forces of production, one that limits the whim of the owners of capital.

This conscious reaction of society, this intervention to undermine the will of the proprietors, which is a consequence of the social development of the forces of production, is an element of the future society that emerges from the old. Other elements are the new cultural and moral values that will develop in this new context that will draw young intellectual forces to fight alongside the proletariat against the hegemony of bourgeois cultural values and ideals. In the same way, the new institutions that are formed, the growing pressure from below to escape from the alienation that capitalism inevitably bears with it even more than its economic exploitation; the grassroots powers that emerge from the struggle, a change in the balance of power both inside the factories and in other centres of social life – all these are elements that the workers' movement can generate if it becomes actively involved in the course of action

---

60   Luxemburg 2006, p. 26.

outlined by Marx more than a century ago in the *Herr Vogt*. Namely, conscious participation in the objective processes unfolding within capitalist society and which because they are contradictory processes are influenced by contradictory alternative tendencies. Only this conscious participation, which rejects the logic of the system and the tendencies towards integration, speeding up the antagonistic logic, namely a new social organisation that adapts productive relations to the social needs of the forces of production, can glue together all the new elements of which we spoke and others that are forming, in a new coherent totality that replaces the old. Certainly, today's ruling class will even oppose this process by force and will attempt to resist by concentrating power in the hands of an increasingly restricted oligarchy. Only when the exacerbation of the contradictions will have fully mobilised the revolutionary will and consciousness of the masses, thereby furnishing them with solid foundations in the present society, will the final battle for power pave the road to socialism. It will almost certainly be a violent confrontation, although other solutions may be possible. However, what must be stressed is that the primary task of a revolutionary party today in developed capitalist countries, is not to prepare for this violent confrontation, but to do the enormous amount of preparatory work without which the violent clash will probably not happen and, if it did, could easily end in defeat.

What we have said here, in Latin America at a time when many Latin American countries are experiencing ferocious reaction, might be misunderstood if we did not underline the fact that our task was to analyse Marx's ideas and that Marx saw socialism triumphing in industrially developed countries. Not that he did not envisage, as we have seen, revolution happening in countries that today are usually termed 'underdeveloped', and which he described as 'on the periphery of capitalism', by which he meant those countries where capitalism was sufficiently developed to subvert the old balance of forces and determine deep social crises, but not enough to produce new ones and give way to a system that is a coherent and self-regulating whole. He focused his attention primarily on developed countries for at least two good reasons. First, because the socialism for which he was fighting presupposed a numerically strong, technically capable, politically developed and mature working class. Secondly, because he thought that socialism could never triumph definitively in the periphery until capitalism had been vanquished in its strongest bastions.

We are now in a phase in which the workers' movement in developed countries seems to be losing its momentum, possibly as a result of the strategy followed (split between reformism and revolutionary wishful thinking), whereas the revolutionary possibilities appear to be greater in the periphery, where social tension is growing. This obliges us to say that since the situations are very different, the methods of action, too, need to be different. We would be digressing from our subject were we to pause to examine in detail the different strategies that we believe necessary in these countries, especially in those where the violent dictatorship of imperialism and its servants leaves no other option but a violent struggle for power.[61] However, we must observe that these power struggles are not necessarily socialist struggles. The term 'socialist' is often used to describe revolutions in underdeveloped countries, but it should be used with reservations, not only because a national element can always be found alongside the social, but also because the lack of many, if not all the premises for socialism, leaves the door ajar to many other possibilities, even after revolution.

We must also add that not even in Latin America are all the situations the same or similar, and that precisely here, in Chile, we are witnessing a struggle that is evolving in profoundly original ways, only broadly similar to those that we have described. A struggle of this nature, in which the use of political power and the pressure of popular forces converge towards a rapid transformation of [socio-economic] structures, constitutes a valuable lesson, whatever the outcome, for the further development of revolutionary strategy. We know that a lot of polemical battles are being waged over this strategy within the Chilean left, and we are certainly in no position to give lessons. Indeed, we came here to learn from your experience. What we would advise is to avoid taking any dogmatic positions or following any particular model. Let us follow Lenin's advice and conduct a concrete analysis of the concrete situation, to then apply the tactics best suited to the situation and within the broad framework of Marxist strategy. Let us end with the hope that the current Chilean experience, a novel experience which is inevitably bound to produce mistakes, with its limitations but also with its successes, with the great obstacles it faces and the even greater courage it is showing in tackling them, can help open up a new road to socialism.

---

61 We have already discussed this problem in the article 'Sviluppo capitalistico e rivoluzione socialista' in *Problemi del Socialismo*, no. 43, 1969.

CHAPTER 12

Marxism and Revolution

At this point, I think it impossible to take up the points one by one to the various points raised by Della Mea as I did last time.* I fear it would again be a dialogue of the deaf, since our arguments are based on different premises.[1] I think it would be better to explain the bases of my ideas so as to clarify my point of view and thus our disagreements.

In the conclusion to my previous response, I mentioned Marx's criticism of the 'revolutionary' positions of Willich and Schapper. Della Mea agrees with me, he agrees with Marx's criticism of Schapper, but he notes that not just the ten or fifty years of which Marx spoke have passed, but more than a hundred; and that the time has come to agree with Schapper. I am sorry for Della Mea, but there has been a misunderstanding, and perhaps one of us has misunderstood Marx's critique.

It seems clear – which is why I recalled it as I did – that Marx's main criticism of Willich and Schapper, that also fits with the evolution of his thought, was not one of chronology but methodology. Marx did not mean to say that revolution, which was impossible in 1850, would be possible in 1900. He meant that revolution, as conceived by Willich, Schapper and many others too, was not possible, and that the method had to change. After the failure of the 1848–9 Revolution, French, German, Italian, Hungarian and other exiles dreamed and laboured under the illusion that they could quickly take up the revolutionary cause once again through conspiracies and uprisings. Marx, on the other hand, was examining the reasons behind the revolution and its defeat. He came to the conclusion, which is fundamental to the development of his revolutionary thought, that revolution cannot simply be the fruit of a subjective will that opposes the capitalist order; it is linked to the existence of objective conditions within capitalism, which produce a crisis in the system: it was the objective strengthening of the capitalist bourgeoisie that led to the defeat of

---

* 'Marxism and Revolution' in *Problemi del socialismo*, October 1966, n. 11.
1 EN: Luciano della Mea was an Italian activist and partisan. He was an editor of major papers and reviews of the Italian Left, and from 1964 a member of the PSIUP. He was extremely politically active in 1968 and was a director of the political journal *Il potere operaio* as well as being a founder of *Lega dei comunisti*. A lively debate took place between Basso and della Mea in the pages of *Problemi del socialismo* between May and October 1966. See L. della Mea, 'Partito e rivoluzione', in *Problemi del socialismo*, May/June 1966.

the 1848–9 revolution and if it does not weaken as a result of another crisis, there can be no return to revolution. From here stems Marx's break with all 1848 revolutionaries, including Willich and Schapper, who thought of revolution without worrying about the structures of society and the balance of forces between the classes. From here stems his estrangement from the Blanquists, who he was initially close to, occasioned especially by the polemic against the French Social Democrats. Marx's condemnation of revolutionary subjectivism and voluntarism was not only valid in 1850 but also fifty years later, and still today.

All subsequent development of Marx's ideas moves in this sense: to be a revolutionary was not to prepare for the seizure of power, much less to prepare for the violent seizure of power and the subsequent dictatorship of the proletariat. Before this can happen, the objective conditions have to mature, i.e. an internal crisis determined by the contradictions present in the development of capitalist society. The subjective conditions, i.e. the proletariat's capacity and determination to exploit the contradictions and the crisis, must also mature so that they can seize power and use it. This close link between the objective and the subjective processes, between the transformation of social structures and the winning of power becomes increasingly clear to Marx. As I mentioned many times, we find it in the 'Preface to *A Contribution to the Critique of Political Economy*', in *Herr Vogt*, and again in his long polemic against Bakunin. In response to Bakunin's theory of the destruction of bourgeois political power, namely the state, Marx maintains that it is not the state that governs society, but capitalist social relations that govern the bourgeois state. In other words, political power depends on social structures. Therefore, the winning of political power cannot be separated from the struggle for the transformation of these structures.

Thus, to be a revolutionary means, first and foremost, fight for these transformations that lay the ground for the seizure of power.

Speaking of his time, Marx pointed to economic crisis or war as the critical moments in which the objective contradictions of capitalist society could explode, leading to a revolutionary rupture. But, as we mentioned, this is not essential. What I think is essential in Marx's revolutionary thought is: 1. That the outbreak of revolution cannot be the result of will alone but must be linked to an objective crisis of capitalist society. 2. That this objective crisis is not external to capitalism but a part of its development, when its contradictions become most acute. 3. That while these contradictions may have different aspects in different situations, they always result from the fundamental contradiction between the forces of production and the relations of production. 4. And, finally, that only a subjective consciousness, the masses' conscious will to intervene can transform a crisis into a revolution. Even now I am more than ever convinced of the validity of these ideas. This is why I absolutely reject all purely subjective conceptions of the revolution that make it depend only on revolutionary determination, regardless of whether there is an acute crisis produced by capitalist contradictions.

What is the relationship between Marx's conception of revolution and the Leninist experience? Once again, I apologise to readers for having to address very complex historical and political issues in such as summary form so must warn the reader against drawing simplistic inferences. If I ever manage to free myself of the burden of day-to-day politics, I hope to conduct a more extensive examination of Marx's revolutionary strategy, in which I shall endeavour to give more exact answers. In brief I think we can say that while Leninist strategy, which led to the triumph of the October Revolution and, subsequently, to the consolidation of the Soviet state, was a brilliant application of Marxist strategy, it cannot be taken as a model since it was developed in specific, practically unique circumstances, very much removed from those of the developed capitalist world we live in today.

Although Marx conceived the socialist revolution as an international revolution, it would require different methods in different countries, depending on the degree of capitalist development. This principle inspired his involvement in the First International. Early on, in a circular of the Communist League, he makes a distinction between industrial countries, like England, and countries that we would now call 'developing', like Germany was then, for which the theory of 'permanent revolution' was developed. Later Marx would speak of a violent path and a peaceful path, depending on the differing power structures. He accepted that in Russia there could be a direct transition from the pre-capitalist stage to the socialist stage, provided that socialist revolution in Russia happened in conjunction with socialist revolution in industrial Europe. Lenin's strategy fits perfectly into the broad framework of Marxist strategy. He exploited a moment of particularly acute crisis in Russia's domestic life, a crisis caused by a long war that exacerbated the contradictions between capitalist development, with its imperialist manifestations, and the backwardness of the general relations of production. He exploited a situation arising from a dual oppression imposed by capitalist development and the backwardness and inadequacy of this development. Marx had noted that this sort of situation was particularly detrimental to the working people of Ireland, and we could make the same observation with regard to the Italian working masses. But in the context of World War I and the strains it placed on Russia, this dual oppression created a particularly explosive mixture. It joined the anti-capitalist revolution of the working masses to that of the peasant masses in the fight against exploitation, backwardness and underdevelopment. At the same time, it made it difficult for a backward capitalism to resist the ferocity of the onslaught.

But although this combination of circumstances led to the Bolsheviks seizing power, it did not open the way to socialist revolution, the transformation of capitalist and pre-capitalist social relations into socialist relations. Lenin, like Marx, believed that the Russian Revolution could follow the path of socialism only if Western Europe did the same, but this did not happen.

After the upheavals of the early post-war years, the working-class movement in the West either succumbed in the struggle with fascism or endeavoured to complete the process of integration into capitalist society, for which reformism had paved the way, and which social democracy would take to the high level it has reached today. Yet it would not be fair to say that the Western workers' movement gave nothing to the Russian revolution, indeed it gave it something essential – Marxist doctrine, the doctrine that inspired and guided not only the revolution but also the efforts to found a socialist society. In this sense, we can say that if the Russian revolution did march towards socialism even when it was left on its own, that does not disprove either Marx's assertions, made almost half a century before, or similar ones made by Lenin, because without the help of the Western working-class movement that had formulated revolutionary doctrine, the Russian Revolution, too, would probably have failed.

It succeeded not only thanks to the assistance of Marxism, not only thanks to the genius of its leaders and the heroism of the masses, but also thanks to the exceptional conditions in which it took place. First, there was the world war, which kept the capitalist powers occupied for the whole first year [of the revolution] and which largely drained them of their energies, making it harder for them to conduct a counter-revolutionary war. Second, Russia was the largest country in the world, and, therefore, the most difficult to subdue militarily (Bela Kun's communist revolution in Hungary, by way of comparison, was easily crushed by invasion). Moreover, the vast resources of the Soviet Union enabled it to survive and develop, despite the surrounding *cordon sanitaire* that was deployed in vain to suppress it.

It is this series of exceptional circumstances that makes the Russian revolution unique, and I confess that I find it difficult to understand how it could have been praised and accepted uncritically as the 'model' to be followed for so many decades. Frankly, I think it would have been easier to understand Stalinism (not the arbitrary excesses, but the essential core of this experience) if it were explained in terms of the exceptional conditions under which the revolution was taking place, especially Russia's backwardness and the absence of the foundations of a socialist society, which stem from advanced technical development. It would be better to admit, frankly, that Russia could not complete the construction of socialism in those years precisely because it first had to lay the foundations, and it was unable to fully develop socialist relations of production because of the backwardness of the forces of production. This would allow the merits of the exceptional historic enterprise to be better appreciated, and to understand its limitations, difficulties, contradictions, its inevitable mistakes and excesses. It would certainly have given the Western working-class movement greater autonomy in the search for a national road to socialism.

Instead, the meaning of this experience has been distorted by holding it up as a model to be followed, leading the Western working-class movement onto the wrong track. To go back to where I started, I think that the Stalinist theory of the differences between bourgeois revolution and socialist revolution has its roots here: if the Russian Revolution were the model to follow, it would have been fair to say, as Stalin did, that while the bourgeois revolution had first transformed the relations of society and production, i.e. the structure of society, and then seized power, the socialist revolution first has to seize power and then violently transform the structure of society. But if we accept, as I think we should, that the Russian experience was successful only because of the coincidence of particular historical circumstances and the strategic genius of Lenin, it would also disprove this general theory of socialist revolution as being appropriate for countries where capitalism is still underdeveloped.

So while a careful study of the Leninist experience would certainly teach us a great deal about our battles today, first of all we need to understand the relationship between the historical conditions in which Lenin worked and the truly 'creative' way he applied the revolutionary Marxist method to those conditions. But we are outside Marxism and far from the spirit of Lenin when, in very different historical circumstances, we advocate emulating that experience to the letter; when we repeat formulas, when we adopt models (such as the Leninist party model) or when we advocate using the same alliance strategy in a social environment in which class division has changed dramatically (the decline in agricultural workers and the growth of the middling layers and above all the specialised workforce).

The problem of the socialist revolution in developed capitalist countries as we enter the final third of the twentieth century, is a new problem for the workers' movement, a problem whose solution we find neither in Mao, Lenin nor even in Marx. There is one fundamental aspect of the problem, the analysis of capitalist society today, that we have to resolve for ourselves. Certainly, Lenin and especially Marx can help us in this task, but we have to be able to apply their lessons 'creatively'.

What we need to do is to understand how the fundamental aforementioned contradiction operates today and discover or trigger within this movement, within the development of neo-capitalist society, moments of crisis, of heightened tension between the forces of production and the relations of production.

Do we still – as Marx thought a century ago – have to wait for economic crises or wars to produce these moments of heightened tension? As I have written, I do not think that we can rule out these possibilities a priori. I do not think that we can say that neo-capitalism will not have its moments of crisis or destructive wars. However, I believe that it would be wrong to focus only on these two possibilities, one of which, a catastrophic crisis, might not occur; and the other, a world war, a war that can lead to revolutionary unrest, we must to try to prevent with all our strength.

Yet without a crisis in the process of capitalist development, without acute tension between the forces of production and the relations of production, it would be hard to envisage a possible revolution in Marxist terms. A subjective appeal to revolutionary will that Della Mea calls for is an appeal that is doomed to failure when the objective conditions are not right. As Marx taught us, the subjective consciousness of the masses is formed through experience and struggle, and a mass revolutionary consciousness cannot fall from the sky when there are no objective conditions driving the revolutionary struggle. In this sense, the appeal to subjectivism is the same as the appeal of Willich and Schapper; it is the same revolutionary method that Marx condemned.

Della Mea disputes my claim that these objective conditions do not exist today. Indeed, he believes that 'at the present stage of capitalism', such conditions are permanently in place; so for this very reason he thinks that today we can speak of how 'socialism is the order of the day [*attualità*]'. As far as I am concerned, I would like to make a distinction with regard to these objective conditions. I think that what is permanent at this stage of capitalism are the objective prerequisites for a socialist system, namely highly developed forces of production manifested in technical progress, greatly increased productivity, a high degree of concentration and the advanced socialisation of the process of production. This is certainly in striking contrast to the capitalist relations of production, and yet this contrast is still not generating the moment of tension and crisis that can trigger the revolutionary rupture. Why?

In my opinion, this is where the strategy followed by the workers' movement can be criticised. It has definitely not been the strategy of intermediate goals, as Della Mea seems to think when he writes that 'more than a few years have now passed since you and … I, with millions of comrades participated in struggles for intermediate goals. The result is plain for all to see in the advance of social democracy and the development of its modern appetites, so enticing in the well-being it offers to the many, if not to everyone, and the power for the few'.

I would like to reiterate what I wrote in the notes to the article by Della Mea, which appeared in issue no. 8.[2] 'Strategy, in this case, means formulating a programme, coordinating short, medium and long term goals, from an overall perspective based on an analysis of social reality, its dynamics, and the balance of existing forces. This is the only serious way to avoid falling into the trap of sterile dogmatism and subaltern empiricism ... The value of a socialist program lies precisely in its capacity to link short-term goals (essentially demands and claims) to medium-term goals (mainly structural reforms and changes in the balance of power) with the final goal of socialist revolution'. This synthesis, this broad perspective, this programmatic coordination is precisely what the workers' movement has lacked over the past quarter-century. During this time, tactics have unfortunately prevailed over strategy, a search for unity over the contents of this unity, a policy of alliances over programmatic objectives, reaction to provocations from the opposition or occasional stimuli over the coordination of struggles and an overall vision. Empiricism – to use a generic and rather imprecise term – has prevailed over revolutionary strategy. It is true that we supported many battles over partial objectives, some of which were very effective. But we never set a serious socialist strategy, a strategy that sees and evaluates each partial objective as just a moment in the progression of actions that can break the balance of capitalist society and trigger a decisive crisis in the not too distant future, depending on the real chances of success and without any idealistic impatience. We have not even conducted a thorough analysis of the society in which we live, which changes before our very eyes and which we risk not understanding. Nor have we defined any intermediate goals, which should involve real structural reforms that can tilt the balance of power towards the working class.

This is the criticism that I have now been levelling for nearly twenty-five years against the Italian workers' movement. If I spoke some time ago in this journal, not without bitterness, of the twenty years lost as a militant socialist, it is precisely because I have never been able to sensitise my party to this issue, which I consider an indispensable premise for every socialist. It is for this very reason that I was not surprised by the capitulation of the PSI, which was already maturing in 1952–3, because this capitulation was the legitimate daughter of that policy.[3] And if, in response to Della Mea, I spoke of 'a serious

---

2   Basso, 'Due risposte', in *Problemi del socialismo*, maggio/giugno 1966, no. 8.
3   EN: Basso is referring to the Italian Socialist Party's steady retreat to ever-more moderate

sign of weakness' in the workers' movement today, it is because I feel that we are taking too long to draw the necessary conclusions from these lessons, too long to overcome the phase of empiricism and the spirit of routine. We need to turn towards an active Marxist strategy.

But the alternative is not between this spirit of routine, which is so hard to die, and revolutionary subjectivism, whether it is manifested in the impatient protests of Della Mea or in the more or less Chinese [Maoist] theories advocated by some small groups of militants today. The Marxist alternative is something else. It involves taking up a struggle that can be driven by the contradictions of society in which we live, with the aim of imposing structural reforms that undermine the foundations of capitalist power so as to gradually take the fundamental contradiction between the forces of production and the capitalist relations of production to breaking point.

In other words, if the revolutionary crisis is perennially postponed, despite the serious contradiction between the forces of production and relations of production, this is because, in the absence of a socialist strategy that can exploit this contradiction, the strong dynamic capabilities of organised capitalism can continuously form new equilibriums – even if still-unstable ones – and gradually integrate the working class.[4]

The strategy I advocate should focus on the conscious intervention of the workers' movement into the contradictory process of capitalist development in order to:

a. Develop the logic inherent to the tendency towards the socialisation of the productive process (intensification of collective action, democratic participation in directing this collective action, formation of counter-powers that can act as the instrument of working-class autonomy in this democratic participation etc.). This would lay the foundations (since the objective premises already exist) for a future socialist society through a transformation of the social structures (intensified collective action) and the balance of power.

b. In the struggle for these objectives, to develop and advance the consciousness of the fundamental contradiction of capitalist society and so the workers' antagonistic consciousness towards capitalist order. In short, we need to develop and advance revolutionary class-consciousness that can be formed only through the conscious intervention of the workers' move-

---

positions, subordinating itself increasingly both to Christian Democracy and to the Italian Communist Party's more pro-Soviet political outlook.

4   See Basso: 'Neocapitalismo e socialisti moderni' in *Problemi del Socialismo*, new series, no. 9, July–August 1966.

ment in the process of capitalist development, in the struggle against the class barriers that continually block collective and democratic action, which must be broken down so that the logic of socialisation can fully unfold.

In my opinion, only coherent action of this kind corresponds to Marx's revolutionary method, because it tends not only to increase and exacerbate the objective contradiction but also – and no less importantly – the subjective consciousness of this contradiction, so as to trigger the tension and crisis that can ignite the spark of revolution. Without this gradual intensification of the conflict, achieved through a series of medium-term goals, I do not see how we can speak, today, of the possibility of a revolution that is not merely the fruit of our optimism or our idealism [...]

CHAPTER 13

Lenin and Marx, Revolutions in the Centre and Revolutions in the Periphery of Capitalism

Just as the term 'Trotskyism' was coined by Trotsky's opponents in the Bolshevik party, so too was the term 'Leninism' coined in 1903 by Lenin's opponents in the Russian Social Democratic Labour Party.* However, soon after Lenin's death, the term was used by his successors to refer to an organic and complete body of writings practically encapsulating the essence of Marxism.

In April 1924, during a lecture given at the Sverdlov University on the principles of Leninism, Stalin offered the famous definition: 'Leninism is Marxism of the era of imperialism and the proletarian revolution. To be more exact, Leninism is the theory and tactics of the proletarian revolution in general, the theory and tactics of the dictatorship of the proletariat in particular'.[1] Before giving this definition, he rejected the opinions of other comrades: 'Some say that Leninism is the application of Marxism to the peculiar conditions of the situation in Russia ... Others say that Leninism is the revival of the revolutionary elements of Marxism of the forties of the nineteenth century, as distinct from the Marxism of subsequent years, when, it is alleged, it became moderate, non-revolutionary'.[2] He admits that both of these definitions contain an element of truth. The meaning and essence of Leninism was a controversial issue at the Fourteenth Party Congress, characterised not only by the struggle against Trotsky but also the clash between Stalin, backed by Bukharin, and Zinoviev. In the article 'In Memory of Lenin', published in Pravda on 13 February 1924, Zinoviev wrote that 'the question of the role of the peasantry is the *fundamental question* of Bolshevism, of Leninism'.[3] In a subsequent article criticising Trotsky ('Bolshevism or Trotskyism') in the 30 November 1924 issue of *Pravda*, i.e. after the aforementioned lectures given by Stalin, he wrote that 'Leninism is Marxism of the era of imperialist wars and of the world revolution, *which began directly in a country where the peasantry predominates*'.[4]

---

* Basso, 'Lenin e Marx, rivoluzioni al centro e rivoluzioni alla periferia del capitalismo' in *Il Segnalatore*, June 1971, no. 1.
1 Stalin, 'The Foundations of Leninism', April 1924, in Stalin 1947, p. 14.
2 Stalin, 'The Foundations of Leninism', in Stalin 1947, p. 13.
3 Zinoviev in Stalin 1947, p. 127.
4 Ibid.

Returning to the subject in his 'On the Problems of Leninism' after his victory at the Fourteenth Congress, Stalin criticised Zinoviev's arguments: 'What does introducing the backwardness of Russia, its peasant character, into the definition of Leninism mean? It means transforming Leninism from an international proletarian doctrine into a product of specifically Russian conditions'.[5] He added that the essence of Leninism was not the question of the role of the peasantry but the dictatorship of the proletariat. It was, of course, Stalin's interpretation that triumphed, first in the Bolshevik Party, and then in the international communist movement. Leninism was accepted as the Marxism of the present epoch, in the sense that the Leninist experience was the complete fulfilment of Marxism as a revolutionary doctrine, a model for all future revolutionary experiences. What I propose to demonstrate in this brief note is precisely the inconsistency of Stalin's interpretation.

Not only Marx and Engels but even Lenin himself always said that class struggle can take many forms. It assumes different theoretical aspects in different historical and social situations. Revolution follows different courses of action and tactics, depending precisely on the different situations and, above all, the different balances of power between social classes. Thus, revolutionary strategy and tactics in a country where 90 percent of the population is rural must necessarily be different from revolutionary strategy and tactics in a country where agriculture does not even account for 10 percent of the population. For a Marxist this would seem a banality. Lenin's main concern, as a Marxist, was certainly not to dictate universal rules of strategy and tactics but to analyse concrete situations and adapt strategy and tactics to the changing balance of power, even if it meant contradicting himself from one day to the next so as not to lose touch with reality. Certainly, he often expressed tactical and contingent needs in the form of universal precepts. When he needed to get a decision accepted, he did not hesitate to put forward general arguments and definitions. In fact, he used them most often when a solution dictated by necessity seemed to be at odds with other categorical statements and solemnly proclaimed principles. We would be very bad Leninists were we incapable of reconstructing the concrete situations in which these kinds of statements were made or arguments put forward, or incapable of understanding the reasons that had dictated a given solution.

Now, Lenin was a true revolutionary, his whole life dominated by a determination to bring down Tsarism and seize power in a predominantly peasant society. All his writings, his analyses, his ideas, his concrete options should be

---

5 Stalin 1947, pp. 124–5.

seen and assessed in this context, namely as a means to an end, to this end. His greatness and universality consist precisely in this, in showing the need for a revolutionary to rationalise each of his actions from the perspective of the end he seeks, to situate his specific action within a concrete historical thread.

Therefore, it is absurd to reduce the wealth of Marx's teachings to the limits of Lenin's experience.

It is impossible to summarise Marx's revolutionary doctrine in a short space; it will have to suffice to recall that his doctrine developed around two elements. The first was the concrete experience of the French Revolution and the other the revolutions of his time, which were not socialist revolutions but democratic and popular revolutions, involving the petty bourgeoisie or the peasants, and often a strong national element. These took place in societies that were still pre-capitalist, where the bourgeoisie had not yet come to power but where there was a strong, determined proletariat who, having helped the bourgeoisie against the old regime and then the petty bourgeoisie against the capitalist bourgeoisie, could eventually seize power for itself, thanks to the tactic of 'permanent revolution'. It was a revolution of this kind that Marx envisaged for Germany at the time when he wrote the *Manifesto*. The other element is the notion of a specifically socialist revolution led by the working class against capitalism, once it had developed its productive potential to the full and exacerbated the antagonism between the forces of production and relations of production. This was something that could only take place in developed capitalist nations, not in pre-capitalist countries. It would involve a revolution in the centre of capitalism ('striking the bourgeoisie to the very heart's core',[6] as Marx described it). The first kind of revolution takes place in the periphery ('in the extremities', as Marx said).[7] However, these phenomena are not independent but related, since even peripheral revolutions are triggered by the expansion of capitalism. The introduction of capitalist relations in peripheral countries upsets old relations and old balances of power, entire social classes ruined by capitalist competition find no adequate compensation in rapid technical developments or improvements of living conditions. In 1850, Marx wrote these words, 'Violent outbreaks must naturally occur rather in the extremities of the bourgeois body than in its heart, since the possibility of adjustment is greater here than there'.[8] He went on to add that revolutions in the extremities of the bourgeois body could eventually follow a socialist path once socialism had triumphed in its heart. In fact, only a highly developed capitalist country has the objective premises for social-

---

6   Marx, *The Manifesto of the Communist Party*, in MECW 6, p. 507.
7   Marx, *The Class Struggles in France 1848 to 1850*, in MECW 10, p. 134.
8   Ibid.

ism and an evolved, politically conscious, technically prepared working class with the initiative and capacity to direct public affairs.

We can summarise Marx's revolutionary conception by saying that, for him, the development of capitalism can be both intensive (in the centre of the system) and extensive (in the periphery). The first accentuates the fundamental contradiction and lays the foundation for the transition to socialism. The second triggers violent upheaval in the periphery, which, as we have seen, can become a permanent revolution and also bring the proletariat to power. When we talk of Marxism we mean both these processes, on the basis of which we can now say that capitalist development in the centre is but the other side of the underdevelopment of the periphery, of countries subjected to relations of economic dependence on capitalist metropoles.

All Lenin's practical activity as a revolutionary, and the overwhelming majority of his writings, centre on the Russian Revolution, a popular democratic revolution in the periphery of capitalism in which the proletariat played a leading role and eventually seized power. It was, in fact, Lenin himself who spoke of the Russian Revolution as breaking the 'weakest link' of capitalism, hence precisely as a revolution in the periphery. Many of his theories (concerning the party, on the seizure of power, on the exercise of seized power, on the dictatorship of the proletariat, etc.) are concrete responses to the problems posed by this type of revolution. For this reason they cannot be applied to socialist revolution in developed capitalist countries. And so, to speak of Leninism as the 'Marxism of the era of imperialism and the proletarian revolution',[9] presenting it as a universally valid, homogeneous body of revolutionary doctrine is, in my opinion, an error which impedes our understanding of the many diverse and much more complex phenomena affecting the socialist revolution in the most advanced capitalist countries. It is these differences that I wish to address in my conclusion.

First, the objective and subjective conditions of revolution are different in the two cases. For Marx, the main driving force of socialist revolution in developed capitalist countries, what we call the capitalist 'centre', is the development of the forces of production. In 1856, he wrote: 'Steam, electricity, and the self-acting mule were revolutionists of a rather more dangerous character than even citizens Barbés, Raspail and Blanqui'.[10] This is all the more important when one considers that only a few years before he had considered Blanqui as the leader of the French revolutionary class. This development of the forces of

---

9   'The Foundations of Leninism', in Stalin 1947, p. 14.
10 Marx, 'Speech at Anniversary of the People's Paper', April 14, 1856, in MECW 14: 655.

production determines a series of contradictions that objectively incorporate tendencies towards socialisation, and it is these objective tendencies, which occur only in developed capitalism, that lay the foundations for socialism and trigger the final crisis. For this crisis actually to happen, and for it to lead to socialism, requires the revolutionary intervention of the proletariat; yet in 1860 Marx described this action as 'conscious participation in the historical process revolutionising society before our very eyes'.[11] Very different is the situation in pre-capitalist countries, where the fundamental contradiction is not yet present, where objective tendencies towards socialism have not yet materialised. The situation in these countries is ripe not for socialist revolution but for popular-democratic revolution, the revolution of the poor and oppressed rather than the revolution of a working class that can assume the leadership of social life. In these countries, the objective factors carry far less weight and so the socialist character of the revolution depends almost entirely on subjective factors. It follows that in a developed capitalist society, a Marxist party must above all focus on the objective social processes, while in a country that is still in the periphery of capitalism, as was Tsarist Russia, a Marxist-Leninist party must prepare to seize political power during a popular democratic revolution and then use the power to build a socialist society. This brings us to another difference. From Marx's revolutionary perspective, revolutionary violence in countries in the capitalist centre functions as a midwife of history, breaking the shackles of the old society to build a new one, the seeds of which are already in place. From Lenin's revolutionary perspective, in a country situated in the periphery of capitalism, it is only after power has been seized that we can begin to lay the foundation of a new society.

Similar considerations can be made about the type and function of the party, which cannot but be different in the two types of society.

Given the era in which he lived, Marx did not have much opportunity to deal seriously with the problem of large mass political parties. However, his whole polemic against secret societies, sects and minority revolutions, all point toward large mass political organisations. In fact, he said, 'the emancipation of the working classes must be conquered by the working classes themselves'[12] and that it is class-consciousness that must guide these workers. The idea of the workers acquiring consciousness from the outside, from intellectuals, as Lenin would have it (who, by the way, was quoting Kautsky *verbatim*) is in stark contrast to Marx. For him, intellectuals and theorists are but spokesmen of the

---

11   Marx, *Herr Vogt*, in MECW 17: 79.
12   Marx, 'Provisional Rules of the Association', in MECW 20: 14.

proletariat, utopians 'so long as the proletariat is not yet sufficiently developed to constitute itself as a class',[13] after which they just have to become aware of the struggle that is taking place before their eyes. In this sense, Marx speaks of proletarian 'spontaneity', understood not as pure spontaneity but as the working class's historical creative capacity (*geschichtliche Selbstätigkeit*). However, Lenin's theory is right if it is framed in terms of the concrete situation in which he operated, that is, Tsarist Russia, where the vast bulk of the population was rural and illiterate, where a small working class had recently been formed and was as yet incapable of achieving a fully developed consciousness by itself. For this reason, the elements of political maturity and revolutionary doctrine had to be imported, not only from outside the working class but also from intellectuals that had emigrated abroad or were inspired by the experience and political maturity of the proletariat in other countries. In this sense, it is true that Leninism, despite Stalin's contrasting position in the above-cited passage, can be seen as the application of Marxism to the original conditions of the Russian people, as a 'Russian translation' of Marxism (I use the word translation not in the literal sense but in the political sense). It can be seen as a translation into a reality that was very different from that of the country where Marx had lived and where he was able to fully develop his doctrine, namely the most economically advanced country of his time. Also accurate is the other claim rejected by Stalin, that Leninism was the 'revival of the revolutionary elements of Marxism of the forties of the nineteenth century',[14] also because in that time Marx was learning about and operating in what were still pre-capitalist countries. Thus, without falling into error by calling Lenin a Blanquist, his conception of the party as one that stands above the masses, a party of a more or less narrow circle of leaders that work clandestinely (as he said at the Second Congress) – the conception of the Bolshevik as a 'Jacobin' of the masses – is strongly reminiscent of the more or less secret leagues and societies in which Marx himself had worked in that period. He even repeats Marx's description of the revolutionary of those years as a modern Jacobin. Marx was to leave that experience behind in the following years thanks to his stay in England. There, he began thinking about other forms of organisation, other methods of struggle for the working class. In Tsarist Russia, however, it was the early Marx that Lenin was applying.

On this point, too, then, we can conclude that Lenin was a great Marxist because he was able to apply Marxist strategy to a particular situation and seize

---

13 Marx, *The Poverty of Philosophy*, in MECW 6: 177.
14 'The Foundations of Leninism', in Stalin 1947, p. 13.

power, something that other socialists before him had failed to do. However, we must also say that his is a particular application of Marxism that cannot be imitated in different historical and social situations.

We could pursue the comparison for another series of problems, ranging from the seizure of power to the exercise of power. Popular democratic revolutions which take place in the periphery of capitalism, like the Russian revolution of 1917 (which only later became a revolution with a socialist aim, though a periodisation of the different stages would be difficult), generally tend to follow traditional methods of seizing power. In these cases, power is still sufficiently identifiable with specific institutions that are above social life, which is still experienced in the form of relatively simple relations. However, in a developed capitalist society, power becomes increasingly embodied in the social structures themselves. The state tends to become a mechanism in a complex machine that drives the whole of society. It acts through a highly structured network of social relations, in which structure and superstructure are increasingly difficult to distinguish, where political and cultural mediation is so intense that it becomes increasingly difficult to understand the real relations, where oppression and violence are part of everyday reality rather than specific state actions. Thus, the problem of the 'seizure of power' takes on completely new and different forms. The workers' movement in the West has not been able to find the right response, as Lenin did in Russia in 1917. However, materially transferring Lenin's experience to the conditions of Western Europe would be an error.

Finally, the same is true for the exercise of power. Lenin can be said to be following in Marx's footsteps in the expression and definition of revolution. But since the Soviet revolution developed in conditions that were completely different from those which Marx imagined – and especially since it had no proletariat that could effectively run its own dictatorship over the exploiting class as a democratic government of the class itself – during the Soviet revolution the very concept of 'dictatorship of the proletariat' gradually assumed, under the pressure of historical necessity, meanings that diverged from the Marxian original, ultimately degenerating into Stalinism. There is no need to go further into this topic, since it is all too familiar.

If my conclusion is to reject Stalin's definition of Leninism and reject the identification of Leninism with Marxism, this does not diminish Lenin's great merits as a revolutionary. He knew how to apply Marx's revolutionary doctrine in a difficult situation and, thanks to his sense of reality and his extraordinary tactical ability, he managed to pilot the boat of revolution through the most difficult waters. Neither does it mean that we should not draw some general lessons from his experience. First, there is his method of concreteness; next, the re-evaluation of will as a necessary moment of socialist revolution; and finally the need to undertake socialist proletarian revolution in developed capitalist countries in close connection with popular-democratic revolutions in pre-capitalist ones. Thus, Lenin teaches us the need for solidarity between the centre and periphery of capitalism, between the emancipation of the working class and emancipation of peasants and farmers. This opens up a vast field for the practical development of revolutionary Marxism, which in the West has tended, and still tends, to degenerate into forms of social democracy.

CHAPTER 14

Marx, Lenin and Rosa Luxemburg

I gladly take the opportunity offered by *Rinascita* to respond not only to Franco De Felice's review of the Letters of Rosa Luxemburg to Karl Kautsky in issue no. 51 of this magazine, but also to Michele Maggi's review of the same book in the 4 December issue of *l'Unità* and Enzo Roggi's criticisms of two of my articles in his review of the *Ulisse* dossier on socialism, in the 1 December issue of *L'Unità*.*

Since there are similarities in some of the criticisms levelled at me, I prefer to address them together, especially in relation to the point subject to most criticism, namely the distinction I attempt to make between Lenin's ideas and Marx's, and between the revolution carried out by Lenin and the one envisaged by Marx. However, I must warn readers that my response, like the other writings I am devoting to these arguments, is based on a general interpretation of Marx's thought and the history of the workers' movement, and as such can be thoroughly expounded only in a book. Since I never seem to have the time to write this book, the fact remains that these single writings can seem incomplete and imperfect, and thus open to the criticism of having neglected or underestimated or simplified one aspect or another. Of course, there may well be shortcomings or simplifications that are intrinsic to my interpretation, irrespective of reasons of space. It will be up to the reader to judge.

However, I find it difficult to imagine any greater simplification that that contained in the current interpretation of what is known as Marxism-Leninism, which goes back to the definition given by Stalin in his lectures at the Sverdlovsk University in April 1924, a few months after Lenin's death. He said, 'Leninism is Marxism of the era of imperialism and proletarian revolution',[1] a definition that Lenin, who was well acquainted with Marxism, would have rejected with all his might. This definition had a precise purpose in Stalin's strategy for gaining power. It was a polemical response to Zinoviev, who had written two months earlier that 'the question of the role of the peasantry is the *fundamental question* of Bolshevism, of Leninism',[2] and that, therefore, Leninism was the theory of a revolution '*began directly in a country where the peasantry pre-*

---

* Lelio Basso, 'Marx, Lenin e Rosa Luxemburg' in *Rinascita*, 7 January 1972, no. 1.
1 'The Foundations of Leninism', in Stalin 1946, p. 14.
2 Zinoviev, in Stalin 1946, p. 126.

dominates'.[3] It was designed to exact the obedience of all communist parties to the Bolshevik Party, heir and guardian of Leninism, that is, to Marxism in the era of imperialism and proletarian revolution.

This definition of Leninism, which reduces Marxism to the confines of Leninist experience, was followed by Stalin's catechetical dogmatisation of Leninism and the reduction of Leninism to Stalinism. It is an open question among scholars whether and to what extent the roots of Stalinism were actually to be found in Leninist theory and practice. I am inclined to believe that they were. Both the one and the other developed from the real conditions of the Russian people, though in Lenin there was a strong element of Western thought, which was missing in Stalin. However, we would not be Marxists if we imagined that the thoughts and actions of these two leaders were not closely tied to the history, struggles, problems, and culture of the Russian people and Russian workers (who were more like peasants than workers); tied, in other words, to the history and culture of a backward country that had been brought into contact with the techniques and ideologies of the industrial world. This does not mean – I hope the reader understands – that Lenin's theories are backward. It only means that he formulated theories and elaborated strategies that were appropriate for this backward country, this people formed mainly of illiterate peasants who needed to be led, and were led, to victory over Tsarism. He did so with a clear understanding that he was responding to a historical situation that was different from the one analysed by Marx.

I hope that it will not be disputed that Marx's ideas were fully developed in England (from the age of 31 until his death), the most capitalist and industrially advanced country in the world at that time, and that all his revolutionary doctrine is based on the great expansion of the forces of production and the conflict that arises between the forces of production and the capitalist relations of production. These conditions were entirely absent from the context of the Soviet revolution, which, therefore, was not a socialist revolution as Marx had envisaged.

I confess that I cannot understand why the communists continue to cling stubbornly to the formula of Marxism-Leninism, a typical product of Stalinism, representing the theoretical foundation of the Stalinist system. The greatness of Lenin is certainly not diminished if we recognise the fact that he led a successful revolution that was outside what Marx hypothesised, and that he defended it in extremely difficult conditions which were very different from

---

[3] Zinoviev, in Stalin 1946, p. p. 10. For a broader discussion of this topic, see my speech at the Zagreb meeting to mark the centenary of Lenin's birth, now republished in *Il segnalatore*, 1971, 1, p. 28 et seq.

those envisaged by Marxist tradition. This can only increase his originality and greatness. Above all, it is much more faithful to his teachings, which are valuable and indispensable. Personally, I think that everything I have learned from Lenin (whether it is a lot or little depends solely on my own capacities, not the wealth of his teachings, which is immense), has been precisely within this historical perspective, that is, referring continuously to the specificity of his work, which is very different from that of Marx. This does not mean, of course, that his work does not also contain lessons of a general nature, only that they have to be understood in a concrete and not abstract fashion.

Let me now turn to what, in my opinion, are the main differences between Marx's thought and Lenin's. This I shall do not so much through a comparison of their works (which, incidentally, I have done several times) but through a historical analysis of the workers' movement and of its thinking, although for reasons of space, I shall be obliged to leave out many details. The workers' movement, in the modern sense, emerged with the rise of modern industry and the factory proletariat; but a revolutionary tradition had already formed that might be described as popular long before. It combined egalitarian utopias (a reaction to early capitalism and the inequality it created), the vaguely democratic aspirations of the social strata crushed by incipient capitalism (artisans, shopkeepers, etc.), memories of and nostalgia for the French Revolution – which was brutally crushed by Thermidor but which would resume its forward march and bear the promised fruits – and a conception of dictatorship (remnant of Robespierre) as a means to implement more advanced projects and reshape society according to reason and justice, etc. Those acquainted with the literature of secret societies and clubs that flourished from the Restoration until 1848 can follow the process of amalgamation of different elements that sometimes coalesce into 'systems' or develop into conspiracies. In any event, they fuelled hopes and shaped revolutionary currents from generation to generation. There are essentially two central ideas behind this popular revolutionary tradition: an ideal society in opposition to the real one and the seizure of power as a means of achieving it; though these two ideas were not always found together.

It would be simplistic to contrast 'Marxism', as a scientific doctrine, to this popular tradition, seen as utopian. Marxism, too, was historically formed and contains several aspects that should be distinguished: its scientific core, a tool used to analyse social reality, which represents a real epistemological break with the past; Marx's practical conception of the proletarian struggle and revolution, which he develops gradually from his experiences in the heart of capitalism, in England; finally, the contributions of his successors, who sometimes enrich these ideas, sometimes debase them, and sometimes apply them to a particular situation. With regard to the practical conception of revolution,

Marx too drew from the popular revolutionary tradition, which we then find extensively present in the Paris Commune and so on, right up to Lenin himself.

Marx's most profoundly original and innovative contribution is his conception of historical materialism, which marks a qualitative leap forward in the doctrine of revolution. This does not simply involve seizing power and imposing a new model of social relations by means of dictatorship; it is a revolution that emerges from the bowels of capitalism itself. It is a long process that accompanies the very development of capitalism. It is driven by the development of the forces of production and the resulting exacerbation of the fundamental contradiction, the ensuing class struggle and growing class-consciousness; these are correlated processes that gradually transform social relations and men, thereby creating within the womb of the old society the elements of the new society and the men to lead it. The seizure of power is undoubtedly an essential and decisive moment in this long and complex historical process that Marx merely outlines. However, it represents neither the start (the construction of socialism does not begin with the seizure of power) nor the end. It is something that depends on the balance of power, which happens when the capitalist system is experiencing an economic or political crisis, when the living conditions of the proletariat have become unbearable. However, the proletariat as a class must be capable of exercising power. Anyone reading Marx unencumbered by dogmatically consecrated formulas cannot fail to appreciate that his whole life was dedicated to furthering his understanding of this historical process. Having started with the example of the French revolution, he gradually moved away from that model in a search for a long-term revolutionary process. The trade unions, cooperatives, the party, the International, universal suffrage, social laws, and so on were all important moments of this process, but the main driver was always the development of class consciousness.

In addition to this Marxian current, another important current formed in Germany. Rather than the growth of consciousness, it emphasised the centralised and disciplined organisation of the masses and leadership from above. Its chief exponent was Ferdinand Lassalle. German Social Democracy, despite its Marxist veneer, is the heir of this concept, and Bebel is its mastermind. These two currents are not rigidly separated or even opposed to each other. Marx also believed in organisation, and the German Social Democrats believed, to some extent, in the need to develop class-consciousness, although in their case it was understood primarily as faith in the party and its leaders. The Marxist veneer was provided by Kautskyism, that is to say, the interpretation of historical materialism in deterministic and evolutionary terms. This gave the masses the certainty of future revolution and, in return, they were asked to put their trust in the party to conduct the struggle, which, to quote Kautsky's famous definition, involved the strategy of attrition (*Ermattungsstrategie*) that in practical terms meant waiting for destiny to be fulfilled and bourgeois society to fall by itself.

Given this situation, what positions were adopted by the two great revolutionary leaders, Lenin and Luxemburg, who came to the forefront of the movement at the end of the last century? Lenin reacted vigorously to the wait and see attitude of the Second International but completely accepted German Social Democracy's line on the party, preferring to focus on organisation and discipline rather than class-consciousness. It is no coincidence that *What is to be Done?* opens with a quote from Lassalle; that the (entirely anti-Marxist) theory of class consciousness being brought to the proletariat from the outside is taken fully from Kautsky; that in the *Two Tactics of Social-Democracy in the Democratic Revolution* Lenin professed full agreement with Bebel, Kautsky and German Social Democracy; and, finally, that his admiration for Bebel comes out once again in the obituary he dedicated to him on the eve of World War I. Lenin's disagreements with Kautsky began only then, while Rosa Luxemburg had, for many years, been denouncing the opportunism of German Social Democracy, of Kautsky and Bebel himself. Having given due space to what are real errors of assessment, Lenin's position can be explained by placing it in its historical context. He led a revolution in a backward country with a newly formed and very thin strata of the working class. He could not wait an entire historical epoch for revolution to mature, since it would require the full development of capitalism, forces of production, and the proletariat's class-consciousness. It was natural for him to focus more on the problems of organisation and leadership from above than the emergence of proletarian class-consciousness from below and the acquisition of a capacity to run their own affairs in a socialist society. It was natural for him to reconnect with the revolutionary tradition that had formed prior to the development of capitalism (as Marx had done in his early years, in the 1840s), rather than to the experience of the mature Marx.

Rosa Luxemburg, conversely, was the only one of Marx's main disciples to try and develop a more faithful form of Marxism, according to which revolution arose from the development of capitalism and the growth of class-consciousness. In this she made some essential contributions (which I have discussed elsewhere), without, of course, resolving the problem of strategy. As long as capitalism remains unvanquished, the problem of revolutionary strategy will never be resolved, despite the valuable lessons of Marx, Luxemburg, Lenin and Mao. It was not by chance that Rosa Luxemburg adopted this perspective, focusing on the growth of class-consciousness rather than tight organisation. She, like Marx, lived in the heart of European capitalism. She, too, like Marx, sought to discover the historical necessity of the collapse of capitalism; that she perhaps sought it in the wrong ways does not mean that she in any way indulged the theory of automatic collapse, which was used to justify the passivity of the Second International. On the contrary, her revolutionary strategy required intense activism and the highest degree of conscious intervention by the proletariat in the revolutionary process. On the other hand, she was fully aware of the ambiguity of history, the two answers that history can give to contradictions: socialism or barbarism.

This is why I continue to think that Rosa Luxemburg, more than Lenin, can help us address the problems of revolutionary strategy in developed capitalist countries. In addition, her explanation of opportunism seems more founded on Marx than Lenin's explanation of labour aristocracies, unless we wish to consider the entire proletariat as an aristocracy, or at least the vast majority of the proletariat of the most advanced capitalist countries.[4] Lenin taught us to break the weakest links, to not underestimate the revolutionary potential of less-developed countries but to solicit their indispensable contributions. In total agreement with Luxemburg, he taught us to see the revolution in a world context. His contribution is fundamental and creative, but it does not amount to the be-all and end-all of Marxism, since it focuses most on aspects that Marx did not develop. We do Marx no honour, but rather betray his memory, if we have him say what he did not say and had no intention of saying. Therefore, I would not say that Lenin and Luxemburg had contrasting ideas but that that they were complementary, as I specifically wrote in the introduction to her political writings.

Moreover, I think I am being faithful to Lenin's teachings even if I have reservations about whether the Leninist revolution was entirely socialist in nature. We all know that when Lenin seized power he did not expect to be able to

---

4 The problem of the opportunism of the social-democratic parties and of the integration of workers' movements in general was something to which Marx and Luxemburg supplied the key but whose importance, in my opinion, they underestimated. In fact, they are the two contradictory aspects linked to the development of capitalism, the other being the growth of class-consciousness (an example of the ambiguity of history). It is precisely the predominance of the aspect of integration that has slowed the revolutionary process in industrially advanced countries, while it has been impossible to import the Leninist revolutionary model, since it is historically linked to different situations. What I am calling for is not a return to Marx, in the sense of seeking the solution to our problems in Marx. This he cannot provide (he can provide a method and guidelines but not specific answers, such as those Lenin was able to find in the realities of his country). I am calling for a simple resumption and analysis of the revolutionary strategy set out by Marx and added to by Luxemburg, so that it can be adapted to the realities of developed capitalist countries. Not only should it be updated to include current developments, but also continually reworked as history progresses.

establish socialism in Russia, because as he noted in his letters, Russia was a backward country in terms of capitalism. By force of circumstances he had to take a different route, since he could not conjure up what Marx considered a prerequisite for socialism: a developed proletariat. The word 'socialism' has changed its meaning over the course of the history of the workers' movement. For Lenin, it signified a historical phase that, in the *Critique of the Gotha Programme*, Marx called the 'first phase of communist society'.[5] In the same work, Marx says that communist society will be preceded by a period of transition characterised by the revolutionary dictatorship of the proletariat. Marx and Engels explained that the dictatorship of the proletariat should follow the forms adopted in the Paris Commune, arising from a revolution that engages the masses directly and solicits their participation (as was characteristic of the Commune) and expressing the most democratic of governments. The coercive force of the state would be applied only to a minority made up of the old ruling class, destined to disappear from history, while society developed the tools of self-government.

This was the natural conclusion of the revolutionary process, as conceived by Marx and Engels for advanced capitalist countries. This was not possible in Lenin's Russia, where the revolution became increasingly elitist and gradually eliminated participation, eventually screening itself behind the shield of the bureaucracy. It would be ridiculous, after over half a century, to attribute this development only to Stalinist degeneration, without pursuing its roots in the conditions of Russia and in the kind of revolution that Lenin had to lead. The fact remains that for Marx and for those who follow his teachings, the kind of revolution and the form of government described above were and remain essential to a socialist society. The crisis of socialism, which I discussed in the *Ulisse* special issue,[6] stems from this: there was a Leninist revolution, but after fifty years we cannot see it as a model for socialism, while the Marx-Luxemburg type of revolution has only been announced and its historical validity has yet to be confirmed, though it is also true that so far no party has seriously made an effort to bring it about.

---

5   Marx, *Critique of the Gotha Programme*, MECW 24, p. 87.
6   EN: These articles, entitled 'La crisi del socialismo' and 'Speranze socialiste', were published in the journal *I Problemi di Ulisse*, special issue 'Quale socialismo', September 1971.

CHAPTER 15

The Transition to Socialism

In the brief introduction to the dossier dedicated to Lenin and Leninism, we said that it represented a first draft of a work devoted to freeing Marx from all the later incrustations and dogmatic utterances of the Second and Third Internationals, and to forming the starting point for a study of all aspects of contemporary society and subsequent developments in the light of a faithful reading of Marx.* The reader may appreciate an explanation for this new dossier, which continues the work above, and is dedicated to the problem of the transition to socialism.

As befits our publication, which has always been non-dogmatic and open to debate, we continue to accept writings that reflect views other than our own, views that may sometimes even be antithetical to our way of thinking on this issue, since they are expressions of currents of thought which exist and which should be examined. The reader will never come across an issue that is lacking in variety, but will be spurred to reflect and decide for themselves; this we believe to be essential precisely for the development of that class consciousness that we believe should not come from the outside and which we consider to be at the basis of any revolutionary vision. The journal's thinking is that which each of us personally expresses – at least as regards the editors, the editorial board being 'pluralistic', to use a word now in fashion though not much to our liking. Naturally, convergences of ideas are also to be found in articles by others, for example, in this issue, there is a contribution by Elmar Altvater.[1] And we are sure that readers will have no difficulty in finding their way around, at least to the extent that the articles are written in a clear language that is accessible to party activists, our main target audience. Although clarity and accessibility are not always easy to achieve, we can assure our readers that we shall always try our best to avoid esoteric language, and apologise in advance if this is not always the case.

The reasons for the choice of topic should be obvious. As we noted last time, Eurocommunism, which now represents the majority of the workers' movement in Italy and large sections of the international proletariat, has not yet

---

* Basso, 'La transizione al socialismo' in *Problemi del socialismo*, January–March, 1977, no. 5.
1 See Altvater, 'L'egemonia Borghese, la logica oggettiva delle compatibilità economiche e l'alternativa del movimento operaio', in *Problemi del socialismo*, January–March, 1977, no. 5.

formulated a revolutionary doctrine, without which, Lenin warned, there can be no revolutionary party. We know that the doctrine comes not from the brains of doctrinaires but from the experiences of a real movement, filtered, of course, through the interpretations of the vanguards. We wish to contribute to this collective effort by offering this first survey of different reflections, which are varied not only in inspiration but also in their perspective. Our personal contribution involves another attempt to return to Marx.

As for the dossier on Lenin, we shall focus only on the main points. What is important for us is to launch the debate, suggest interpretations and therefore offer prospects for research and action, which so far have been neglected. In this way we hope to contribute as far as possible – not only personally but as a journal – to the elaboration of a doctrinal foundation for a new revolutionary strategy for developed capitalist countries and, thus, also for their transition to socialism.

First, we wish to leave no room for a frequent misunderstanding when Marxists begin to discuss the transition to socialism. There comes to mind at once a sentence in the *Critique of the Gotha Programme* where Marx speaks of the dictatorship of the proletariat as a transitional regime. Today Eurocommunist parties have abandoned the use of this expression without explaining why. It might have been better to clarify the meaning it had for Marx, and then see whether it is still acceptable to us. Marx only speaks of the dictatorship of the proletariat in two short periods of his life: in the years immediately following the defeat of the 1848–9 revolution and after the defeat of the Commune. In these two periods Marx collaborated with the Blanquists, the heirs of the Babouvist tradition and proponents of Jacobin dictatorship. On both occasions this collaboration was short-lived. It is very likely that the words 'Dictatorship of the proletariat' are the result of these two circumstances. Marx accepted the Blanquist view that the failure of the revolution was also due to the lack of a strong central power, a dictatorship. Without this, a regime that has just emerged from profound social upheaval and with no solid foundations would find it difficult to withstand the counter-offensive of forces that had dominated society until then. However, unlike the Blanquists, Marx rejects the idea that a dictatorship formed by a secret council of conspirators or some central committee can substitute for the class. If there must be a dictatorship, it must be the dictatorship of the proletariat, a class that seizes power only when it is ready to exercise it, one that exercises it on the basis of broad-based internal democracy without delegating its powers to others. This regime is a 'dictatorship' in the sense that until its power is consolidated, the representatives of the bourgeoisie must be deprived of their political rights, because their economic power, their cultural hegemony and past power would allow them, especially at a time of upheaval and unrest, to disrupt genuine democratic participation and force the victorious masses back to their previous condition of wage slavery.

This interpretation is the result of a thorough analysis of all the passages in which Marx mentions 'the dictatorship of the proletariat': carried out through a study of the conditions of the time when these texts were written and the corresponding Blanquist positions, and an examination of the research conducted on this issue by other authors, including [Hal] Draper, whose work is fundamental. The conclusion of this study might well be that the expression used by Marx could imply criticism of the Blanquists, who propounded 'revolutionary dictatorship', whereas Marx is saying 'yes a dictatorship, but let it be of the proletariat'. We do not know, however, if Marx remained faithful to this view until his death. After his death, Engels watered things down considerably, justifying Draper's view, which was that, in reality, dictatorship here is synonymous with domination, *Herrschaft*. Instead, we believe that for Marx the two terms did not coincide. Instead, dictatorship is a moment of accentuated dominance.

But whatever opinion you may have in that regard, it is clear that in addition to being short-lived, this dictatorial phase that follows the seizure of power is a phase of revolutionary transformation of capitalist society into communist society; a phase in which profound upheavals, expropriations, radical changes in the structures of society would inevitably be accompanied by turmoil and upheaval that had to be checked as much as possible.

When we speak now of the transition to socialism, we are not referring to that phase, still far in the future, but the one that precedes and leads to the seizure of power. Capitalist society is not some eternal model. It is, as Marx wrote, a historical and transitory social formation, which, in a sense, is always in a period of transition because it is permanently unstable. Essentially, we have before us two problems. First, how does this transition process come about, by what forces is it driven, in what conditions does it take place? Second, do these conditions exist today; are these forces in operation today?

We are not, of course, claiming to have the definitive answer; we are merely suggesting an interpretation of Marx. But first of all, having dispensed with that worthless distinction that dominated the Second International between 'reformers' and 'revolutionaries', the first being those who thought socialism would come about through a series of reforms, and the second instead only through the violent seizure of power. It is a worthless distinction from a Marxian standpoint because a simple accumulation of reforms that do not meet certain requirements will never bring about socialism, and the violent seizure of power alone cannot create socialism unless the foundations have previously been laid within capitalist society. As Marx sees it, the revolutionary process, the process of transition from capitalism to socialism includes two phases. One involves laying these foundations, building the elements of a future society whose conditions have already been created by the process of capitalist development. In the second phase, thanks to the development of the objective and subjective conditions, the workers' movement can finally take power and free the nascent elements of the new society that emerge from the old structures that continue to try to suffocate them.

The crucial point for an interpreter of Marx is precisely to understand the course of the first phase, which, in our opinion, is precisely the stage that we are now in. In a passage of the French edition of *Capital*, Marx says that: 'The development of contradictions of a historical mode of production is the only historical way towards its dissolution and transformation. Therein lies the secret of the historical movement which doctrinaires, utopians and socialists do not want to understand'.[2] Hence, it is only the development of the inherent contradictions and the fundamental contradiction in particular, that drives the process. This fundamental contradiction is, as we know, the one between the increasingly social character of the forces of production and the private nature of the relations of production. These concepts are well-enough known that we need not dwell on them. As the forces of production grow, which it is indispensable – for capitalism – that they do, their social character increases, setting in motion processes and creating forms of social aggregation that are incompatible with the private dominance and exploitation of these forces of production.

One can easily interpret a proposition of this sort in deterministic fashion, especially since Marx often yields to the temptation of referring to the end of capitalism as a 'natural necessity'. This deterministic interpretation, which was extensively developed by Kautsky, enabled the leaders of German Social Democracy and a broad current of self-styled 'Marxists' of the Second International, to proclaim themselves revolutionaries merely because they believed in the inevitable victory of the social character of the forces of production, and therefore of socialism; so that all the workers' movement had to do was to prepare for the day of collapse.

But all Marx's teachings, even in the early 'Theses on Feuerbach', insist on the need for a dialectical interaction between this objective process (which also takes place independently of the will of the proletariat) and the proletariat's revolutionary praxis (the subjective action of class struggle). In a passage I have often cited from one of Marx's less well-known books, the *Herr Vogt*, he describes the revolutionary process as the conscious participation of the workers' movement in the objective processes taking place before our eyes. It is clear

---

2 TN: this translation is drawn from Chattopadhyay 2016, p. 182.

then that Marx excludes any deterministic interpretation of the revolutionary process. Without the conscious intervention of the masses, the development of the immanent antagonisms could lead not to the victory of socialism, but to a generalised catastrophe. Engels' succinct rallying cry 'Socialism or barbarism' perfectly encapsulates this Marxian concept.

It must be clear, though, that while it is true that objective development cannot by itself bring about the victory of socialism, the same must be said for the subjective action of the proletariat. If subjective action is arbitrary, if the goals are limited or badly thought out, if they do not fit into the development of the objective processes, then class struggle may just lead to a mere improvement in living standards within capitalist society, without minimally destroying its foundations or creating new socialist relations of production. We have seen that it is only by developing the contradictions inherent in society that the workers' movement can determine the transition from the capitalist social formation to socialism, even though, as Marx said (readers, please take heed), 'the doctrinaires ... do not want to understand'. They did not want to understand then, and they do not want to understand even now.

What happens if the workers' movement acts without following the objective development of contradictions? That is to say, if the workers' movement does not employ the social development of the forces of production to compel capitalist society to release the elements of a new structure, new kinds of social relations forming the foundations of a new social structure, which cannot arise merely from a sense of equity and justice but only on the basis of historical necessity? Throughout a life consumed by revolutionary passion, Marx did not stop to examine this aspect of the problem. He preferred to work on the optimistic assumption that the processes set in motion by the forces of production ('steam, electricity, and the self-acting mule', he wrote, 'were revolutionists of a rather more dangerous character than even citizens Barbés, Raspail and Blanqui') would coincide with the class action of the proletariat, whose function is revolutionary.[3]

But history proved him wrong and the revolution, which he awaited so anxiously, never happened where he expected. How did this profound divergence from Marx's predictions come about? What happened? What happened was that the actions of the workers' movement did not support the objective developments we mentioned; they did not follow the spontaneous process of socialisation. On the other hand, capitalism, far from being in decline as Marx had hoped, still had one great opportunity – to exploit the Third World.

---

3 Marx, 'Speech at Anniversary of the People's Paper', in MECW 14, p. 655.

Thus it was able to continue expanding while the forces of production continued developing within it. In the 'Preface to the *Critique of Political Economy*', Marx himself taught us that a social formation does not decline until it has exhausted its capacity to create new forces of production. In the last century, this capacity had certainly not waned, also partly due to the fact that the workers' movement – I repeat – had made no attempt to strike at the heart of capitalism. It was only concerned with enjoying a better life within it.

We can summarise our argument by saying that three forces act in capitalist society: the forces of production, which are the revolutionary forces; the workers' movement, which should act on them but has not in fact done so; and the relations of production, which are the forces of conservation and which have, as Marx well explained in *Capital*, a capacity for self-reproduction. If the first two forces act at the same time, in the sense of the above-quoted sentence from Herr Vogt, the victory of socialism at the historical level will be guaranteed. However, if they do not coincide, if the process initiated within capitalist society by the immanent antagonisms is not directed towards socialism by the conscious will of the proletariat, it will again be the capitalist relations that prevail enabling the system to survive.

As we have said, Marx did not elaborate on this aspect of the problem. He realised that in England, which was then the most advanced country and closer to revolution from a Marxian perspective, the proletariat was gradually losing its revolutionary drive. However, he attributed this 'opportunism' to the privileged situation of the English proletariat, thanks to the huge profits that British capitalism made in international markets. In fact, today we can say that this was not a simple case of the opportunism of the labour aristocracies but a phenomenon of general working-class integration into the capitalist system. This naturally first developed in England and then spread throughout the workers across Western society, where no revolutionary politics has been seriously undertaken. This capacity for integration was none other than a manifestation of the conservative force of the relations of production, which always tend towards self-reproduction, taking on the semblance, even in the minds of the workers, of a natural phenomenon, as Marx noted in *Capital*.

Hardly any of Marx's disciples have progressed any further along the path he opened for the transition to socialism. Only Rosa Luxemburg extended the analysis. If it is true that the fundamental contradiction permeates the whole of society, if it is true that the conflict between the forces of production and relations of production is manifested at all times and in every act of the process of social development, we must conclude that every moment of this process contains within it an antithesis, two possible directions, ambiguities of choice.

It is precisely this ambiguity of the historical process that Luxemburg focused on, returning to the Marxian dialectic that his epigones had consigned to the attic.

We have thoroughly examined the theme of the ambiguity of history in the thoughts of the Polish revolutionary in an anthology of writings by and about Rosa Luxemburg, soon to be published by Mondadori.[4] We would refer any readers interested in the strategy we are proposing to this book.

In the polemic against Bernstein that she wrote at the turn of the century, Rosa not only reiterated the Marxian thesis of the unity and interaction of the objective revolutionary process (*Umwälzungsprozess*) and the workers' movement's conscious subjective intervention (*bewusste Teilnahme*), but also clarified the internal dialectic of the objective phase (forces of production – relations of production). A book she wrote a few years later, *The Mass Strike*, focuses instead on the internal dialectic of the subjective phase (spontaneity-consciousness and class-party) and draws conclusions that can generally speaking be accepted as completely valid. But we can say that all her work is characterised by a dramatic sense of the ambiguity of history.

Without analysing at any great length the socialising action of the forces of production and the conservative relations of production, Rosa illustrates their presence very effectively in every moment of history. If the driving force behind capitalist development and the overcoming of capitalism is the fundamental antagonism, there must be an incidence of this antagonism permanently operating in the course of its development. 'World politics', she wrote in her response to Bernstein, using the terminology of the time, which today would be called 'imperialism', 'and the workers' movement. Each is only a different aspect of the present phase of capitalist development'.[5] Two different, contradictory aspects of the same development, ever-present within it, two forces that impress antagonistic movements and tendencies upon development. Thus, even everyday action is a battlefield in the campaign to achieve the ultimate goal. In fact, every day men are called to resolve this ambiguity, so that from the contradictory womb of development may emerge a partial objective, an immediate response that marks a step forward along the road leading either to the triumph of imperialism or to the triumph of socialism.

This idea is repeated several times in her writings, but we find it most clearly expressed in *The Crisis in the German Social Democracy*: 'Historic development

---

4 Basso (ed.) 1977.
5 Luxemburg 2008, p. 87.

moves in contradictions, and for every necessity puts its opposite into the world as well. The capitalist state of society is doubtless a historic necessity, but so also is the revolt of the working class against it. Capital is a historic necessity, but in the same measure is its grave digger, the Socialist proletariat. The world rule of imperialism is a historic necessity, but likewise its overthrow by the proletarian international. Side by side the two historic necessities exist, in constant conflict with each other'.[6]

No Marx scholar, not even Marx himself, had before then described the global historical process as the arena of this daily conflict and hence where every aspect of society, every institution, every event is affected by the simultaneous presence of two opposing tendencies that lacerate society, two historical necessities which vie for dominance. 'Our historical necessity', adds Rosa, 'enters into its full rights the moment that the other – bourgeois class domination – ceases to be the bearer of historical progress, when it becomes an obstacle, a danger to the further development of society'.[7]

If socialism is to be found at the end of this long journey that the workers' movement must undertake, following the route mapped-out by the objective contradictions, it is clear that a party or a movement cannot describe itself as revolutionary just because it aims for and prepares for the seizure of power. It must have the capacity to recognise and follow, each day, the path that leads to socialism, a process which, as Marx indicated, can last an entire historical epoch. Here lies the fundamental importance of another of Luxemburg's theses, which she defended with tenacity: the unity of daily struggle and final goal. Not only had Bernstein, the theorist of revisionism, declared that for him the movement was everything and the end goal was nothing, but also that the praxis of the workers' movement had almost always been dominated by a *de facto* separation between daily action, focused on simple improvements in living standards unconnected to any socialist consideration, and revolutionary aspiration. Marx and Luxemburg taught us that this road will never lead to socialism. If everyday action is not placed in the broader context of general progress towards socialism, part of the coordination of all the socialist elements that are being created by the internal antagonism of society, if it does not aim to become the point of crystallisation for all socialising tendencies expressed by both the development of the forces of production and the development of class consciousness, there will only be immediate practical benefits but no step forward along the road to socialism. Quite the reverse, it will clear the way for

---

6 Luxemburg 1919, p. 123.
7 Ibid.

the conservative and consolidating action of the relations of production, and, therefore, the integration of the working class into the system.

At this point, we should turn to another question: are the conditions now in place to allow the workers' movement to resist the lure of integration and finally set off along the path of socialism? I think they are, but it is a very broad area of discussion and it will have to be addressed at a later date. For now we shall content ourselves with having framed the problem theoretically within our interpretation of Marx's thought.

PART 4

Marxism, a Science of Revolution
(Selected Writings from Lelio Basso, Socialismo
e rivoluzione, Feltrinelli, Milan, 1980)

CHAPTER 16

Socialism as the Emancipation of Man

The third and by far the most important level of Marxian analysis in terms of dehumanisation regards capitalist society itself, to which Marx devoted the best years of his life.*[1] The conclusion he reached was that the degree of dehumanisation and alienation would become so unbearable that capitalism could not possibly survive. At the same time, the social development of the forces of production, advanced by capitalist society itself, would lead to a demand for a similarly free development of the human person.

The thesis of the persistence of Marx's notion of alienation as an element underpinning the ideas he presents in *Capital* as well, something which continues to be contested by both Marxist traditionalists and structuralist philosophers, is gaining ground among the most observant and perceptive exponents of Marx's thought.

The superficiality and erroneousness of the interpretations, formulated mainly by dogmatic Marxists, that see Marx's insistence on alienation and humanist issues in the *Manuscripts* of 1844 as an indiscretion of his Hegelian youth, are borne out by the fundamental orientation of the analyses contained in the *Grundrisse* and *Capital*. Marx wished to uncover and explain an economic mechanism and its limits, which perpetuate inhuman relations – relations of universal mystification – in order then to go on to indicate ways in which it could be transcended, such as to establish new and more human social relations. So naturally Marx returned to the category that best expresses the complexity of these inhuman relations, the category of alienation.[2]

Our aim is to follow Marx's steps, basing our analysis primarily on *Capital* and the *Grundrisse*, as well as other writings, so as to show how even his *mag-*

---

* 'Il socialismo come emancipazione dell'uomo', chapter two of *Socialismo e rivoluzione*, Feltrinelli, Milan 1980.
1 EN: Basso is referring to what he calls Marx's third period, which for him coincides with the highest phase of his theoretical development.
2 Vranicki 1971, p. 177. Lukács, too, maintained there was continuity in Marx's basic conception of the problem of man throughout his writings, as 'can be seen from the well-known and oft-quoted words from the Preface to the *Critique of Political Economy* in which bourgeois society is described as the last manifestation of the "pre-history of human society"' (Lukács 1971, p. 190).

num opus is to be read in this light. It is not a treatise on political economy but a 'critique' of political economy that aims to show the substance of the social relations behind the data and the categories of bourgeois 'science'. 'It comes to the surface here', writes Marx in *Capital*, 'in a purely economic way – i.e., from the bourgeois point of view, within the limitations of capitalist understanding, from the standpoint of capitalist production itself, that it has its barrier, that it is relative'.[3] In this sense, *Capital* is primarily a work of sociology, economic sociology, political perhaps, but primarily of the sociology of knowledge, because it offers us guidance in looking at life beyond economic schema, that is to say, bourgeois schema. If Marx's above-cited cautions were not to be heeded, the ultimate meaning of the book would remain incomprehensible.[4]

---

3   Marx, *Capital*, Volume III, MECW 37, p. 258.
4   Marx scholars do not always realise that to understand his ideas, consideration must also be given to his unpublished writings. It was the circumstances of his life, the poverty which forced him to earn a living by writing newspaper articles, the illnesses that forced him into long periods of inactivity, his political commitments, which absorbed much of his time in one of the most fruitful periods, that prevented him from publishing any other fundamental work apart from *Capital*. However, we know that he himself considered it an annoying duty to devote so much time to 'economic filth'. He planned other works, certainly no less important, as can be seen from his projects for which we have his notes. As he wrote to J. Dietzgen, 'When I have cast off the burden, I shall write a "Dialectic". The true laws of dialectics are already contained in Hegel, though in a mystical form. What is needed is to strip away this form' (Marx to Joseph Dietzgen, London, 9 May 1868, in MECW 43, p. 31). But not only was *Capital* conceived as part of a much wider work – and only in that framework can its true meaning be found – but it, too, was never finished. Marx published only Book I during his lifetime and left a vast mass of manuscripts. It was from these that Engels drew material for Book II and Book III, according to his own criteria and neglecting hundreds of other pages that only later came to light. And there is no doubt that as these pages come to light – the *Grundrisse* primarily but also other materials – the true Marx will become increasingly clear. Nevertheless, we still have enough material to establish what Marx meant by the words 'critique of political economy', used as a title in 1859 and subtitle in 1867: political economy is the bourgeois science that explains and justifies production, circulation, distribution and consumption processes that take place in bourgeois society as natural processes. The task of Marx's critique is precisely to demystify this science, highlighting the real social relations, which are also extra-economic relations. It is in this sense that we have spoken of sociology and sociology of knowledge. On this point, we believe we can agree with M. Rubel, who explains the purpose and significance of *Capital* as follows: 'A scientific act, *Capital* is directed against a science whose pretext is the wealth of nations and the raison d'être of the enslavement of the "largest and most miserable class". Political economy, for Karl Marx, was the science of evil, the theory of the dominant social order … To explain so as to expose the plight of labour exploitation; to disabuse; to tear this veil that is the ideology justifying the exploitation of man by man – that was Marx's ambition as a *critic* of political economy'. And later: 'And to criticise political economy, we must consider it in its relationship with society as a whole' (Rubel 1963, pp. XVIII and LXV).

Of course, we do not wish to deny the fundamental importance of Marxian economic analysis, but let us not forget that, for Marx, the economy was the anatomy of civil society, and he studied anatomy in order to study, understand and treat the social body as a whole and so men above all.[5] It would therefore be difficult to read *Capital* and claim to understand its meaning without having grasped Marx's method and the principles of his sociology of knowledge, which are a clarification and a deepening of what we previously said about the 'world upside-down' and the inversion of the subject-object relationship. In other words, his analysis and criticism of capitalism are founded on the principle that upside-down relations produce an upside-down consciousness of the world. They give us the appearance of reality, hiding the true essence of the processes. Ideology is used to give a mask of eternity to an existence that is factual, historical and transitory. The great revolutionary strength of *Capital* lies precisely in this demonstration of the historical origin and transitory nature of capitalism and, therefore, the historical necessity of overcoming it. However, at the root of the upside-down relations created by capitalism is the process of dehumanisation and alienation.

In the following pages of this chapter we shall be obliged to make continuous and extensive use of quotations from Marx, precisely because we know how much resistance our interpretation may come up against and we want to support it not with a few scattered sentences but with a systematic presentation of all the salient points of Marx's analysis. Anticipating our conclusions, we wish to show that the ultimate aim of the analysis of surplus labour and surplus value is not to denounce the capitalists' thieving from the workers but to highlight a dehumanisation mechanism (objectification of the product, antagonism towards and domination over the producer). The latter deprives workers of control over the production process by transforming living labour into dead labour, 'fetishising' goods and 'reifying' human relationships. It perpetuates these reified relations so as to increase continuously the domination and oppression of capital, of dead labour over living workers.[6] Consequently, Marx openly assigns revolution the task of re-humanisation. This was also true of his early writings, but now it is based on a materialist conception of history and not on philosophical abstractions. What in the *Manuscripts* was a sort of

---

5 Roman Rosdolsky notes that 'the essential result of Marx's *Critique of Political Economy* consists in, namely, the proof that economics, "*is not concerned with things, but with relations between people, and in the last instance between classes*"; but these relations "are always *bound to things and appear as things*" (Engels)' (Rosdolsky 1977, pp. 442–3).

6 'Capital is dead labour, which, vampire-like, only lives by sucking living labour, and lives the more, the more labour it sucks' (*Capital*, I, MECW 35, p. 241).

fusion, if not a simple juxtaposition of the philosophical-anthropological heritage of Hegel and Feuerbach on the one hand, and capitalist economy on the other, becomes in *Capital* a synthesis, in which Ricardo and Hegel contribute to the creation of a materialist conception that goes beyond both and gives us an explanation of the laws that govern the development of capitalist society, laws which also govern the birth of a new society.

Demystification of the Capitalist Relation between Living Labour and Objectified Labour

Before addressing the issue more directly, we should say a few words about the aforementioned demystifying character of Marxian analysis. Without this demystification it would be impossible to understand reality. In his analysis of social reality, Marx sets out from the premise that one must distinguish the phenomenal form (*Erscheinungsform*) from the hidden substratum (*verbogene Hintergrund*); and while 'the phenomenal forms appear directly and spontaneously as current modes of thought; the latter must first be discovered by science'.[7] '[T]he relationship of capital actually conceals the inner connection behind the utter indifference, isolation, and estrangement in which they place the labourer vis-á-vis the conditions of realising his labour'.[8]

> On the one hand, the value, or the past labour, which dominates living labour, is incarnated in the capitalist. On the other hand, the labourer appears as bare material labour-power, as a commodity. Even in the simple relations of production this inverted relationship necessarily produces certain correspondingly inverted conceptions, a transposed con-

---

[7] MECW 35, p. 542. The Italian translation speaks of *rapporto sostanziale* [essential relation] where we prefer to translate *verbogene Hintergrund* with *substrato nascosto* (hidden substrate). See also the following passages. 'These imaginary expressions, arise, however, from the relations of production themselves. They are categories for the *phenomenal forms* of *essential relations*. That in their appearance things often represent themselves in inverted form is pretty well known in every science except Political Economy' (p. 537). 'It should not astonish us, then, that vulgar economy feels particularly at home in the estranged [The German word *Entfremdung* is usually translated as 'alienated' – LB] outward appearances of economic relations in which these *prima facie* absurd and perfect contradictions appear and that these relations seem the more self-evident the more their internal relationships are concealed from it, although they are understandable to the popular mind' (*Capital*, Vol. III: MECW 37, p. 804).

[8] *Capital*, Vol. III, MECW 37, p. 88.

sciousness which is further developed by the metamorphoses and modifications of the actual circulation process.[9]

It is, therefore, this inversion of relations that produces inverted notions and the mystification of consciousness, and ensures the enslavement of the workers. 'This phenomenal form, which makes the actual relation invisible, and, indeed, shows the direct opposite of that relation, forms the basis of all the juridical notions of both labourer and capitalist, of all the mystifications of the capitalistic mode of production, of all its illusions as to liberty, of all the apologetic shifts of the vulgar economists'.[10] Thus one of the foundations underlying social order is precisely this mystification, which inverts the reality of things.

How does this inverted relationship present itself? Let us again hear from Marx:

> ... under the capitalist mode of production and in the case of capital, which forms its dominant category, its determining production relation, this enchanted and perverted world develops still more ... With the development of relative surplus-value in the actual specifically capitalist mode of production, whereby the productive powers of social labour are developed, these productive powers and the social interrelations of labour in the direct labour-process seem transferred from labour to capital. Capital thus becomes a very mystic being since all of labour's social productive forces appear to be due to capital, rather than labour as such, and seem to issue from the womb of capital itself.[11]

But this process does not just occur in the already formed capitalist relation, but already in the very process of constitution of the capitalist relation, in the encounter between the capitalist, the owner of the money to be transformed into livelihood and means of production, and the worker, owner of labour-power who, according to bourgeois economics, achieves the simple exchange of goods, an exchange of 'equivalents'. But what creates the capitalist relation is not the exchange of goods, but the character of isolation, alienation, and fetishism.

> [W]hat stamps money or commodities with the *character of capital* from the outset, even in the first process before they have actually been con-

---

9 MECW 37, p. 49.
10 *Capital*, Vol. I, MECW 35, p. 540.
11 *Capital*, Vol. III, MECW 37, p. 814.

verted into *capital*, is neither their nature as money nor their nature as commodities, nor is it the material use value these commodities have of serving as means of subsistence and means of production, but the circumstance that this money and these commodities, these means of production and subsistence, confront labour capacity which has been denuded of all objective wealth as *independent powers*, personified in those who own them. The material conditions necessary for the realisation of labour are therefore themselves alienated from the worker, and appear rather as fetishes endowed with a will and a soul of their own, and *commodities* figure as the *buyers of persons* ... It is not a case of the worker buying means of subsistence and means of production, but of the means of subsistence buying the worker, in order to incorporate him into the means of production.[12]

That being said, the very moment that the relation is constituted, it naturally not only preserves but aggravates the situation. Capital 'is merely the products of labourers turned into independent powers, products as rulers and buyers of their producers, but rather also the social forces and the future form of this labour, which confront the labourers as properties of their products'.[13] Therefore, it is the process of alienation that determines the inversion of relations and conceptions. It is '[t]he changed form of the conditions of labour, i.e., alienated [*Entfremdung*] from labour and confronting it independently [*ihr gegenüber verselbständigte*], whereby the produced means of production are thus transformed into capital',[14] so that ultimately 'the cause may appear as an effect and the effect as a cause'.[15] 'As, in religion, man is governed by the products of his own brain, so in capitalistic production, he is governed by the products of his own hand'.[16] He could not have expressed more succinctly and effectively the parallel between religious alienation and capitalist alienation, highlighting the essential similarity of the processes despite their historical diversity.

This inevitably brings to mind a similar comparison that Marx makes in the *Manuscripts*:

---

12   MECW 34, p. 411.
13   MECW 37., p. 802. The version we have provided corresponds to the Institute of Marx-Engels-Lenin Institute Moscow, rather than Engels' truncated version. [TN: it is also true of the MECW version cited here].
14   MECW 37, p. 811.
15   MECW 37, p. 855.
16   MECW 35, p. 616.

The more the worker spends himself, the more powerful becomes the alien world of objects which he creates over and against himself, the poorer he himself – his inner world – becomes, the less belongs to him as his own. It is the same in religion. The more man puts into God, the less he retains in himself. The worker puts his life into the object; but now his life no longer belongs to him but to the object. Hence, the greater this activity, the more the worker lacks objects. Whatever the product of his labour is, he is not. Therefore, the greater this product, the less is he himself. The alienation of the worker in his product means not only that his labour becomes an object, an external existence, but that it exists outside him, independently, as something alien to him, and that it becomes a power on its own confronting him. It means that the life which he has conferred on the object confronts him as something hostile and alien.[17]

And just as in religion one must overcome alienation by re-appropriation, which is at once a gaining conscious awareness and a practical overturning, so too in the face of capitalist alienation one must resolve the contradiction critically, dissipating 'this false appearance and illusion, this mutual independence and ossification of the various social elements of wealth, this personification of things and conversion of production relations into entities, this religion of everyday life'.[18] One must uncover the hidden connections, understand 'the inner nature of capital, just as the apparent motions of the heavenly bodies are not intelligible to any but him who is acquainted with their real motions, motions which are not directly perceptible by the senses',[19] and take back possession of the production process and so build a socialist society.

The Dehumanising Character of Capitalism

This introduction will allow us to better grasp the meaning of capitalism as Marx sees it: as a historical process that was rooted in the preceding social formation and which generates the seeds of the next social formation.

From the very beginning, capitalism showed its dehumanising character. In fact, it came about through a series of combined processes that led on the one hand to primitive accumulation and on the other to the formation of 'free workers' who no longer have their own means of work and were thus compelled to

---

17   Marx, *Economic and Philosophical Manuscripts of 1844*, MECW 3, p. 272.
18   MECW 37, p. 817.
19   Engels, *Anti-Dühring*, MECW 25, p. 199.

sell their labour-power. For Marx the separation of the worker from his means of work is not only an economic fact but above all a social and human fact. These men, stripped of the tools of their craft or the implements they used to cultivate the land, which they no longer possess, are forced to give up even their personal work, that is their independent capacity to realise a project of their own. Marx stresses the fact that the possession of tools is linked to craftsmanship and vice versa. In this way, like in small-scale agriculture, the worker preserves a direct relationship with his work and with his product, while not participating in the control of the collective processes that are beyond him. Therefore, on the individual level, he is still able to express his own personality in his work. Even with capitalism, as long as the artisan can retain ownership of his tools, 'labour still as his own; definite self-sufficient development of one-sided abilities',[20] and although labour becomes only 'half artistic', it is labour that is 'half end-in-itself'. 'The principle of developed capital is precisely to make special skill superfluous, and to make manual work, directly physical labour, generally superfluous both as skill and as muscular exertion; to transfer skill, rather, into the dead forces of nature',[21] thus killing the very personality of the worker as a creator. Capitalism replaces quality with quantity and, therefore, people with things.[22]

These observations obviously do not induce Marx to preach a return to the Middle Ages, to craftsmen's guilds and manual skill, that is to say, the autonomy of the individual worker. The development of modern industry has finally laid the foundations for common collective control over the social labour process, i.e. for the total emancipation of man and the total, free and conscious development that forms his supreme aspiration.

Marx says that the original fullness of social relations can exist because 'it is the bond natural to individuals within specific and limited relations of production', in which 'the single individual seems to be developed more fully, because he has not yet worked out his relationships in their fullness, or erected them

---

20   Marx 1993, p. 497.
21   Marx 1993, p. 587.
22   'Now, this is not an isolated fact. On the contrary, it is capitalist society's fundamental social phenomenon: the transformation of qualitative human relations into the *quantitative attributes of inert things*, the expression of social labour used to produce certain goods as *value*, as the *objective quality of these goods*, a reification which thereafter gradually extends to the psychic life of men, so that abstractness and quantity prevail over concreteness and quality ... In the conscience of producers, commerce and the capitalist economy tends to replace use-value with exchange-value, and human and significant relations with universal and abstract relations between buyers and sellers. It thus tends to replace quality with quantity in human life in general' (Goldmann 1959, pp. 1447–9).

as independent social powers and relations opposite himself'.[23] 'Universally developed individuals, whose social relations as their own communal relations, are hence also subordinated to their own communal control, are no product of nature, but of history'.[24]

Yet his refusal of capitalist alienation is such that this return to the past, which he rejects in favour of industry, is less objectionable in the case of agriculture, in which case only the problem of the re-humanisation of labour leads him to make the following type of observation: 'the capitalist system works against a rational agriculture, or that a rational agriculture is incompatible with the capitalist system (although the latter promotes technical improvements in agriculture), and needs either the hand of the small farmer living by his own labour or the control of associated producers'.[25] It is clear that the only reason why Marx prefers the 'control of associated producers', and even earlier the 'work of the small farmer' to the technical development offered by capitalism, is that both these forms offer the possibility of exercising control over one's own work, personal work carried out in accordance with a plan (collective in the first case, individual in the other). What they both have in common is that labour is 'human'.[26] As for industrial labour, Marx's fundamental thesis is that we have to go through capitalist dehumanisation before we can get to communist humanisation [...]

The Leap from the Realm of Necessity to the Realm of Freedom

There are two famous texts in which Marx himself anticipates some aspects of future society: *The Civil War in France* and the *Critique of the Gotha Programme*. In the first he simply analyses the first historical attempt to build a new society, highlighting how its aim was taking the path he proposed, which is the society's desire to reclaim the powers usurped by the state. In the second book he is principally concerned with criticising the programme adopted by the continent's foremost workers' party by demolishing certain absurd or dangerous statements rather than outlining his own future programme. Beyond these statements, references to communist society contained in his writings

---

23 Marx 1993, p. 162.
24 Ibid.
25 K. Marx, *Capital*, vol. III, MECW 37, p. 123.
26 For the 'human' character of the agricultural worker, see Engels' letter to Paul Ernst of 5 June 1890: 'The lower middle-class Norwegian is the son of a free peasant and, such being the case, is a *man* compared with the degenerate German philistine' (MECW 48, p. 505).

always revolve around the themes of overcoming alienation, conscious control over the social production process, and the free development of all. To quote from *Capital*, 'a community of free individuals', 'carrying on their work with the means of production in common, in which the labour-power of all the different individuals is consciously applied as the *combined* labour-power of the community ... production by freely associated men, consciously regulated by them in accordance with a settled plan'.[27] It is clear that 'the means of production in common', i.e. the socialisation of the means of production, are not ends in themselves. They are only the means through which can arise the force of social labour, of a communal plan, of a community of free individuals that is the master of its own social movement. That this is also the ultimate meaning of *Capital* is clear from what Marx himself says. In a letter to Kugelmann he refers approvingly to the opinion Joseph Dietzgen had of him: 'You express for the first time in a clear and irresistible scientific form, what henceforth will be the conscious tendency of historical development, to subordinate to human conscience the natural strength, so far blind, of the social process of production'.[28]

In the opening address of the International, the goal of the workers' movement is briefly but clearly spelt out: 'social production controlled by social foresight' is opposed, as the 'economy of the working class', to the 'the blind rule of the supply and demand laws'.[29] Not only are the two elements of foresight, of planning, of targeted production and of collective participation returned to production (which has already been done by capitalism) but also to foresight; and the blind rule of external forces returns as a negative element to be removed – ultimately resulting in the producers' victory over the product that dominated them in the capitalist system.

In *Anti-Dühring*, Engels summarises this process of de-alienation and re-appropriation that we have traced throughout Marx's writings:

> With the seizing of the means of production by society, production of commodities is done away with, and, simultaneously, the mastery of the product over the producer. Anarchy in social production is replaced by systematic, definite organisation. The struggle for individual existence disappears. Then, for the first time, man, in a certain sense, is finally marked off from the rest of the animal kingdom and emerges from mere

---

27 *Capital*, I, MECW, 35, p. 90.
28 TN: Dietzgen's letter is quoted in Marx 1941, p. 56. The letter to Kugelmann in which he refers to Dietzgen's opinion is from 7 December 1867.
29 Marx, 'Inaugural Address to the International Working Men's Association', MECW 21, p. 330.

animal conditions of existence into really human ones. The whole sphere of the conditions of life which environ man, and which have hitherto ruled man, now comes under the dominion and control of man who for the first time becomes the real, conscious lord of nature because he has now become master of his own social organisation. The laws of his own social action, hitherto standing face to face with man as laws of nature foreign to, and dominating him, will then be used with full understanding, and so mastered by him. Man's own social organisation, hitherto confronting him as a necessity imposed by nature and history, now becomes the result of his own free action. The extraneous objective forces that have hitherto governed history pass under the control of man himself. Only from that time will man himself, with full consciousness, make his own history – only from that time will the social causes set in movement by him have, in the main and in a constantly growing measure, the results intended by him. It is the humanity's leap from the kingdom of necessity to the kingdom of freedom.[30]

In a passage from *Capital* quoted above, Marx spoke of the advent of the future society as a leap from the realm of necessity to the realm of freedom. The terms may be different from Engels', but the concept is the same.

In fact, the realm of freedom actually begins only where labour which is determined by necessity and mundane considerations ceases; thus in the very nature of things it lies beyond the sphere of actual material production. Just as the savage must wrestle with Nature to satisfy his wants, to maintain and reproduce life, so must civilised man, and he must do so in all social formations and under all possible modes of production. With his development, this realm of physical necessity expands as a result of his wants; but, at the same time, the forces of production which satisfy these wants also increase. Freedom in this field can only consist in socialised man, the associated producers, rationally regulating their interchange with Nature, bringing it under their common control, instead of being ruled by it as by the blind forces of Nature; and achieving this with the least expenditure of energy and under conditions most favourable to, and worthy of, their human nature. But it nonetheless still remains a realm of necessity. Beyond it begins that development of human energy, which is an end in itself, the true realm of freedom, which, however, can blossom forth only with this realm of necessity as its basis. The shortening of the working-day is its basic prerequisite.[31]

---

30 Engels, *Anti-Dühring*, MECW 25, p. 270.
31 *Capital*, Vol. III, MECW 37, p. 807. This is in line with ideas already expressed in the *Mani-*

The development of human energy, which is an end in-itself, is the true realm of freedom.[32] According to Marx, this and nothing else is communist society. In an interview for the *Chicago Tribune* a few years before his death, Marx was asked if the ultimate goal of the workers' movement was the 'supremacy of labour'. Marx corrected the reporter by replying that it was 'the emancipation of labour'.[33] We can then endorse E. Kamenka's conclusion that for Marx, communism

> is not merely a vision of economic plenty or social security ... To the end of his life, through the 'economic filth' that he waded through so conscientiously and unwillingly, Marx remained the philosopher, the apostle, and the predictor of freedom ... To master nature and to overcome human alienation – in these achievements lies the key to the freedom of man. Capitalism has done the former; socialism, Marx believed, would accomplish the latter.[34]

Needless to say, though, that the meaning of the word 'freedom' for Marx is, as it is for myself, quite different from the one it has for bourgeois liberals. It is not just a sphere of independent activity that belongs to the individual and cannot be touched by the state; rather, it means conscious and free participation in the collective control of the process of construction of a common future in a society free from class domination.

Marx and Engels' radical statements expressing the advent of a new society only acquire their full meaning once we understand them as signalling a profound and radical break with bourgeois society and its institutions: 'the end of prehistory';[35] 'a leap from the kingdom of necessity to the kingdom of freedom'; 'extinction of the state', and others. These should not be seen as just emphatic

---

festo: 'In bourgeois society, therefore, the past dominates the present; in communist society the present dominates the past' (MECW 6, p. 499).

32 As concerns Ricardo's expression '*production for the sake of production*', Marx writes that this 'means nothing but the development of human productive forces, in other words the *development of the richness of human nature as an end in itself*' (*Theories of Surplus Value*, II, MECW 31, p. 347).

33 The interview appeared in *The Chicago Tribune*, 5 January 1879. MECW 24, p. 572.

34 Kamenka 1967, pp. 111–12.

35 'The bourgeois relations of production are the last antagonistic form of the social process of production – antagonistic not in the sense of individual antagonism but of an antagonism that emanates from the individuals' social conditions of existence – but the productive forces developing within bourgeois society create also the material conditions for a solution of this antagonism. The prehistory of human society accordingly closes with this social formation' ('Preface to the *Critique of Political Economy*', in MECW 29, pp. 263–4).

expressions or propaganda, but as a clear reference to the fact that the socialist revolution will, for the first time in history, give men the possibility of jointly dominating the forces of production and building their future together, each developing their potentialities. In short, it will radically reverse the process of dehumanisation that capitalism is driving to its furthest depths.

CHAPTER 17

The Scientist and the Revolutionary

The Contrast between the Impatience of the Revolutionary and the Composed Analysis of the Scientist*

So far, we have sought to reconstruct the coherent and systematic Marxian conception of the revolutionary process, but we cannot ignore the fact that our reconstruction of a long process might seem to contradict many statements made by Marx himself about the imminence of a revolutionary crisis. We must therefore examine the reasons for this contradiction that threatens to undermine our entire argument, especially since proponents of revolution in the short term have often used Marx's statements.

Frederick Engels provides the answer in the eulogy to his friend when he speaks of Marx as having two souls: one that of a man of science and another that of a revolutionary, the latter forming the greater part of the man.[1] We believe that these two souls were not perfectly balanced and that the revolutionary prevailed over the scientist, so that, in a sense, his revolutionary passion ultimately affected the clarity of his scientific analysis. Perhaps this passion was for the best, since it made him realise the need for revolution in the analysis of the historical process. But it was this same passion that, for most of his life, led him to preserve the illusion of the imminence of revolution, despite the considerations in his theories.

We know that this statement of ours contradicts orthodox Marxism, which tends to present Marx's ideas as a compact block with no cracks, a coherent system developed over time and coherently continued first by Kautsky and then by Lenin. We do not accept any of these claims and for this very reason we have set about expounding our own arguments.

---

* 'Lo scienziato e il rivoluzionario', fourth chapter of *Socialismo e rivoluzione*, Feltrinelli, Milan, 1980.
1 'Such was the man of science. But this was not even half the man. Science was for Marx a historically dynamic, revolutionary force … For Marx was before all else a revolutionist. His real mission in life was to contribute, in one way or another, to the overthrow of capitalist society and of the state institutions which it had brought into being, to contribute to the liberation of the modern proletariat, which he was the first to make conscious of its own position and its needs, conscious of the conditions of its emancipation' (Frederick Engels, 'Speech at the Graveside of Karl Marx', Highgate Cemetery, London 17 March 1883, in Marx and Engels 1968, pp. 429–30).

Even Rosenberg had already noticed a crack in the theory. 'During the nineties', he writes, 'Engels, then an old man, made the same mistake that he, together with Marx, had made fifty years earlier. In his own revolutionary ardour he overestimated the fighting power of the existing popular parties'.[2] Being both a militant and a scientist is not easy, as is confirmed by Marx's daughter, Jenny, who, speaking of Flourens, says: 'He is a most extraordinary mixture of a *savant and homme d'action*'.[3] Finally, is it not Marx himself who attaches vital importance to revolutionary ardour, seeing it not simply in psychological terms but as a constitutive phase of revolutionary success? 'The English have all the *material* necessary for the social revolution', he wrote in a context that we shall examine later. 'What they lack is *the spirit of generalisation* and *revolutionary ardour*'.[4] And so while, according to Marx, the British lack of revolutionary ardour prevented them from transforming the existing material preconditions into actual revolution, it was just such a strong revolutionary passion that led Marx to presume the existence of objective conditions that had not yet developed. However, with his extraordinary capacity for analysis and intuition of historical developments, he foresaw their nature and role.[5]

In any event, it is natural that despite his formidable intellect Marx was swayed by the influences of his time and of when his views were formed. While, by studying the course of history, he was able to analyse the past and present and draw from this the knowledge of the dynamic processes that would operate in the future, thus allowing him to predict the course of the development of capitalist society up its demise, he was unable to go beyond his experience when it came to the practical methods for the transition from capitalism to socialism. The historical experiences that strongly influenced his cultural and political formation were the industrial revolution and the French Revolution and its aftermath.

---

2 Rosenberg 1939, p. 297. A Soviet writer, V.S. Vygodsky wrote, 'the theoretical work of Marx was always subordinate to the interests of the working class, the interests of the proletarian revolution' (Vygodsky 1974, p. 7).

3 Jenny Marx to Ludwig and Gertrud Kugelmann, London, 8 May 1870, in MECW 43, p. 559.

4 Marx, 'Confidential Communication on Bakunin', 28 March 1870, in MECW 21, p. 118. [TN: MECW 21 dates this 3 November 1864. This however appears to be a mistake since it appears in the volume dated 1867–70 and contrasts with the Italian edition, which has the date of 28 March 1870 as well as the Marxist Internet Archive: https://www.marxists.org/archive/marx/works/1870/03/28.htm (last accessed 12/04/2017)].

5 A scholar of the First International, Miklòs Molnàr, has also highlighted the tension in Marx between the theorist and the militant revolutionary: 'So, the febrile years 1870–2 were at the same time those of the last surge of a man who wanted to be a militant revolutionary but had to resign himself to the role of theorist' (Molnàr 1963, p. 128).

The former, which started in England at the time Marx's views were being formed, gradually spread to the continent, especially France and Belgium, where Marx spent the years from 1843 to 1848. Although these countries had not yet experienced all the overwhelming effects that the industrial revolution had produced in England, Engels, who in those years had formed a close bond of friendship and fruitful cooperation with Marx, was experiencing it at close hand in England, describing its effects in dramatic and unforgettable terms. This was to make a deep impression on Marx, who thus came to foresee a future of growing poverty and ever-greater misery. It was the tragic contradiction of productive development and consequent wealth, such as had never before been seen in history, accompanied by the increasingly miserable condition of the masses, which appeared to be in worse conditions than slaves. Hegel, the master to whom Marx owed his philosophical initiation, had understood this contradiction and had tried to express it and resolve it philosophically with dialectics.[6]

Having stripped it of its Hegelian mystical veil, dialectics became for Marx a way not to resolve contradictions amongst ideas but the way reality manifests itself through the contradictions within the historical process. He saw, before his very eyes, the gathering pace of the contradictions between the accumulation of wealth and the despair of poverty, the limitless creative capacity of man and increasing technological resources accompanied by a condition of degradation and inhumanity to which the majority of men were condemned. There was, finally, a contradiction not only between the ruling class and oppressed class but between two ways of life, two cultures, two worlds whose coexistence was becoming impossible. In his novel *Sybil*, Disraeli wrote 'Two nations; between whom there is no intercourse and no sympathy; who are as ignorant of each other's habits, thoughts, and feelings, as if they were dwellers in different zones, or inhabitants of different planets'.[7] Two utterly different nations, two incompatible worlds, and yet inextricably conjoined within the dynamics of the same society, producing continuous torment, crises, wars, revolutions and bitter social struggles. A society that could be rationally justified only in the conception of a historical process that progressed through antagonisms, struggles and continuous tension, and where there were moments of only

---

6 'Hegel discovered the schism in the middle-class society, that sprang from the ruins of the old patriarchal order. He drew attention to the contrast between the small minority which grew ever richer and the great majority which steadily became more and more impoverished. This contrast seemed to him to proceed from an unalterable natural law'. (Rosenberg 1934, p. 6).
7 Disraeli 1926, p. 67.

apparent calm while the contradictions persisted and were working to destroy existing orders and pave the way for another.

The new industrial world is born and develops in the midst of lacerating contradictions, 'after infinite pangs',[8] in the words of Carlyle. In this process, driven by objective contradictions, Marx discovers the revolutionary process taking place in a *continuum*, not just in periodic explosions; this *continuum* is not always evident to contemporaries but it never abandoned its subterranean labour of mining and erosion. It is this identification of the objective foundations of the revolutionary process that led him to describe other socialist writers as utopians, because they based their socialism and their revolutionary expectations on subjective opinions.

As a result of his direct experience of this historical process as well as his great erudition, Marx came to formulate, long before he was able to analyse the laws of the development of capitalist society in England, his more general conception of the historical process and identify its fundamental mechanisms. *The German Ideology* and then the *Poverty of Philosophy* are his first formulations of this materialist conception of history, which he would later summarise in the 1859 Preface. The same backdrop can also be seen in the *Manifesto*, which is both a monument raised to the creative and revolutionary genius of the bourgeoisie, who inaugurated a new era in world history, and the announcement of its coming end as a result of its own internal contradictions.

But how will this end come about? By what means will the rule of the bourgeoisie be transformed into a classless society? What stage of the revolutionary process will spark off the revolutionary crisis? What will trigger the change from one society to another? Will the revolutionary will of the oppressed be enough to make it happen, to leap from process to change? It is in answer to these questions that revolutionary impatience gains the upper hand and prevails over the proper analysis of situations, over what should have been the legitimate conclusions of a scientist. The man of science would, in fact, answer that the leap is only possible when the objective processes are in place, when the old ruling class has exhausted its historical function and has become an obstacle to further development of the forces of production, when the embryo of the new society has already formed within the womb of the old. But, spurred on by his enthusiasm, the revolutionary in him foreshortens the times and skips through some stages. He marches towards revolution without waiting for the circumstances to ripen, believing perhaps the moment was ripe when it was not.

---

8   TN: from Carlyle 1907, vol. 4, p. 368.

In a sense, it was precisely because the times were not ripe that led Marx to this erroneous conclusion. In fact, we now know the road to socialism in Western capitalist society is troubled and difficult. We also know that an advanced society can provide a wide range of tools for the struggles of the proletariat. But, in Marx's formative period, it would have been impossible to speak of trade union struggles, of universal suffrage, the commons, workers' control, structural reform and so on. It would have been impossible to identify a chain of partial objectives that could have completed the different stages of social development of the forces of production and introduced the elements of the new society in the womb of the old.

Hence Marx was able to recognise that the underlying mechanisms of capitalist development continued the dialectical process of the preceding course of history and was thereby able to read capitalism's death sentence inscribed within the bosom of a contradictory society. But these contradictions had not yet reached breaking point, and had not yet produced all the political and social crises that, albeit with the inevitable errors, difficulties and regressions could feed the creative initiative of the proletariat that could make the revolution possible. He could not learn from experience to distinguish the slow processes of transformation, the winding and drifting path of conflicting forces. He managed to direct the proletariat in the direction of the main road, but not the details of the routes to follow along their hard march of history; nor the straight line from one social formation to another, the shortest route between two formations; it was the revolutionary leap forward, revolution in the classical sense of the word, the violent confrontation for the seizure of power – experience suggested no other way of radically transforming society, as Marx himself had said in the abovementioned passage from the *Ideology*.[9]

But even more than the lack of a different experience, it was the historical experience of the French Revolution itself that led Marx to this outlook.

The Sources of His Erroneous Assessment of the Imminence of the Revolution

Let us pause to examine the erroneous assessment of the phase of capitalist development. Particularly illuminating, in this regard, are the pages in the *Manifesto* dedicated to the bourgeoisie. They seem to have been written

---

9 'The revolution is necessary, therefore, not only because the ruling class cannot be overthrown in any other way'. See *The German Ideology*, in MECW 5, p. 53.

today. So clear is Marx's analysis that he manages to penetrate even the secrets of the future, not by virtue of a power of divination but simply because he understood the mechanisms that dictate and will dictate the course of history. Let us read these passages, which seem a description of today's multinationals.

> Modern industry has established the world market, for which the discovery of America paved the way. This market has given an immense development to commerce, to navigation, to communication by land. This development has, in its turn, reacted on the extension of industry; and in proportion as industry, commerce, navigation, railways extended, in the same proportion the bourgeoisie developed, increased its capital, and pushed into the background every class handed down from the Middle Ages ... The need of a constantly expanding market for its products chases the bourgeoisie over the entire surface of the globe. It must nestle everywhere, settle everywhere, establish connexions everywhere. The bourgeoisie has through its exploitation of the world market given a cosmopolitan character to production and consumption in every country. To the great chagrin of Reactionists, it has drawn from under the feet of industry the national ground on which it stood. All old-established national industries have been destroyed or are daily being destroyed. They are dislodged by new industries, whose introduction becomes a life and death question for all civilised nations, by industries that no longer work up indigenous raw material, but raw material drawn from the remotest zones; industries whose products are consumed, not only at home, but in every quarter of the globe. In place of the old wants, satisfied by the production of the country, we find new wants, requiring for their satisfaction the products of distant lands and climes. In place of the old local and national seclusion and self-sufficiency, we have intercourse in every direction, universal inter-dependence of nations ... The bourgeoisie, by the rapid improvement of all instruments of production, by the immensely facilitated means of communication, draws all, even the most barbarian, nations into civilisation ... It compels all nations, on pain of extinction, to adopt the bourgeois mode of production; it compels them to introduce what it calls civilisation into their midst, i.e., to become bourgeois themselves. In one word, it creates a world after its own image ... The bourgeoisie keeps more and more, doing away with the scattered state of the population, of the means of production, and of property. It has agglomerated population, centralised the means of production, and has concentrated property in a few hands. The necessary consequence of this was political centralisation ... Subjection of Nature's forces to man, machinery,

application of chemistry to industry and agriculture, steam-navigation, railways, electric telegraphs, clearing of whole continents for cultivation, canalisation of rivers, whole populations conjured out of the ground – what earlier century had even a presentiment that such productive forces slumbered in the lap of social labour?[10]

It is hard to believe that this is a picture of the world a hundred and thirty years ago. Consider the fact that a country like Italy emerged just thirty years ago from a period of almost total national closure, autarky. Nevertheless, the processes that would lead to these developments in capitalism were already in place a hundred and thirty years ago.

The same could be said of the passages that Marx dedicates to the destruction of the old moral and social values, submerged by total desecration and replaced by the 'naked self-interest' and by 'callous cash payment'. Today, of course, the desecration of old values has been completed. Today, 'personal worth' has been 'sacrificed to exchange value'.[11] Today, with prince consorts and prime ministers being bought off by multinationals, with corruption and consumerist cravings spreading everywhere, we can say that these pages of the *Manifesto* describe bourgeois society exactly as it is today.

The reasons for Marx's mistaken revolutionary predictions, which unfortunately have exerted a negative influence on subsequent 'Marxism', lies in this tendency to anticipate the stages of bourgeois development, and therefore also its contradictions and their consequences. We find this confirmed two years later, in an article for the journal *Neue Rheinische Zeitung – Ökonomische – politische Revue*, in which he comments on the 1851 Great Exhibition of London.[12] In his article, Marx cannot fail to recognise the great triumph of the English bourgeoisie, which after the revolution had affirmed its undisputed leadership over other nations. In his view, however, this aspect of the triumph of the bourgeoisie cannot be disassociated from the announcement of its approaching ruin.

'This exhibition was announced by the English bourgeoisie already in 1849, with the most impressive cold-bloodedness, at a time when the whole Continent was still dreaming of revolution. For this exhibition, they have summoned all their vassals from France to China to a great examination, in which they

---

10   Marx, *Manifesto of the Communist Party*, in MECW 6, pp. 486 ff.
11   Marx, *Manifesto of the Communist Party*, in MECW 6, p. 487.
12   David Landes, the historian of the Industrial Revolution, notes that 'It is something of a commonplace that the Crystal Palace Exposition in 1851 marked the apogee of Britain's career as the "workshop of the world"' (Landes 2003, p. 124).

are to demonstrate how they have been using their time; and even the omnipotent Tsar of Russia feels obliged to order his subjects to appear in large numbers at this great examination. This great world congress of products and producers is quite different in its significance from the absolutist Congresses of Bregenz and Warsaw ... This exhibition is a striking proof of the concentrated power with which modern large-scale industry is everywhere demolishing national barriers and increasingly blurring local peculiarities of production, society and national character among all peoples. By putting on show the massed resources of modern industry in a small concentrated space, just at a time when modern bourgeois society is being undermined from all sides, it is also displaying materials which have been produced, and are still being produced day after day in these turbulent times, for the construction of a new society'.[13]

Here is the root of the distortions in the arguments Marx deployed to give a scientific basis to his prediction of the coming revolution. We have already highlighted, several times, Marx's profound originality compared to all the utopians who came before and after him. He discovered that it is capitalist development itself that produces the elements of the future society and creates the conditions for revolution. Marx always rightly insisted on this aspect of his theory, which his readers could not readily grasp, accustomed as they were to conceiving the revolution in the spirit of pure voluntarism. 'Meyer's letter', Marx wrote to Kugelmann, 'gave me great pleasure. However, he has partly misunderstood my exposition. Otherwise he would have seen that I depict *large-scale industry* not only as the mother of the antagonism, but also as the producer of material and intellectual conditions for resolving these antagonism, though this cannot proceed *along pleasant lines*'.[14] Years later, writing to [Carlo] Cafiero to thank him for his *Compendium of Capital*,[15] he pointed out that there was 'an apparent gap in the views set out in your preface, which is that there is no proof that the *material conditions* indispensable to the emancipation of the proletariat are engendered in spontaneous fashion by the progress of capitalist production'.[16]

This relationship between capitalist development and intensification of contradictions, and the mounting tension in the class struggle, is also emphasised by Engels, who noted in a letter to Lessner dated 4 April 1869, on the

---

13   Marx and Engels, 'Review, May to October [1850]' in *Neue Rheinische Zeitung. Politisch-ökonomische Revue*, MECW 10, pp. 499–500.
14   Marx to Ludwig Kugelmann, London, 17 March 1868, in MECW 42, p. 551.
15   EN: Cafiero was an Italian anarchist and early populariser of *Capital*.
16   Marx to Carlo Cafiero, London, 29 July 1879, in MECW 45, p. 366.

improvement of the economic situation, that in the reaction to the years 1848–9 he and Marx had predicted 'the enormous industrial development of the last 18 years and declared this would result in a sharpening of the contradictions between labour and capital, and more acute class struggle'.[17]

Reading these writings, it seems that Marx and Engels saw capitalist development and the revolutionary process progressing in tandem and at the same rate, so that the death of capitalism would occur at the very moment of its apogee. It is clear that this reasoning does not account for the resistance offered from the beginning by the principle of totality, which reabsorbs the subversive forces and reintegrates the centrifugal forces, and thus of the capacity – expressed by the logic of the relations of production – to delay and preserve. Marx knew all this very well and had also explained it in his books. Indeed, he had often insisted on this conflict between forces of production and relations of production, in which the latter did not play a merely passive role. He had indeed written that the relations of production would even end up preventing or slowing down the further development of the forces of production. Only at that point would the social formation lose its raison d'être and its decline be historically justified.

But could it have been imagined, in the penultimate quarter of the nineteenth century, that the bourgeoisie would no longer be capable of developing new forces of production, despite the great crisis of 1857 and the subsequent long depression of 1873 and the following years? Was it not precisely in those years that Marx witnessed before his very eyes a flourish of new discoveries and new technical applications, extolling their virtues in his speeches and writings? He never wrote that the bourgeoisie had exhausted its capacity to create new forces of production but he attempts to give a scientific explanation to the imminence of the revolution. We are at the end of 1858, the crisis has just passed, the bourgeoisie has resumed its expansion and Marx had finished writing his *Critique of Political Economy*. In the preface, he set out one of the fundamental principles of his materialist interpretation of history: 'No social order is ever destroyed before all the productive forces for which it is sufficient have been developed'. To justify his hopes, Marx uses a concept that is a little different, that the bourgeoisie has exhausted its historical task, if not its creative capacity, but it was he who sets out what this historical task was.

He acknowledges the triumph of the bourgeoisie, but for him this apogee is again attended by collapse.

---

17   Engels to Friederich Lessner, Manchester, 4 April 1869, in MECW 43, p. 252.

> There is no denying that bourgeois society has for the second time experienced its 16th century, a 16th century which, I hope, will sound its death knell just as the first ushered it into the world. The proper task of bourgeois society is the creation of the world market, at least in outline, and of the production based on that market. Since the world is round, the colonisation of California and Australia and the opening up of China and Japan would seem to have completed this process. For us, the difficult question is this: on the Continent revolution is imminent and will, moreover, instantly assume a socialist character. Will it not necessarily be crushed in this little corner of the earth, since the movement of bourgeois society is still, in the ascendant over a far greater area?[18]

This letter reveals *prima facie* the Achilles heel of his position: it would have been difficult to demonstrate the reasons to believe in the imminence of revolution on the Continent. A few years earlier Marx had explained that a revolution would break out only after a crisis; but the crisis had been overcome without revolutions. In fact, in the same letter Marx speaks of 'the optimistic turn taken by world trade at this moment'. It is true that he adds the revolution to have begun with the convening of the 'notables' to St. Petersburg, even the most ardent of revolutionaries would not have ventured to speak of an impending revolution on the continent on the basis of such slight evidence. In truth, Marx *deduced* the revolution from the premises of his arguments, but these premises did not stand up. One premise was that the bourgeoisie had the task of creating a world market, and this contradicted, as we said, the contemporary assertion that a social formation must create all the forces of production of which it is capable. The second premise was that the world market was already formed, 'at least in its broad outlines', whereas we must recognise that the world market has yet to be completely formed, despite the unimaginable progress made in this direction over the past 120 years.

We hope that the above has shown and proved that there was a flaw in Marx's theory of the imminence of the revolution, and that, therefore, we are justified in distinguishing between Marx's scientific analysis, which retains its validity and which still offers many lessons, and his flawed reasoning dictated by revolutionary passion, which has only served to fuel misguided interpretations of his ideas.

---

18   Marx to Engels, London, 8 October 1858, in MECW 40, p. 347.

Relationship between Revolution-as-Process and Revolution-as-Leap

We can now better understand a problem that has caused endless controversy within the workers' movement: what is the relationship between the development of capitalism and the revolutionary crisis itself, between the long process that precedes it and the revolutionary leap? The traditional division of the workers' movement into revolutionaries (i.e. supporters of the leap) and reformists (i.e. proponents of a process which does not have to be revolutionary) has its theoretical roots in the absence of dialectical spirit. For Marx, 'unavoidable evolution turn into a revolution';[19] which is to say, at a certain point the process turns into a leap. In other words, 'evolution' for Marx is *Umwälzungsprozess*, the process of continuous upheaval caused by the contradictions of capitalist society during which the proletariat's *Revolutionären Praxis* comes into play, directing the process towards a socialist outcome. By the time the objective and subjective processes have reached a sufficient degree of development, the contradictions will have become so obvious as to cause a revolutionary crisis. It is at this point that the leap takes place.

Rosa Luxemburg clearly illustrated this relationship between revolution-as-process and revolution-as-leap. She argued against those who wanted to isolate the revolutionary process from the revolutionary leap and reduce Marxism to daily reformist activities and passive expectation of the revolution, as well as against those who wanted to isolate the leap from the process and reduce Marxism to subjectivism, Blanquism, adventurism.[20] She emphasised the necessary link uniting daily struggle with the final goal, so that daily struggle becomes a true revolutionary process and does not degenerate into reformism.[21] She also

---

19   Marx to Henry Mayers Hyndman, London, 8 December 1880, in MECW 46, p. 49.
20   '... the moment you abandon the point of view of totality, you must also jettison the starting point and the goal, the assumptions and the requirements of the dialectical method. When this happens revolution will be understood not as part of a process but as an isolated act cut off from the general course of events. If that is so it must inevitably seem as if the revolutionary aspects of Marx are really just a relapse into the primitive period of the workers' movement, i.e. Blanquism' (Lukács 1971, p. 29).
21   'Instead of spontaneous revolutions, revolts, and barricades, after each of which the proletariat relapsed once more into its dull passiveness, there came the systematic daily struggle, the utilization of bourgeois parliamentarianism, mass organizations, the welding of the economic with the political struggle, of socialist ideals with stubborn defence of most immediate interests. For the first time the cause of the proletariat and its emancipation were led by the guiding star of scientific knowledge ... The theoretical works of Marx gave to the working class of the whole world a compass by which to fix its tactics from hour to hour, in its journey toward the one unchanging goal' (Luxemburg 1919, p. 9).

adds that in the context of this doctrine of revolution-as-process, the qualitative leap, acute revolutionary crisis and the subsequent catastrophe of bourgeois society, are not outside capitalist development but part of it. Capitalist development cannot be a peaceful process towards continuous progress because it harbours within itself the permanent contradiction that results in the revolutionary process that shadows it. 'Catastrophes are not in contrast to development but are a phase of it' that only the petty bourgeoisie can understand 'as an imperceptible process of different phases and degrees of development that merge into one another entirely peacefully'.[22]

In June 1919, a student of Rosa Luxemburg's teachings, the minister of culture of the Hungarian revolutionary government [Georg] Lukács, gave an explanation of the qualitative leap that culminates in revolution in a lecture given at the inauguration of the Institute for Research into Historical Materialism in Budapest. 'This leap', he said, 'does not consist of one unique act which without a transition brings about with lightning speed this, the greatest transformation in the history of mankind ... The leap is rather a lengthy, arduous process. Its essence is expressed in the fact that on every occasion *it denotes a turning in the direction of something qualitatively new* ... And it is just as vital to keep in mind the fact that it is a leap as that it is a process'.[23]

---

22 Luxemburg, 'Erörterungen über die Taktik' in *Sächsische Arbeiterzeitung* of 19 October 1868, now in Luxemburg 1970, p. 259.
23 Lukács 1971, p. 250 and p. 252.

Bibliography

Andreucci, F. and T. Detti (ed.) 1975, *Il movimento operaio italiano. Dizionario biografico (1853–1943)*, Vol. 1, Rome: Editori Riuniti.

Balibar, E. 1995, *The Philosophy of Marx*, London: Verso.

Basso, Lelio 1968, '*Stato e Rivoluzione* cinquant'anni dopo' (*State and Revolution* fifty years later), in *Problemi del Socialismo*, 26.

Basso, Lelio 1971, 'Lenin e Marx, rivoluzione al centro e rivoluzioni periferia del capitalismo' [Lenin and Marx, the revolution at the centre and the periphery of the capitalist revolution], in *Il Segnalatore*, 1.

Basso, Lelio 1973a, *Introduzione a Rosa Luxemburg una vita per il socialism*, Milan: Feltrinelli.

Basso, Lelio 1973b, 'Società e stato nella dottrina di Marx' in *Problemi del socialism*.

Basso, Lelio 1976a, *Rosa Luxemburg e lo sciluppo del pensiero marxista*, Milan: Franco Angeli.

Basso, Lelio 1976b, Marxismo e democrazia nei paesi dell'Europa occidentale, Milan: Angeli.

Basso, Lelio (ed.) 1977, *Per conoscere Rosa Luxemburg*, Milan: Mondadori.

Basso, Lelio 1980, *Socialismo e rivoluzione*, Feltrinelli: Milan.

Basso, Lelio, Guido Carandini et al. 1977, *Stato e teorie marxiste*, Milan: Mazzotta.

Carlyle, Thomas 1907, 'Count Cagliostro' in *Critical and Miscellaneous Essays: Collected and Republished*, Vol. 4, London: Chapman & Hall.

Chattopadhyay, Paresh 2016, *Marx's Associated Mode of Production*, New York: Palgrave MacMillan.

Disraeli, Benjamin 1926, *Sybil or the Two Nations*, Oxford: Oxford University Press.

Laclau, Ernesto and Chantal Mouffe 1985, *Hegemony and Socialist Strategy: Towards a Radical Democratic Politics*, London: Verso.

Garin, E. 1955, *Cronache di filosofia italiana (1900–1943)*, Bari: Laterza.

Garin, E. 1965, 'Antonio Labriola e i saggi sul materialismo storico', in A. Labriola, *La concezione materialistica della storia*, Bari: Laterza.

Gentile, Giovanni 1899, *La filosofia di Marx*, Pisa: E. Spoerri.

Giorgi, Chiara 2015a, 'Socialismo/comunismo: questione terminologica e implicazioni politiche', *Parole chiave*, 2015, 52 ('socialismo').

Giorgi, Chiara 2015b, *Un socialista del Novecento. Uguaglianza, libertà e diritti nel percorso di Lelio Basso*, Roma: Carocci.

Giorgi, Chiara 2018, La 'critica vivente di una società in movimento': una lettura novecentesca del Capitale. In Giorgi, Chiara (ed.) Rileggere il capitale, Roma: Manifestolibri.

Girardin, C. 1972, 'Sur la théorie marxiste de l' Eta', in *Temps Modernes*, 314/315.

Goldmann, L. 1959, 'La réification' in *Les Temps Modernes*, March.
Guastini, Riccardo 1981, Appunti su lelio basso interprete di marx, Milan: Franco Angeli.
Favilli, Paolo 1996, *Storia del marxismo italiano. Dalle origini alla grande guerra*, Milan: Franco Angeli.
Hölderlin, Friedrich 1990, *Hyperion and Selected Poems*, edited by E. Santner, Continuum: New York.
Kamenka, E. 1967, 'Marxian Humanism and the Crisis in Socialist Ethics', in *Socialist Humanism*, edited by Eric Fromm, London: The Penguin Press.
Labriola, Antonio 1976, *La concezione materialistica della storia*, Rome: Laterza.
Landes, D.S. 2003, *The Unbound Prometheus. Technological change and industrial development in Western Europe from 1750 to the present*, Cambridge: Cambridge University Press.
Leone, Enrico 1923, *Anti-Bergson*, Naples: La Luce del Pensiero.
Lukács, György 1971, *History and Class Consciousness: Studies in Marxist Dialectics*, Cambridge, MA: MIT Press.
Luporini, Cesare 1973, 'Il marxismo e la cultura italiana del Novecento', in *Storia d'Italia*, Vol. V, n. 2, I documenti, Turin: Einaudi.
Luxemburg, Rosa 1919, *The Crisis in the German Social Democracy. The Junius Pamphlet The Junius Pamphlet*, New York: The Socialist Publication Society.
Luxemburg, Rosa 1967, *Scritti Politici*, Rome: Editore Riuniti.
Luxemburg, Rosa 1970, *Gesammelte Werke*, volume 1/1, Dietz Verlag: Berlin.
Luxemburg, Rosa 1971, *Lettere ai Kautsky*, Rome: Editori Riuniti.
Luxemburg, Rosa 1972a, *Gesammelte Werke*, volume 1/2, Dietz Verlag: Berlin.
Luxemburg 1972b, *The accumulation of Capital. An-Anticritique*, New York: Monthly Review Press.
Luxemburg, Rosa 1976, 'Foreword to the Anthology: *The Polish Question and the Socialist Movement*', in *The National Question: Selected Writings by Rosa Luxemburg*, London: Monthly Review Press.
Luxemburg, Rosa 2003, *The Accumulation of Capital*, Routledge: London and New York.
Luxemburg, Rosa 2004, *The Rosa Luxemburg Reader*, New York: Monthly Review Press.
Luxemburg, Rosa 2008, *Reform or Revolution*, in *The Essential Rosa Luxemburg*, Chicago: Haymarket Books.
Marramao, Giacomo 1971, *Marxismo e revisionismo in Italia dalla "Critica sociale" al dibattito sul leninismo*, Bari: De Donato.
Marx, Karl 1941, *Marx Letters to Kugelmann*, London: Lawrence & Wishart.
Marx, Karl 1992a, 'Concerning Feuerbach' in *Early Writings*, edited by Rodney Livingstone and Gregor Benton, London: Penguin.
Marx, Karl 1992b, *The First International and After: Political Writings Three*, Harmondsworth: Penguin.
Marx, Karl 1993, *Grundrisse*, translated by Martin Nicolaus, London: Penguin.

BIBLIOGRAPHY

Marx, Karl 1996, *Later Political Writings*, Cambridge: Cambridge University Press.

Marx, Karl and Friedrich Engels 1968, *Selected Works in One Volume*, Lawrence & Wishart, London.

Marx, Karl and Friedrich Engels 1969, *Selected Works*, Vol. 1, Moscow: Progress Publishers.

Marx, Karl, and Friedrich Engels 1977, *Selected Works in Three Volumes*, Vol. 3, Moscow: Progress Publishers.

Marx, Karl and Friedrich Engels 1975, *Marx and Engels Collected Works*, Vol. 5, London: Lawrence & Wishart.

Mezzadra, Sandro 2018, In the Marxian Workshops. Producing Subjects, London, New York: Rowman & Littlefield International.

Molnàr, Miklòs 1963, *Le déclin de la Première Internationale, La Conférence de Londres de 1871*, Geneva.

Miliband, Ralph 2009, *The State in Capitalist Society*, London: Merlin Press.

Miliband, Ralph 2015, *Class War Conservativism and Other Essays*, London: Verso.

Mondolfo, R. 1975, *Umanismo di Marx. Studi filosofici 1908–1966*, Turin: Einaudi.

Monina, G. (ed.) 2005, *Il Movimento di unità proletaria (1943–1945)*, Rome: Carocci.

Monina, G. 2016, *Lelio Basso, leader globale. Un socialista nel secondo Novecento*, Roma: Carocci.

Poulantzas, Nicos 1973, *Political Power and Social Classes*, London: NLB.

Rosenberg, A. 1934, *A History of Bolshevism. From Marx to the First Five-Year Plan*, Oxford: Oxford University Press.

Rosenberg, A. 1936, *A History of the German Republic*, Methuen & Co., London.

Rosenberg, A. 1939, *Democracy and Socialism. A contribution to the Political History of the Past 150 Years*, London: G. Bell & Sons.

Rubel, M. 1963, *Oeuvres de Karl Marx*, Paris: Gallimard.

Sala, Mercedes (ed.) 2005, *La Comune di Parigi nella Biblioteca Basso*, Florence: L.S. Olschki.

Salvati, M., and C. Giorgi (eds.) 2003, *Scritti scelti. Frammenti di un percorso politico e intellettuale (1903–1978)*, Rome: Carocci.

Stalin, J. 1947, *Problems of Leninism*, Moscow: Foreign Languages Publishing House.

Vranicki, Predrag, 1971, *Storia del marxismo*, Rome: Einaudi.

Vygodsky, V.S., 1974, *Introduzione ai 'Grundrisse' di Marx*, Florence.

Zilli, V. 1970, 'Lenin e l'elaborazione della formula "Dittatura democratica del proletariato e dei contadini"' [Lenin and the phrase 'democratic dictatorship of the proletariat and peasantry'] in *Il Politico*, 3.

Index

agriculture 23, 91, 113, 147, 181, 192
Althusser, Louis 125
antagonisms 16, 97–98, 148, 167, 175, 184, 188, 193
Anti-Dühring 114, 133, 179, 182–83
Avanti 25–26, 31, 64

Bakunin, Mikhail 121, 133, 138, 187
Balibar, Étienne 7, 13–14
barbarism 86, 159
Basso, Luca 18
Bebel, August 72, 77, 157–58
Bergson, Henri 34
Bernstein, Eduard 7, 70, 72, 77, 90, 167–68
Bismarck, Otto 100
Blanqui, Louis Auguste 100, 149, 165
Bobbio, Norberto 4
Bolshevik Party 72, 147, 155
Bolshevism 146, 154
Bonacchi, Gabriella 11
Bonaparte, Louis 110, 113, 123
bourgeoisie 12, 15–16, 32, 39, 46, 69, 96–97, 111, 118–20, 122–23, 125–28, 148, 162, 189–92, 194–95
bourgeois state 50, 64–65, 69, 94, 100, 111, 115, 138
Bukharin, Nikolai 146
bureaucracy 19, 112–13, 123, 160

capitalism 19–22, 70–72, 78, 89–90, 100–105, 127–30, 134–35, 137–38, 141–42, 148–50, 152–53, 157–60, 163–65, 175, 179–82
class consciousness 2, 14, 22, 40, 72–73, 83, 89, 104, 117, 157, 168
class struggle 6, 8–9, 15, 20, 26–27, 40, 78, 80, 83, 98–99, 102, 118–19, 127–28, 130, 164–65
Commune, Paris 21, 27, 44, 132, 157, 160
communism 37, 45, 184

democracy 3, 15, 23–27, 49, 51, 53, 64–66, 91, 116
Die Rote Fahne 74
Dietzgen, Joseph 174, 182
Disraeli, Benjamin 188

empiricism 143–44
Engels, Frederick 5, 19, 94–95, 101, 110–12, 117–22, 124, 132–33, 160, 163, 174–75, 178–79, 183–84, 186–88, 193–95
exploitation 19, 117, 140, 164, 174, 191

factories 22–23, 53–55, 61, 131, 134
factory legislation 16, 134
fascism 3–4, 9, 23, 27, 58, 65, 102, 106, 140
Favilli, Paolo 5
First International 139, 187
First World War 1, 24, 27, 44, 49, 53, 56, 90
Frankfurt School 19
freedom 3, 8–9, 21, 27, 33, 36–37, 41, 73, 96, 116, 119, 131, 133, 181, 183–84
French Revolution 11, 35, 51, 148, 156–57, 187, 190

Garin, Eugenio 5, 6, 7
Gentile, Giovanni 5, 7–8, 31, 33
Giorgi, Chiara 15, 21, 49
Goethe, Johann Wolfgang von 36–37
Gotha Programme 95, 122, 131, 133, 160, 162

Hegel, G.W.F. 7, 9–10, 40, 44, 174, 176, 188
history 6, 27–28, 32, 40, 42–45, 86, 94–95, 102, 119, 121, 154–55, 159–60, 183, 187–91
Hölderlin, Friedrich 35–36

idealism 5, 7, 13, 33, 42–43, 45, 145
imperialism 73, 78, 83, 85–86, 90–91, 136, 167
industry 129, 181, 191–92
Italian Socialist Party 23, 27–28, 31, 143

Jogisches, Leo 74–75

Kamenka, E. 184
Kant, Immanuel 7, 33–34, 40
Kautsky, Karl 7, 77, 83–84, 158, 164, 186
Kugelmann, Ludwig 182, 193

labour 14, 20, 50, 128–29, 132, 175–81, 183, 194
labour aristocracies 88, 159, 166
Labriola, Antonio 5–7, 14, 44, 62, 110
Landes, David 192

Lassalle, Ferdinand   157, 158
Latin America   27, 135–36
Lenin, Vladimir   7, 62, 72–73, 76, 83, 89, 91–92, 94, 105, 108–10, 136, 140–41, 146–47, 149–62
Leninism   108, 146–47, 149, 151–52, 154–55, 161
Liebknecht, Karl   73, 74–75
Lukács, György   17, 71, 73, 75, 79, 83, 173, 196–97
Luporini, Cesare   7, 8
Luxemburg, Rosa   1–2, 11–12, 15, 17–18, 67–69, 73–74, 77–81, 83–85, 87–91, 105, 134, 154, 158–59, 167–68, 196–97
Lynd, Robert   117

Marramao, Giacomo   4, 5, 6, 7, 14
Martov, Julius   91
Marx, Karl   1, 3–5, 7–22, 33–45, 78–85, 93–125, 127–35, 137–42, 146–66, 168–69, 173–75, 177–84, 186–90, 192–96
　Civil War in France   21, 110–11, 113, 115, 119, 122, 124–25, 128, 130–33, 181
　Communist Manifesto   122
　German Ideology   95, 110–12, 114–15, 120–21, 189–90
　Grundrisse   14, 20, 173–74
　Herr Vogt   81, 102, 104, 135, 138, 150, 164, 166
　Philosophical Manuscripts   179
　Poverty of Philosophy   95, 97, 99, 121, 151, 189
Marx, Jenny   187
Marxism   4–8, 10, 17, 33–34, 42, 46–47, 77, 108–11, 139–41, 145–47, 149, 151–52, 154–56, 158–59, 196
Marxism-Leninism   60, 108, 154–55
Mehring, Franz   73, 75, 124
Meyer, Ernst   73
Mezzadra, Sandro   7, 14–15, 18
Miliband, Ralph   117, 120
Mondolfo   1, 4–5, 43
Monina, Giancarlo   23, 27
Mussolini, Benito   123

Napoleon III   118, 122–23, 126–27
nationalisations   101, 105
nationalism   23, 91
Noske, Gustav   75

Papini, Giovanni   31
peasantry   146–47, 154
Petrarch, Francesco   31
philosophy   4–8, 31–34, 93, 95, 97, 99, 121, 151, 189
Poulantzas, Nico   120, 123, 127–28
proletariat   6–11, 13–14, 32–34, 43, 45–46, 73–74, 83–88, 101–2, 127–30, 146–47, 149–52, 157–60, 162–66, 190, 196

reformism   5–6, 17–18, 40, 107, 135, 140, 196
revolution   1–3, 10–12, 15–16, 18–19, 22–24, 70–72, 78–80, 87–91, 103–4, 108–9, 131–32, 135–41, 145–60, 186–90, 192–96
revolutionary   1–2, 5, 13, 79, 135, 138, 147–49, 151–52, 163–66, 168, 186–87, 189, 191, 193, 195–97
Ricardo, David   176
Robespierre, Maximilien   156
Roggi, Enzo   154
Rubel, Maximilien   174
Ruge, Arnold   35–36, 38
Russian Revolution   50, 61, 72, 74, 140–41, 149, 152

Salvati, Mariuccia   49
Second International   1–2, 4, 69, 71, 91, 158–59, 163–64
self-government   3, 24, 52, 54, 56, 115, 131–32, 160
social democracy   49, 58, 70, 73, 77, 79, 140, 143, 153
socialisation   20, 23, 25, 45, 55–57, 83, 91, 134, 144–45, 150, 165, 182
socialism   3–8, 21–25, 31–33, 39, 42–46, 70–71, 86–87, 90–91, 128–36, 140–42, 150, 159–60, 163–66, 168, 183–85
socialist society   3–4, 11, 22, 25–26, 101, 127–28, 132, 140, 144, 150, 158, 160, 179
social relations   2–3, 7–8, 14, 16, 24–25, 94, 98, 115, 122, 124, 152, 157, 165, 174, 180–81
Sorel, Georges   34, 44
Stalin, Joseph   108, 141, 146–47, 149, 151, 154–55
state   10, 12, 15–16, 19, 23–24, 26, 35, 42, 49–50, 94–101, 103–15, 117–35, 138, 181, 184
Stirner, Max   40

strategy   16, 21, 79–80, 84, 89, 91, 93, 99–100, 106, 135–36, 142–44, 147, 158, 167
syndicalism   33

totality   3, 17–18, 70–72, 76–79, 82, 87–89, 98, 117, 120, 125, 194, 196
Tronti, Mario   7
Trotsky, Leon   146
Trotskyism   146

unions   3, 7, 16, 27, 52–54, 65, 80, 88

Vietnam War   27
Vygodsky, David   18

war   1, 64–65, 70–74, 77–78, 85–86, 90–91, 114, 119, 138, 142, 188
Willich, August   137–38, 142
workers   22–27, 41–42, 44–45, 50–56, 64–66, 74–75, 81–84, 88–89, 93, 102–9, 141–44, 154–56, 159–61, 164–69, 177–82
world market   106, 108, 191, 195
World War II   18, 91, 116

Zasulich, Vera   129–30
Zetkin, Clara   73
Zimmerwald   73
Zinoviev, Grigory   146, 154–55

Printed in the United States
By Bookmasters